1st Workshop on Document-grounded Dialogue and Conversational Question Answering (DialDoc 2021)

Online
5 August 2021

ISBN: 978-1-7138-3314-7

Printed from e-media with permission by:

Curran Associates, Inc.
57 Morehouse Lane
Red Hook, NY 12571

Some format issues inherent in the e-media version may also appear in this print version.

Association for Computational Linguistics
209 N. Eighth Street
Stroudsburg, Pennsylvania 18360

Phone: 1-570-476-8006
Fax: 1-570-476-0860

acl@aclweb.org

Additional copies of this publication are available from:

Curran Associates, Inc.
57 Morehouse Lane
Red Hook, NY 12571 USA
Phone: 845-758-0400
Fax: 845-758-2633
Email: curran@proceedings.com
Web: www.proceedings.com

DialDoc 2021

The 1st Workshop on Document-grounded Dialogue and Conversational Question Answering

Proceedings of the Workshop

August 5, 2021
Bangkok, Thailand (online)

Preface

DialDoc Workshop focuses on Document-grounded Dialogue and Conversational Question Answering where system responses or answers are based on the relevant content in the associated documents. Such dialogue and conversational question answering systems have the potential to access heterogeneous knowledge in document content dynamically via natural language interactions. In addition, there is a vast amount of written and visual document content created by individuals and organizations to present their knowledge to the world in broad applications. Thus, there is a substantial demand of building personal assistive conversational systems based on documents in many different domains. This area also attracts great attentions from researchers and practitioners in various fields.

There are significant individual research threads that show promises in dialogue and QA models over different kinds of knowledge in document content, including (1) unstructured content such as text passages; (2) semi-structured content such as tables or lists; (3) multimedia such as images and videos with associated textual descriptions; (4) or structured data specified by schema such as RDFa or Microdata in the webpages. The purpose of this workshop is to invite researchers to bring their individual perspectives on the document-grounded dialogue and conversational question answering and advance the related AI research in joint effort. We also organize a Shared Task on modeling goal-oriented information-seeking dialogues that are grounded in the associated documents.

This Shared Task focuses on building goal-oriented information-seeking conversation systems. The goal is to teach a dialogue system to identify the most relevant knowledge in the given document for generating agent responses in natural language. It includes two subtasks: the first subtask is to predict the grounding span for next agent response given the context; the second subtask is to generate agent response in natural language given the context. There are a total of 23 teams that participated Dev-Test phase. For final test phrase, 11 teams submitted to the leaderboard of Subtask 1, and 9 teams submitted to the leaderboard of Subtask 2. Many submissions outperform baseline significantly. For the first task, the best system achieved 67.1 Exact Match and 76.3 F1 score. For the second subtask, the best system achieved 41.1 SacreBLEU score and highest rank by human evaluation.

In this workshop, we have research track and technical system track for Shared Task. There are a total 22 submissions, including 14 submissions to research track and 8 submissions to technical system track, among which, there are 5 non-archival submissions. The workshop program features all 19 accepted papers with another 8 ACL finding papers from ACL main conference. The paper presentations are either as posters or talks in virtual format. We are also fortunate to have great invited talks by Jonathan Berant, Danqi Chen, Dilek Hakkani-Tur, Verena Rieser, Jason Weston, William Wang Yang and Scott (Wen-tau) Yih.

Finally, we would like to thank our program committee members, invited speakers, ACL workshop chairs. We are also thankful to IBM Research for sponsoring the Shared Task competition.

Organizing Committee

Song Feng, IBM Research
Siva Reddy, McGill University and MILA
Malihe Alikhani, University of Pittsburgh
He He, New York University
Yangfeng Ji, University of Virginia
Mohit Iyyer, University of Massachusetts Amherst
Zhou Yu, Columbia University

Program Committee

Amanda Buddemeyer, University of Pittsburgh
Asli Celikyilmaz, Microsoft Research
Chengguang Tang, Alibaba DAMO
Chulaka Gunasekara, IBM Research AI
Danish Contractor, IBM Research AI
Dian Yu, Tencent
Diane Litman, University of Pittsburgh
Ehud Reiter, University of Aberdeen
Elizabeth Clark, University of Washington
Eunsol Choi, University of Texas at Austin
Hanjie Chen, University of Virginia
Hareesh Ravi, Rutgers University
Hui Wan, IBM Research AI
Ioannis Konstas, Heriot-Watt University
Jiwei Li, SHANNON.AI
Jonathan Herzig, Tel-Aviv University
Matthew Stone, Rutgers University
Mert Inan, University of Pittsburgh
Michael Johnston, Interactions
Minjoon Seo, KAIST
Mo Yu, IBM Research AI
Peng Qi, Stanford University

Ravneet Singh, University of Pittsburgh
Ryuichi Takanobu, Tsinghua University
Seokhwan Kim, Amazon Alexa AI
Shehzaad Dhuliawala, Microsoft Research Montreal
Srinivas Bangalore, Interactions
Vaibhav Adlakha, McGill and Mila
Xiaoxiao Guo, IBM Research AI

Invited Speakers

Jonathan Berant, Tel-Aviv University
Danqi Chen, Princeton University
Dilek Hakkani-Tur, Amazon Alexa AI
Verena Rieser, Heriot-Watt University
Jason Weston, Facebook AI Research
William Wang Yang, University of California, Santa Barbara
Scott (We- tau) Yih, Facebook AI Research

Table of Contents

Conference Program

Thursday, August 5, 2021

8:00–8:05 Openning Remark

8:05–8:40 Invited talk I: Jonathan Berant

8:40–9:15 Invited talk II: Verena Rieser

9:15–10:05 Paper lightning talk I

10:05–10:30 Coffee break

10:30–11:05 Invited talk III: Jason Weston

11:05–11:30 Shared task overview

11:05–11:30 *DialDoc 2021 Shared Task: Goal-Oriented Document-grounded Dialogue Modeling*
Song Feng

11:30–12:30 Poster session I

11:30–12:30 *SeqDialN: Sequential Visual Dialog Network in Joint Visual-Linguistic Representation Space*
Liu Yang, Fanqi Meng, Xiao Liu, Ming-Kuang Daniel Wu, Vicent Ying and James Xu

11:30–12:30 *A Template-guided Hybrid Pointer Network for Knowledge-based Task-oriented Dialogue Systems*
Dingmin Wang, ziyao chen, Wanwei He, Li Zhong, Yunzhe Tao and Min Yang

11:30–12:30 *Automatic Learning Assistant in Telugu*
Meghana Bommadi, Shreya Terupally and Radhika Mamidi

Thursday, August 5, 2021 (continued)

11:30–12:30 *Combining Open Domain Question Answering with a Task-Oriented Dialog System*
Jan Nehring, Nils Feldhus, Harleen Kaur and Akhyar Ahmed

11:30–12:30 *CAiRE in DialDoc21: Data Augmentation for Information Seeking Dialogue System*
Yan Xu, Etsuko Ishii, Genta Indra Winata, Zhaojiang Lin, Andrea Madotto, Zihan Liu, Peng Xu and Pascale Fung

11:30–12:30 *Technical Report on Shared Task in DialDoc21*
Jiapeng Li, Mingda Li, Longxuan Ma, Wei-Nan Zhang and Ting Liu

11:30–12:30 *Cascaded Span Extraction and Response Generation for Document-Grounded Dialog*
Nico Daheim, David Thulke, Christian Dugast and Hermann Ney

11:30–12:30 *Ensemble ALBERT and RoBERTa for Span Prediction in Question Answering*
Sony Bachina, Spandana Balumuri and Sowmya Kamath S

11:30–12:30 *Q^2: Evaluating Factual Consistency in Knowledge-Grounded Dialogues via Question Generation and Question Answering*
Or Honovich, Leshem Choshen, Roee Aharoni, Ella Neeman, Idan Szpektor and Omri Abend

12:30–13:30 Lunch break

13:30–14:05 Invited talk IV: Danqi Chen

14:05–14:55 Paper lightning talk II

14:55–15:30 Invited talk V: Dilek Hakkani-Tur

Thursday, August 5, 2021 (continued)

15:30–16:30 Poster session II

15:30–16:30 *WeaSuLπ: Weakly Supervised Dialogue Policy Learning: Reward Estimation for Multi-turn Dialogue*
Anant Khandelwal

15:30–16:30 *Summary-Oriented Question Generation for Informational Queries*
Xusen Yin, Li Zhou, Kevin Small and Jonathan May

15:30–16:30 *Document-Grounded Goal-Oriented Dialogue Systems on Pre-Trained Language Model with Diverse Input Representation*
Boeun Kim, Dohaeng Lee, Sihyung Kim, Yejin Lee, Jin-Xia Huang, Oh-Woog Kwon and Harksoo Kim

15:30–16:30 *Team JARS: DialDoc Subtask 1 - Improved Knowledge Identification with Supervised Out-of-Domain Pretraining*
Sopan Khosla, Justin Lovelace, Ritam Dutt and Adithya Pratapa

15:30–16:30 *Building Goal-oriented Document-grounded Dialogue Systems*
Xi Chen, Faner Lin, Yeju Zhou, Kaixin Ma, Jonathan Francis, Eric Nyberg and Alessandro Oltramari

15:30–16:30 *Agenda Pushing in Email to Thwart Phishing*
Hyundong Cho, Genevieve Bartlett and Marjorie Freedman

15:30–16:30 *Can I Be of Further Assistance? Using Unstructured Knowledge Access to Improve Task-oriented Conversational Modeling*
Di Jin, Seokhwan Kim and Dilek Hakkani-Tur

15:30–16:30 *Open-Retrieval Conversational Machine Reading*
Yifan Gao, Jingjing Li, Michael Lyu and Irwin King

15:30–16:30 *Empathic Conversations Grounded in News Stories: Dataset and Modeling of Empathy and Distress*
Damilola Omitaomu, Shabnam Tafreshi, Sven Buechel, Chris Callison-Burch, Lyle Ungar, Anneke Buffone and João Sedoc

15:30–16:30 *A Multi-Passage Knowledge Selector for Information-Seeking Dialogues*
Zeqiu Wu, Bo-Ru Lu, Hannaneh Hajishirzi and Mari Ostendorf

Thursday, August 5, 2021 (continued)

16:30–17:05 Invited talk VI: William Wang Yang

17:05–17:40 Invited talk VII: Scott (Wen-tau) Yih

DialDoc 2021 Shared Task: Goal-Oriented Document-grounded Dialogue Modeling

Song Feng
IBM Research AI
sfeng@us.ibm.com

Abstract

We present the results of Shared Task at Workshop DialDoc 2021 that is focused on document-grounded dialogue and conversational question answering. The primary goal of this Shared Task is to build goal-oriented information-seeking conversation systems that can identify the most relevant knowledge in the associated document for generating agent responses in natural language. It includes two subtasks on predicting agent responses: the first subtask is to predict the grounding text span in the given document for next agent response; the second subtask is to generate agent response in natural language given the context. Many submissions outperform baseline significantly. For the first task, the best-performing system achieved 67.1 Exact Match and 76.3 F1. For the second subtask, the best system achieved 41.1 SacreBLEU and highest rank by human evaluation.

1 Introduction

Goal-oriented conversational systems could assist end users to query information in documents dynamically via natural language interactions. Meanwhile, there is a vast number of documents in which individuals and organizations choose to present their interests and knowledge to the world for broad applications. Thus, it attracts a lot of attentions from researchers and practitioners from different fields. There have been significant individual research threads that show promises in handling heterogeneous knowledge embedded in the documents (Talmor et al., 2021), including (1) unstructured content such as text passages (CoQA (Reddy et al., 2019), QuAC (Choi et al., 2018), ShARC (Saeidi et al., 2018), DoQA (Campos et al., 2020), Doc2Dial (Feng et al., 2020)); (2) semi-structured content such as tables or lists (SQA (Iyyer et al., 2017), HybridQA (Chen et al., 2020)); (3) multimedia such as images and videos with associated textual descriptions (RecipeQA (Yagcioglu et al., 2018), PsTuts-VQA (Colas et al., 2020), MIMOQA (Singh et al., 2021)) Despite these recent advances, the challenge remains for handling multi-turn queries of complex dialogue scenarios (Ma et al., 2020; Feng et al., 2020) and then respond based on the most relevant content in documents of various types from wide domains. As a step forward, we propose a shared task and competition to invite researchers to bring their individual perspectives and advance the field in joint effort.

We introduce DialDoc 2021 Shared Task, which focuses on building goal-oriented information-seeking dialogue that are grounded in textual content. In particular, the goal is to develop a dialogue system to comprehend multi-turn queries and identify the most relevant knowledge in the associated document for generating agent responses in natural language. It includes two subtasks for predicting agent response. The first subtask (Subtask 1) is to predict the grounding text span in the given document for next agent response; the second subtask (Subtask 2) is to generate agent response in natural language given the contexts. The dataset used for the task is a goal-oriented document-grounded dialogue dataset Doc2Dial (Feng et al., 2020). We hosted the leaderboards for Dev-Test and Test phase on `eval.ai` for two subtasks respectively. There are a total of 23 teams that participated Dev-Test phase. For final test phrase, 11 teams submitted to the leaderboard of Subtask 1, and 9 teams submitted to the leaderboard of Subtask 2. For the first task, the best system achieved 67.09 Exact Match and 76.34 F1. For the second subtask, the best system achieved 41.06 sacrebleu and rank the best by human evaluation.

In this work, we first describe the dataset and the two subtasks. Then, we provide a summary of the evaluation results from participating systems.

Proceedings of the 1st Workshop on Document-grounded Dialogue and Conversational Question Answering, pages 1–7
August 5–6, 2021. ©2021 Association for Computational Linguistics

2 Dataset

We use Doc2Dial dataset [1] introduced in Feng et al. (2020), which contains 4793 goal-oriented dialogues and a total of 488 associated grounding documents from four domains for social welfare: `dmv`, `va`, `ssa`, and `studentaid`. In this dataset, dialogues contain the scenarios when agent ask follow-up questions for clarification or verification based on dialogue-based and document-based context. Each turn is annotated with (1) grounding span from the associated document, (2) dialogue act, e.g., *query*, *respond* and (3) speaker role, either *agent* or *user*.

For developing models, we divide the data into training, validation and test split based on the number of dialogues. For evaluating the models, we provide a dev-test set which contains about 30% test dataset. The final test set also includes dialogue and document data from an unseen domain *cdccovid* that is not in the training, validation or dev-test set. The dialogues of unseen domain were collected in the same data collection process as published Doc2Dial dataset. Table 1 presents the number of dialogues ('dials'), total turns ('turns') of all dialogues and total turns for prediction ('predicts') in each data split.

#	train	val	test-dev	test
dials	3474	661	198	787
turns	44149	8539	1353	5264
predicts	20431	3972	198	787

Table 1: Statistics of dialogue data of different data splits.

3 Task Description

This Shared Task focuses on building goal-oriented information-seeking dialogue systems. The goal is to teach a dialogue system to identify the most relevant knowledge in the associated document for generating agent responses in natural language. It includes two subtasks on predicting agent response. The agent can either provide an answer or ask follow-up question. Here we only consider the cases that use queries are answerable.

3.1 Subtask 1

This subtask is to predict the grounding span of next agent response. The input current turn, dialogue history and one associated document; the output is a text span. The evaluation is based on token-level F1 and exact match score (Rajpurkar et al., 2018).

3.2 Subtask 2

This subtask is to generate the next agent utterance. The input is current turn, dialogue history and the document context; the output is utterance in natural language. The evaluation is based on SacreBLEU (Post, 2018). We also perform human evaluation on the top three submissions with highest SacreBLEU for determining the final rank.

Human evaluation We ask human annotators to rank a group of three utterances from the three submissions based on *relevance* and *fluency* given document context and dialogue history. *relevance* is used to measure how well the generated utterance is relevant to grounding span as a response to the previous dialogue turn(s). *fluency* indicates whether the generated utterance is grammatically correct and generally fluent in English. We randomly select 100 generated turns where the utterances are not all the same. We collect five judgements per group.

4 Baseline

Subtask 1 The baseline model for Subtask 1 is based on BERT-QA (Devlin et al., 2019). For each token, it computes the probabilities of start and end positions by a linear projection from the last hidden layers of the BERT model. Then it multiplies the scores of the start and end positions for estimating the probability of the corresponding span. As a baseline, we fine-tune BERT-base on Doc2Dial dataset where the input is dialogue query and the associated document context. The dialogue query is the concatenation of dialogue turns in reverse order.

Subtask 2 The task is formulated as an end-to-end text generation task. The baseline approach for Subtask 2 is based on sequence-to-sequence model BART by (Lewis et al., 2020). We fine-tune the pre-trained BART model (`bart-cnn-large`) on Doc2Dial dataset. The source input consists of current turn, dialogue history along with document title and content that are separated by special tokens. The target output is next agent utterance.

[1] `https://doc2dial.github.io/file/doc2dial_v1.0.1.zip`

5 Shared Task Submissions

We hosted the leaderboards [2] for Dev-Test and Test phase for the two subtasks on `eval.ai`. The Dev-Test and Test phase lasted three months and one week respectively. There are a total of 23 teams that participated Dev-Test phase. For final Test phrase, 11 teams submitted to the leaderboard of Subtask 1, and 9 teams submitted to the leaderboard of Subtask 2. Among the best-performing systems, some teams utilize additional data for augmentation for pre-training (e.g., CAiRE (Xu et al., 2021), SCIR-DT (Li et al., 2021)), some teams employ neural retrievers for obtaining most relevant document passages (e.g., RWTH (Daheim et al., 2021) and ER). For the first task, the best system achieved 67.1 Exact Match and 76.3 F1. For the second subtask, the best system achieved 41.1 sacrebleu and rank the best by human evaluation. Next, we provide a brief summary of the work by 8 teams as listed in Table 2, who submitted their technical system papers.

5.1 ER

ER[3] participates Subtask 1. It introduces a model that leverages the structure in grounding document and dialogue context. It applies a multi-passage reader model based on transformer-based encoder to encode each passage concatenated with dialogue context and document title. It optimizes both passage selection, start and end position selection with gold knowledge passage during training. The final submission is an ensemble of 12 models and achieves the best results for Subtask 1.

5.2 SCIR-DT

SCIR-DT (Li et al., 2021) participates Subtask 1. Their methods include data augmentation, model pretraining/fine-tuning, postprocessing, and ensemble. For data augmentation, they use back-translation and synonym substitution to obtain 5 times of document and dialogue data, which are then paired into 25 times data. They use the augmented data for pretraining BERT and RoBERTa with whole word masking technique and doc2dial data for fine-tuning BERT, RobERTa and ELECTRA. The ensemble method selects the most probably rank span based on the linear combination of ranking results per model and learn the hyperparameter for inference. The team ranks 2nd based on the average of normalized F1 and EM scores used for the final evaluation.

[2] https://eval.ai/web/challenges/challenge-page/793/overview

[3] The submission is non-archival.

Team	Affiliation
CAiRE	The Hong Kong University of Science and Technology
ER	Anonymous
JARS	Carnegie Mellon University
KU_NLP	Konkuk University & Kangwon National University
RWTH	RWTH Aachen University
SB_NITK	National Institute of Technology Karnataka
Schlussstein	Carnegie Mellon University Bosch Research Pittsburgh
SCIR-DT	Harbin Institute of Technology

Table 2: Participating teams and affiliations.

5.3 KU_NLP

KU_NLP (Kim et al., 2021) participates both tasks. For Subtask 1, they adopt pretrained RoBERTa as backbone and predict dialogue act and span jointly. For Subtask 2, they include several tokens and embeddings based on document structure into input representation for BART. Instead of random order of the training instances, they propose to apply curriculum learning (Xu et al., 2020) based on the computed task difficulty level for each task respectively. The final submission on Subtask 2 is based on the span prediction by a single model. It achieves best SacreBLEU and human evaluation results.

5.4 RWTH

RWTH (Daheim et al., 2021) participates both tasks. For Subtask 1, it applies BERTQA with additional span-based specifics in their approach. First, they restrict start and end position only to the begin and end of sub-clauses since Doc2Dial dataset is based on preprocessed spans. In addition, they consider modeling the joint probability of a span inspired by Fajcik et al. (2020). The final submission is the ensemble of multiple models, where the probability of a span is obtained by marginalizing the joint probability of span and model over all models. For Subtask 2, they propose to cascade over all spans where they use top N (=5) spans as a approximation. The probability is computed jointly. The generation model is trained with cross-entropy using an n-best list obtained from the separately trained selection model.

5.5 CAiRE

CAiRE (Xu et al., 2021) participates both tasks. They utilize data augmentation methods and several training techniques. For the first task, it uses QA data such as MRQA shared task dataset (Fisch et al., 2019) and conversational QA data such as CoQA (Reddy et al., 2019) for pretraining RoBERTa with multi-task learning strategy and the models are fine-tuned on Doc2Dial dataset. For the second task, they pretrain BART on Wizard-of-Wikipedia dataset (Dinan et al., 2019). Then they fine-tune the model using the knowledge prediction results from the first task. The final submission is based on the ensemble of multiple models where the best span is determined by the majority vote by models.

5.6 SB_NITK

SB_NITK (Bachina et al., 2021) participates Subtask 1. They also adapt data augmentation approaches that utilize additional Question Answering dataset such as SQuAD 2.0 (Lee et al., 2020), Natural Questions (Kwiatkowski et al., 2019) and CORD-19 (Wang et al., 2020) for pretraining several models including RoBERTa, ALBERT and ELECTRA. Then they experiment with different combinations of ensemble models. The final submission is based on the ensemble of ensemble ALBERTA and RoBERTa using all three additional datasets.

5.7 JARS

JARS (Khosla et al., 2021) participates in Subtask 1. It also uses transformer-based QA models, for which it pretrains on different Question Answering datasets such as SQuAD, different subsets of MRQA-2019 training set along with conversational QA data such as CoQA and QuAC. The experiments suggest that conversational QA datasets are more helpful comparing to QA datasets. They compare three different ensemble methods and use the highest average probability score for span prediction based on multiple models.

5.8 Schlussstein

Schlussstein (Chen et al., 2021) submit to both subtasks. For Subtask 1, they pretrain BERT on datasets such as SQuAD and CoQA before finetuning on Doc2Dial. To incorporate longer document content in Doc2Dial dataset, they also experiment with longer document stride and observe performance improvement. For Subtask 2, it pretrains BART model on CoQA dataset before fine-tuning it on Doc2Dial dataset.

	Team	Exact_Match	F1
1	ER	67.1 (61.8)	76.3 (73.1)
2	SCIR-DT	63.9 (59.1)	75.6 (71.6)
3	RWTH	63.5 (58.3)	75.9 (73.2)
4	CAiRE	60.7 (-)	75.0 (-)
5	KU_NLP	58.7 (58.7)	73.4 (73.4)
6	SB_NITK	58.6 (-)	73.4 (-)
7	JARS	53.5 (52.6)	70.9 (67.4)
-	baseline	35.8 (35.8)	52.6 (52.6)

Table 3: Participating teams of Subtask 1. The rank is based on the average of normalized average of F1 and EM scores.

Rank	Team	SacreBLEU
1	KU_NLP	41.1 (41.1)
2	RWTH	40.4 (39.1)
3	CAiRE	37.7 (-)
4	SCIR-DT	30.7 (-)
-	baseline	17.6 (17.6)

Table 4: Participating teams and evaluation results on test set of Subtask 2.

6 Results

Subtask 1 We present the evaluation results on final Test phase of Subtask1 from 7 participating teams in Table 3. The submissions are ordered based on the average of normalized F1 and EM scores. All submissions of Test Phase outperform BERT-base baseline by large margin. The scores in parentheses are by single models. All other results except the ones by KU_NLP are based on various ensemble methods, which further improve the performances significantly in most cases.

Subtask 2 Table 4 presents the evaluation results on final test set of Subtask 2 from 4 participating teams. We performance human evaluations on the top three submissions based on SacreBLEU scores. We use three different ways to compute majority vote to get the aggregated results: (1) we consider the rank if it is agreed among at least three annotators; (2) we consider the rank if it is agreed among at least two annotators; (3) we also use the aggregation results provided by Appen platform, which takes consideration of annotator's historical performances.

7 Conclusion

We presented the results of 1st DialDoc 2021 Shared Task, which included two subtasks on document-grounded goal-oriented dialogue modeling. We received submissions from a total of 17 teams during entire phase for Subtask 1, and 9 teams for Subtask 2. All submissions during final Test phase outperformed baselines by a large margin for both subtasks. By organizing this shared task, we hope to invite researchers and practitioners to bring their individual perspectives on the subject, and to jointly advance the techniques toward building assistive agents to access document content for end users by conversing.

Acknowledgements

We would like to thank Luis Lastras, Sachindra Joshi, Siva Reddy and Siva Sankalp Patel for a lot of helpful discussions on organizing this shared task. We thank `eval.ai` for their help and support on hosting the leaderboards on their platform. Finally, we are thankful to IBM Research AI for sponsoring the shared task and competition.

References

Sony Bachina, Spandana Balumuri, and Sowmya Kamath S. 2021. Ensemble albert and roberta for span prediction in question answering. In *Proceedings of the 1st Workshop on Document-grounded Dialogue and Conversational Question Answering*. Association for Computational Linguistics.

Jon Ander Campos, Arantxa Otegi, Aitor Soroa, Jan Deriu, Mark Cieliebak, and Eneko Agirre. 2020. DoQA - accessing domain-specific FAQs via conversational QA. In *Proceedings of the 58th Annual Meeting of the Association for Computational Linguistics*, pages 7302–7314, Online. Association for Computational Linguistics.

Wenhu Chen, Hanwen Zha, Zhiyu Chen, Wenhan Xiong, Hong Wang, and William Yang Wang. 2020. HybridQA: A dataset of multi-hop question answering over tabular and textual data. In *Findings of the Association for Computational Linguistics: EMNLP 2020*, pages 1026–1036, Online. Association for Computational Linguistics.

Xi Chen, Faner Lin, Yeju Zhou, and Kaixin Ma. 2021. Building goal-oriented document-grounded dialogue systems. In *Proceedings of the 1st Workshop on Document-grounded Dialogue and Conversational Question Answering*. Association for Computational Linguistics.

Eunsol Choi, He He, Mohit Iyyer, Mark Yatskar, Wentau Yih, Yejin Choi, Percy Liang, and Luke Zettlemoyer. 2018. QuAC: Question answering in context. In *Proceedings of the 2018 Conference on Empirical Methods in Natural Language Processing*, pages 2174–2184, Brussels, Belgium. Association for Computational Linguistics.

Anthony Colas, Seokhwan Kim, Franck Dernoncourt, Siddhesh Gupte, Zhe Wang, and Doo Soon Kim. 2020. TutorialVQA: Question answering dataset for tutorial videos. In *Proceedings of the 12th Language Resources and Evaluation Conference*, pages 5450–5455, Marseille, France. European Language Resources Association.

Nico Daheim, David Thulke, Christian Dugast, and Hermann Ney. 2021. Cascaded span extraction and response generation for document-grounded dialog. In *Proceedings of the 1st Workshop on Document-grounded Dialogue and Conversational Question Answering*. Association for Computational Linguistics.

Jacob Devlin, Ming-Wei Chang, Kenton Lee, and Kristina Toutanova. 2019. BERT: Pre-training of deep bidirectional transformers for language understanding. In *Proceedings of the 2019 Conference of the North American Chapter of the Association for Computational Linguistics: Human Language Technologies, Volume 1 (Long and Short Papers)*, pages 4171–4186, Minneapolis, Minnesota. Association for Computational Linguistics.

Emily Dinan, Stephen Roller, Kurt Shuster, Angela Fan, Michael Auli, and Jason Weston. 2019. Wizard of wikipedia: Knowledge-powered conversational agents. In *International Conference on Learning Representations*.

Martin Fajcik, Josef Jon, Martin Docekal, and Pavel Smrz. 2020. BUT-FIT at SemEval-2020 task 5: Automatic detection of counterfactual statements with deep pre-trained language representation models. In *Proceedings of the Fourteenth Workshop on Semantic Evaluation*, pages 437–444, Barcelona (online). International Committee for Computational Linguistics.

Song Feng, Hui Wan, Chulaka Gunasekara, Siva Patel, Sachindra Joshi, and Luis Lastras. 2020. doc2dial: A goal-oriented document-grounded dialogue dataset. In *Proceedings of the 2020 Conference on Empirical Methods in Natural Language Processing (EMNLP)*, pages 8118–8128, Online. Association for Computational Linguistics.

Adam Fisch, Alon Talmor, Robin Jia, Minjoon Seo, Eunsol Choi, and Danqi Chen. 2019. MRQA 2019 shared task: Evaluating generalization in reading comprehension. In *Proceedings of the 2nd Workshop on Machine Reading for Question Answering*, pages 1–13, Hong Kong, China. Association for Computational Linguistics.

Mohit Iyyer, Wen-tau Yih, and Ming-Wei Chang. 2017. Search-based neural structured learning for sequential question answering. In *Proceedings of the 55th Annual Meeting of the Association for Computational Linguistics (Volume 1: Long Papers)*, pages 1821–1831, Vancouver, Canada. Association for Computational Linguistics.

Sopan Khosla, Justin Lovelace, Ritam Dutt, and Adithya Pratapa. 2021. Team jars: Dialdoc subtask 1 - improved knowledge identification with supervised out-of-domain pretraining. In *Proceedings of the 1st Workshop on Document-grounded Dialogue and Conversational Question Answering*. Association for Computational Linguistics.

Boeun Kim, Dohaeng Lee, Yejin Lee, Harksoo Kim, Sihyung Kim, Jin-Xia Huang, and Oh-Woog Kwon. 2021. Document-grounded goal-oriented dialogue systems on pre-trained language model with diverse input representation. In *Proceedings of the 1st Workshop on Document-grounded Dialogue and Conversational Question Answering*. Association for Computational Linguistics.

Tom Kwiatkowski, Jennimaria Palomaki, Olivia Redfield, Michael Collins, Ankur Parikh, Chris Alberti, Danielle Epstein, Illia Polosukhin, Matthew Kelcey, Jacob Devlin, Kenton Lee, Kristina N. Toutanova, Llion Jones, Ming-Wei Chang, Andrew Dai, Jakob Uszkoreit, Quoc Le, and Slav Petrov. 2019. Natural questions: a benchmark for question answering research. *Transactions of the Association of Computational Linguistics*.

Gyeongbok Lee, Seung-won Hwang, and Hyunsouk Cho. 2020. SQuAD2-CR: Semi-supervised annotation for cause and rationales for unanswerability in SQuAD 2.0. In *Proceedings of the 12th Language Resources and Evaluation Conference*, pages 5425–5432, Marseille, France. European Language Resources Association.

Mike Lewis, Yinhan Liu, Naman Goyal, Marjan Ghazvininejad, Abdelrahman Mohamed, Omer Levy, Veselin Stoyanov, and Luke Zettlemoyer. 2020. BART: Denoising sequence-to-sequence pretraining for natural language generation, translation, and comprehension. In *Proceedings of the 58th Annual Meeting of the Association for Computational Linguistics*, pages 7871–7880, Online. Association for Computational Linguistics.

Jiapeng Li, Mingda Li, Longxuan Ma, Weinan Zhangy, and Ting Liu. 2021. Technical report on shared task in dialdoc21. In *Proceedings of the 1st Workshop on Document-grounded Dialogue and Conversational Question Answering*. Association for Computational Linguistics.

Longxuan Ma, Wei-Nan Zhang, Mingda Li, and Ting Liu. 2020. A survey of document grounded dialogue systems (dgds). *arXiv preprint arXiv:2004.13818*.

Matt Post. 2018. A call for clarity in reporting BLEU scores. In *Proceedings of the Third Conference on Machine Translation: Research Papers*, pages 186–191, Brussels, Belgium. Association for Computational Linguistics.

Pranav Rajpurkar, Robin Jia, and Percy Liang. 2018. Know what you don't know: Unanswerable questions for SQuAD. In *Proceedings of the 56th Annual Meeting of the Association for Computational Linguistics (Volume 2: Short Papers)*, pages 784–789, Melbourne, Australia. Association for Computational Linguistics.

Siva Reddy, Danqi Chen, and Christopher D. Manning. 2019. CoQA: A conversational question answering challenge. *Transactions of the Association for Computational Linguistics*, 7:249–266.

Marzieh Saeidi, Max Bartolo, Patrick Lewis, Sameer Singh, Tim Rocktäschel, Mike Sheldon, Guillaume Bouchard, and Sebastian Riedel. 2018. Interpretation of natural language rules in conversational machine reading. In *Proceedings of the 2018 Conference on Empirical Methods in Natural Language Processing*, pages 2087–2097, Brussels, Belgium. Association for Computational Linguistics.

Hrituraj Singh, Anshul Nasery, Denil Mehta, Aishwarya Agarwal, Jatin Lamba, and Balaji Vasan Srinivasan. 2021. MIMOQA: Multimodal input multimodal output question answering. In *Proceedings of the 2021 Conference of the North American Chapter of the Association for Computational Linguistics: Human Language Technologies*, pages 5317–5332, Online. Association for Computational Linguistics.

Alon Talmor, Ori Yoran, Amnon Catav, Dan Lahav, Yizhong Wang, Akari Asai, Gabriel Ilharco, Hannaneh Hajishirzi, and Jonathan Berant. 2021. Multimodal{qa}: complex question answering over text, tables and images. In *International Conference on Learning Representations*.

Lucy Lu Wang, Kyle Lo, Yoganand Chandrasekhar, Russell Reas, Jiangjiang Yang, Doug Burdick, Darrin Eide, Kathryn Funk, Yannis Katsis, Rodney Michael Kinney, Yunyao Li, Ziyang Liu, William Merrill, Paul Mooney, Dewey A. Murdick, Devvret Rishi, Jerry Sheehan, Zhihong Shen, Brandon Stilson, Alex D. Wade, Kuansan Wang, Nancy Xin Ru Wang, Christopher Wilhelm, Boya Xie, Douglas M. Raymond, Daniel S. Weld, Oren Etzioni, and Sebastian Kohlmeier. 2020. CORD-19: The COVID-19 open research dataset. In *Proceedings of the 1st Workshop on NLP for COVID-19 at ACL 2020*, Online. Association for Computational Linguistics.

Benfeng Xu, Licheng Zhang, Zhendong Mao, Quan Wang, Hongtao Xie, and Yongdong Zhang. 2020. Curriculum learning for natural language understanding. In *Proceedings of the 58th Annual Meeting of the Association for Computational Linguistics*, pages 6095–6104, Online. Association for Computational Linguistics.

Yan Xu, Etsuko Ishii, Genta Indra Winata, Zhaojiang Lin, Andrea Madotto, Zihan Liu, Peng Xu, and Pascale Fung. 2021. Caire in dialdoc21: Data augmentation for information-seeking dialogue system. In *Proceedings of the 1st Workshop on Document-grounded Dialogue and Conversational Question Answering*. Association for Computational Linguistics.

Semih Yagcioglu, Aykut Erdem, Erkut Erdem, and Nazli Ikizler-Cinbis. 2018. RecipeQA: A challenge dataset for multimodal comprehension of cooking recipes. In *Proceedings of the 2018 Conference on Empirical Methods in Natural Language Processing*, pages 1358–1368, Brussels, Belgium. Association for Computational Linguistics.

SeqDialN: Sequential Visual Dialog Networks in Joint Visual-Linguistic Representation Space

Liu Yang[1], Fanqi Meng[2], Xiao Liu[3], Ming-Kuang Daniel Wu[4], Vicent Ying[4]
Xianchao Xu[1]
[1]Intel China Research Center
[2]University of Science and Technology of China
[3]University of California, Davis
[4]Stanford University
{liu.y.yang, james.xu}@intel.com, farrell@mail.ustc.edu.cn
xioliu@ucdavis.edu, danielwu@alumni.stanford.edu
vhying@stanford.edu

Abstract

The key challenge of the visual dialog task is how to fuse features from multimodal sources and extract relevant information from dialog history to answer the current query. In this work, we formulate a visual dialog as an information flow in which each piece of information is encoded with the joint visual-linguistic representation of a single dialog round. Based on this formulation, we consider the visual dialog task as a sequence problem consisting of ordered visual-linguistic vectors. For featurization, we use a Dense Symmetric Co-Attention network (Nguyen and Okatani, 2018) as a lightweight vison-language joint representation generator to fuse multimodal features (i.e., image and text), yielding better computation and data efficiencies. For inference, we propose two Sequential Dialog Networks (SeqDialN): the first uses LSTM (Hochreiter and Schmidhuber, 1997) for information propagation (IP) and the second uses a modified Transformer (Vaswani et al., 2017) for multi-step reasoning (MR). Our architecture separates the complexity of multimodal feature fusion from that of inference, which allows simpler design of the inference engine. On VisDial v1.0 test-std dataset, our best single generative SeqDialN achieves 62.54% NDCG[1] and 48.63% MRR[2]; our ensemble generative SeqDialN achieves 63.78% NDCG and 49.98% MRR, which set a new state-of-the-art generative visual dialog model. We fine-tune discriminative SeqDialN with *dense annotations*[3] and boost the performance up to 72.41% NDCG and 55.11% MRR. In this work, we discuss the extensive experiments we have conducted to demonstrate the effectiveness of our model components. We also provide visualization for the reasoning process from the relevant conversation rounds and discuss our fine-tuning methods. The code is available at https://github.com/xiaoxiaoheimei/SeqDialN.

1 Introduction

Visual Dialog has attracted increasing research interest as an emerging field, bringing together aspects of computer vision, natural language processing, and dialog systems. In this task, an AI agent is required to hold a meaningful dialog with humans in natural, conversational language about visual content. Specifically, given an image, a dialog history, and a query about the image, the agent has to ground the query in image, infer context from history, and answer the query accurately (Das et al., 2017).

Our work is inspired by the use of visual-linguistic joint representation to erase the modality gap, where we embed the visual signals into the text snippets for each dialog round. In this way, we convert a visual dialog into an ordered vector sequence, where each vector is the joint visual-linguistic representation of a specific dialog round. Rather than using ViLBERT (Lu et al., 2019), we chose Dense Symmetric Co-Attention (Nguyen and Okatani, 2018) as a lightweight joint visual-linguistic representation generator. In contrast to VisDial-BERT (Murahari et al., 2019), which concatenates all rounds of the dialog history into a single textual input for ViLBERT(Lu et al., 2019), we keep each dialog round separate. Keeping this inherent sequential structure from the visual dialog allows us to reason across the dialog history to find the most query-relevant dialog rounds. By viewing visual dialog task as a vector sequence, We propose two sequential networks to tackle the problem.

Fig. 1 illustrates a conceptual overview

[1]Normalized Discounted Cumulative Gain

[2]Mean Reciprocal Rank

[3]Relevance scores for 100 answer options corresponding to each question on a subset of the training set, publicly available on visualdialog.org/data

Proceedings of the 1st Workshop on Document-grounded Dialogue and Conversational Question Answering, pages 8–17
August 5–6, 2021.

of the proposed method. The visual features and language embeddings are learned from two independent domains. They are fed into the Dense Symmetric Co-Attention Network (Nguyen and Okatani, 2018) to produce a **visual-linguistic vector sequence** in the joint visual-linguistic feature space. Our baseline model, the Information Propagation Network (SeqIPN), which uses a LSTM (Hochreiter and Schmidhuber, 1997) to summarize the visual-linguistic sequence, outperforms other well-known baselines (Das et al., 2017; Lu et al., 2017), on NDCG metric by a large margin > 0.5. Multi-step reasoning network (SeqMRN) is based on Transformer (Vaswani et al., 2017). We expect the multi-head attention mechanism of Transformer better captures the relationship within the visual linguistic sequence. We achieve multi-step reasoning by stacking several Transformers to refine attentions in high level semantic space. SeqMRN outperforms VisDial-BERT (Murahari et al., 2019) by $> 1.5\%$ on NDCG when trained with comparable amount of data, while using 30% less parameters. The pipeline in Fig.1 facilitates the combination of different word embeddings and SeqDialN models. In this work, we compare two kinds of pre-trained word representations: GloVe(Pennington et al., 2014) and DistilBert (Sanh et al., 2019). The ablation test shows that SeqMRN with DistilBert embedding yields the best performance. Further experiment reveals SeqDialN sets a new state-of-the-art **generative** visual dialog model.

VLDialog and NDCGFinetune(Murahari et al., 2019; Qi et al., 2019b) tune with *dense annotations*[3]. Training on the *dense annotation*[3] makes these models perform very well on the NDCG metric but poorly on the others because the *dense annotation*[3] dataset doesn't correlate well with the original ground-truth answer to the question (Murahari et al., 2019). In this work, we propose a reweighting method to mitigate the damage to non-NDCG metrics in fine-tuning process, which make our best model outperform (Murahari et al., 2019; Qi et al., 2019b,a) on MRR by a large margin at the cost of a little lower NDCG than them.

The main contributions of this paper is three fold. (1) We formulate the visual dialog task as reasoning from a sequence in the joint visual-linguistic representation space. (2) We propose two sequential networks to tackle the visual dialog task in the joint visual-linguistic representation space. (3) We set a new state-of-the-art **generative** visual dialog model.

2 Related Work

2.1 VQA

VQA focuses on providing a natural language answer given an image and a free-form, open-ended question. Attention mechanisms have been deeply explored in VQA related work. In deep networks, the attention mechanism helps refine semantic meanings at different levels. SANs (Yang et al., 2016) create stacked attention networks, producing multiple attention maps in a sequential manner to imitate multi-step reasoning. (Lu et al., 2016) introduces co-attention between image regions and words in the question. (Yu et al., 2017) utilizes image-guided attention to extract the language concept of an image and then combines this with a novel multi-modal feature fusion of image and question.

Recently, Dense Co-Attention Network (DCN) (Nguyen and Okatani, 2018) proposes a symmetric co-attention layer to address VQA tasks. DCN is "dense symmetric" because it makes each visual region aware of the existence of each question word and vice versa. This fine-granularity co-attention enables DCN to discriminate subtle differences or similarities between vision and language features. In this work, we use DCN as the generator of joint visual-linguistic representation.

2.2 Visual Dialog

Previous research has tackled the visual dialog task from various theoretical perspectives. Early baselines include Late Fusion, Hierarchical Recurrent Encoder, and Memory Networks (Das et al., 2017). (Guo et al., 2019) proposes a two-stage method which filters out the obviously irrelevant answers in primary stage, then re-ranks the rest answers in synergistic stage. (Guo et al., 2019) won the visual dialog challenge[4] in 2018. Several models try to leverage the dialog structure to conduct explicit reasoning. GNN (Zheng et al., 2019) abstracts visual dialog as a fully connected graph where each node represents a single dialog round and each edge represents semantic dependency of the two connected nodes. Recursive Visual Attention(RvA) (Niu et al., 2019) designs sub-networks to infer the stopping condition when

[4]visdial/challenge2020

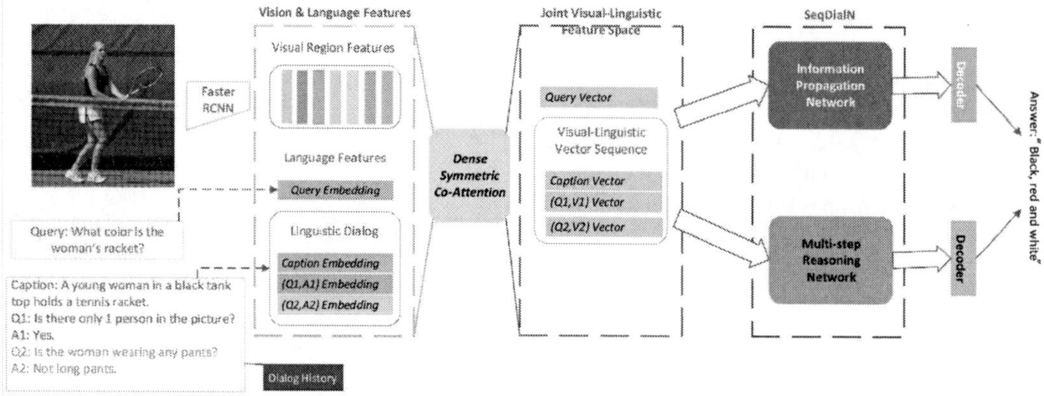

Figure 1: Conceptual architecture of sequential visual dialog network (SeqDialN).

recursively traversing the dialog stack to resolve visual co-reference relationships. RvA won the visual dialog challenge[4] in 2019 by fine-tuning with *dense annotations*[3]. ReDAN (Gan et al., 2019) develops a recurrent dual attention network to progressively update the semantic representations of query, vision, and history, making them co-aware through multiple steps to achieve multi-step reasoning. ReDAN (Gan et al., 2019) achieves 64.47% NDCG on the VisDial v1.0 test-std set, is still the highest score among all published work trained **without** *dense annotations*[3].

Based on ViLBERT (Lu et al., 2019), recent VisDial-BERT (Murahari et al., 2019) leverages the joint visual-linguistic representation to tackle visual dialog task. By fine-tuning with *dense annotations*, VisDial-BERT (Murahari et al., 2019) achieves state-of-the-art NDCG (74.47%) using a discriminative model. However, its non-NDCG performance is significantly lower. Futhermore, it's not easy to deploy a discriminative model in real applications. Similar performance degradation occurs to P1P2 (Qi et al., 2019a), which also trained with *dense annotations*[3].

3 Approach

The visual dialog task (Das et al., 2017) is formulated as follows: at time t, given a query Q_t grounded in image I, and dialog history (including the image caption C) $H_t = \{C, (Q_1, A_1), \cdots, (Q_{t-1}, A_{t-1})\}$ as additional context. For discriminative task, the goal is to rank 100 candidate answers $A_t = \{A_t^1, A_t^2, \cdots, A_t^{100}\}$. For generative task, the goal is to generate an answer in natural language. The task requires the agent to predict the ground truth answer and rank other feasible answers as high as possible.

As illustrated in Fig. 1, we rely on Faster-RCNN (Ren et al., 2015) to extract features corresponding to salient image regions (Anderson et al., 2018). The vision feature of image I is represented as $F_I \in R^{n_v \times d_v}$, where $n_v = 36$ being the number of object-like region proposals in the image and $d_v = 2048$ being the dimension of the feature vector. Q_t and each item in H is padded or truncated to the same length d_l. Thus, each sentence S is represented as $F_S \in R^{d_l \times d_e}$, where d_e being the dimension of the word embedding. To facilitate further discussion, we denote d_h as the dimension of the hidden state throughout this section.

3.1 Visual Dialog as Visual-Linguistic Vector Sequence

Dense Co-Attention Network (DCN) (Nguyen and Okatani, 2018) proposes using contents in sub-grids of a convolutional neuron network as visual region features. However, we turn to use Faster R-CNN proposals (Ren et al., 2015; Anderson et al., 2018) because people usually talk about objects in their conversations, so Faster R-CNN proposals better suit for the purpose of object identification. Given an image I with vision feature $F_I \in R^{n_v \times d_v}$ and a sentence S with embedding $F_S \in R^{d_l \times d_e}$, we define $DCN(I, S) \in R^{d_h}$ the Dense Co-attention (Nguyen and Okatani, 2018) representation of I and S. We define an instance of t round visual dialog by a tuple $D = (I, H_t, Q_t)$. Using DCN, we convert dialog history H_t into the visual-linguistic vector sequence $\widehat{H}_t$ as:

$$\begin{aligned} &\widehat{C} = DCN(I, C) \\ &\widehat{L}_i = DCN(I, (Q_i, A_i)), i = 1, \cdots, t-1 \quad (1) \\ &\widehat{H}_t = \{\widehat{C}, \widehat{L}_1, \cdots, \widehat{L}_{t-1}\} \end{aligned}$$

Let $\widehat{Q}_t = DCN(I, Q_t)$, the original visual dialog then turns into a new tuple $\widehat{D} = (\widehat{H}_t, \widehat{Q}_t)$ in the joint visual-linguistic representation space. Note that the sequential structure of $\widehat{H}_t$ is exactly the same as that of H_t and image I no longer exists in $\widehat{D}$ as an explicit domain.

To facilitate discussion in section 3.2, we define the question history $\mathcal{Q}_t$ by:

$$\begin{aligned} \widehat{Q}_i &= DCN(I, Q_i), 1 \leq i \leq t \\ \mathcal{Q}_t &= \{\widehat{Q}_1, \cdots, \widehat{Q}_{t-1}, \widehat{Q}_t\} \end{aligned} \tag{2}$$

Note, $\mathcal{Q}_t$ includes the visual-linguistic vector of the query Q_t.

3.2 SeqIPN: Information Propagation Network

As illustrated in Fig. 2, Information Propagation Network is a 2-layer LSTM. After converting the visual dialog into a tuple $\widehat{D} = (\widehat{H}_t, \widehat{Q}_t)$ in the joint visual-linguistic representation space, we apply a LSTM to the visual-linguistic vector sequence $\widehat{H}_t$ and use the hidden state at time t as the summary of visual-linguistic history. Specifically:

$$R_L = LSTM(\widehat{H}_t)[t],\ R_L \in R^{d_h} \tag{3}$$

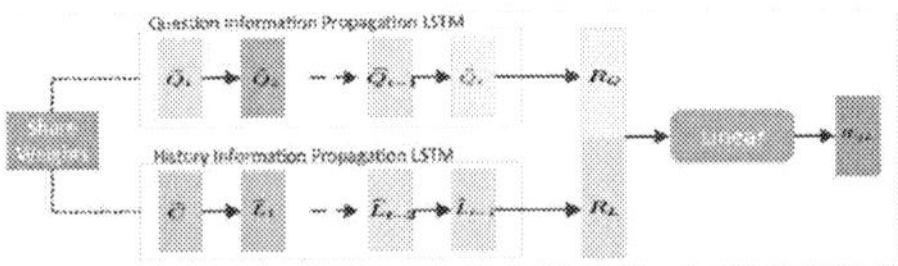

Figure 2: Architecture of Information Propagation Network (SeqIPN)

We apply the same LSTM to question history $\mathcal{Q}_t$ and use $\widehat{Q}_t$'s hidden state R_Q as the context aware query. Experiment shows introducing R_Q can slightly drop the MRR ($< 1\%$) but increase NDCG a lot ($> 1.5\%$). The observation can be explained as R_Q is the query distorted by LSTM, which fools the discriminator and results in the MRR drop. However, the impact is controllable because LSTM's forget gate makes the impact of previous questions gradually fade away along the propagation. On the other hand, R_Q collects more semantic information to broaden the scope of candidate answers, which results in the NDCG increase.

$[R_L, R_Q] \in R^{2d_h}$ is linearly projected to $R_{QL} \in R^{d_h}$ as the final representation of $\widehat{D}$. R_{QL} is fed into the decoder to predict answer.

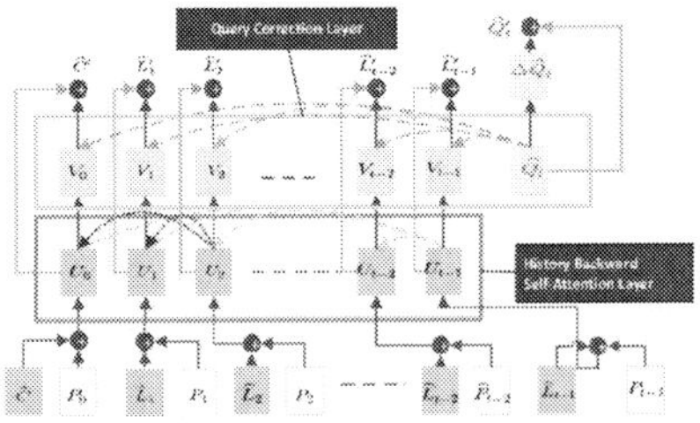

Figure 3: Conceptual architecture of Multistep Reasoning Network (SeqMRN).

3.3 SeqMRN: Multi-step Reasoning Network

Transformer (Vaswani et al., 2017) was originally developed for sequence to sequence task using an encoder-decoder architecture.In this work, we modify Transformer's encoder by replacing its self-attention with the decoder's masked self-attention, while keeping other modules unchanged. We focus on the modifications to enable multi-step reasoning via Transformer. For simplicity, we define three functions $Query(), Key()$, and $Value()$. Given a vector $\boldsymbol{v} \in R^{d_h}$, $Query(\boldsymbol{v}), Key(\boldsymbol{v})$, and $Value(\boldsymbol{v})$ are vectors in R^{d_h} and represent $\boldsymbol{v}$'s query, key, and value described in (Vaswani et al., 2017) respectively.

Fig. 3 is a conceptual architecture of the proposed Multi-step Reasoning Network(SeqMRN). $\{P_0, \cdots, P_{t-1}\}$ are position features defined in (Vaswani et al., 2017). Given dialog tuple $\widehat{D} = (\widehat{H}_t, \widehat{Q}_t)$, the position aware visual-linguistic sequence $\mathcal{U}_t$ is defined by:

$$\begin{aligned} \mathcal{U}_t &= \{U_0, U_1, \cdots, U_{t-1}\} \\ U_0 &= \widehat{C} + P_0 \\ U_i &= \widehat{L}_i + P_i,\ 1 \leq i \leq t-1 \end{aligned} \tag{4}$$

3.3.1 History Backward Self-Attention Layer

As illustrated in Fig. 3, this layer applies masked self-attention within the position aware sequence $\mathcal{U}_t$. This layer allows a single dialog round to gather relevant information from **previous** conversations and embed the information into its own representation.

Specifically, for $U_i, 0 \leq i \leq t-1$, its attention logits with respect to all the other rounds of dialog is defined by:

$$\boldsymbol{\tau}^i : \tau^i_j = \begin{cases} Key(U_j)^T Query(U_i) & j \leq i \\ -\infty & i < j \end{cases} \tag{5}$$

where $\boldsymbol{\tau}^i \in R^t$. Then, the context aware visual-linguistic sequence $\mathcal{V}_t$ is defined by:

$$\boldsymbol{w}^i = softmax(\boldsymbol{\tau}^i/\sqrt{d_h}),\ \boldsymbol{w}^i \in R^t$$
$$\mathcal{V}_t = \{V_0, \cdots, V_{t-1}\} : V_i = \sum_{j=0}^{t-1} \boldsymbol{w}^i[j] \cdot U_j \tag{6}$$

3.3.2 Query Correction Layer

In this layer, the query $\widehat{Q}_t$ renews its knowledge about the context based on $\mathcal{V}_t$. The attention weights reflect how $\widehat{Q}_t$ distributes its focus over $\mathcal{V}_t$, which enables reasoning across the dialog history.

Specifically, the query's attention logits with respect to $\mathcal{V}_t$ is defined by:

$$\boldsymbol{u} : u_j = Key(V_j)^T Query(\widehat{Q}_t)/\sqrt{d_h} \quad 0 \le j \le t-1 \tag{7}$$

However, we don't want history information in $\mathcal{V}_t$ to overpower the query's own semantic meaning, thus we augment $\widehat{Q}_t$ by self-attention weight u_q:

$$u_q = Key(\widehat{Q}_t)^T Query(\widehat{Q}_t)/\sqrt{d_h} \tag{8}$$

Then, the query's correction $\triangle\widehat{Q}_t$ is defined as:

$$\boldsymbol{w} = softmax([\boldsymbol{u}; u_q]), \boldsymbol{w} \in R^{t+1}$$
$$\triangle\widehat{Q}_t = \sum_{i=0}^{t-1} w_i V_i + w_t \widehat{Q}_t \tag{9}$$

Note that Question Correction Layer keeps $\mathcal{V}_t$ unchanged. Contrary to SeqIPN, we don't use question history $\mathcal{Q}_t$ in SeqMRN because attention mechanism can make $\widehat{Q}_t$ indistinguishable from other questions in $\mathcal{Q}_t$.

3.3.3 Multi-step Reasoning

History Backward Self-Attention Layer and Question Correction Layer form the building blocks of our proposed Multi-step Reasoning Network. As illustrated in Fig. 3, residual connection is used.

$$\widehat{Q}'_t = \widehat{Q}_t + \triangle\widehat{Q}_t$$
$$\widehat{C}' = V_0 + U_0 \tag{10}$$
$$\widehat{L}'_i = V_i + U_i, 1 \le i \le t-1$$

where the results $\widehat{Q}'_t$, $\widehat{C}'$ and $\widehat{L}'_t$ are vectors in R^{d_h}.

We have refined the dialog tuple $\widehat{D} = (\widehat{H}_t, \widehat{Q}_t)$ to be a new tuple $\widehat{D}' = (\widehat{H}'_t, \widehat{Q}'_t)$, where $\widehat{H}'_t = \{\widehat{C}', \widehat{L}'_1, \cdots, \widehat{L}'_{t-1}\}$. Members in $\widehat{D}'$ are more environment aware than their corresponding members in $\widehat{D}$. We achieve multistep reasoning by stacking several such building blocks to progressively refine $\widehat{D}$. We consider $\widehat{L}'_{t-1}$ of the last block as the summary of dialog history and consider $\widehat{Q}'_t$ of the last block as the context aware query. We project $[\widehat{Q}'_t; \widehat{L}'_{t-1}]$ to $R_{QL} \in R^{d_h}$ as the final representation of $\widehat{D}$.

3.4 Decoder Module

3.4.1 Discriminative Decoder

For each candidate anwer $A_t^j \in A_t$, a LSTM is applied to A_t^j to obtain its representation $R_j \in R^{d_h}$. The score of A_t^j is defined by $s_j = R_j^T R_{QL}$. Like (Guo et al., 2019), we optimize the N-pair loss (Sohn, 2016):

$$\mathcal{L}_D = log(\sum_{j=1}^{100} exp\frac{s_j - s_{gt}}{\tau}) \tag{11}$$

where s_{gt} is the score of the ground truth answer, and we set $\tau = 0.25$.

3.4.2 Generative Decoder

Inspired by attention based NMT (Luong et al., 2015), we develop an attention based decoder. The decoder is a LSTM initialized by R_{QL}. At time t, we compute similarity weights between current hidden state and the hidden states of previous timestamps instead of directly using the hidden state to generate the distribution over vocabulary. Then, the distribution is generated based on the weighted sum of hidden states.

3.5 Reweighting Method in Fine-tuning with Dense Annotations

VisDial v1.0 training dataset provides a subset named *dense annotations*[3] which contains 2K dialog instances. For each instance in *dense annotations*, two human annotators assign each of its candidate answer with a relevance score based on the ground-truth answer. (Qi et al., 2019b) finetunes with *dense annotations* using a generalized cross entropy loss:

$$\mathcal{L}_G = -\sum_{j=1}^{100} y_j log(softmax(\boldsymbol{s})[j]) \tag{12}$$

where $\boldsymbol{s}$ is the score vector of candidate answers, y_j is the relevance score label of the jth candidate answer. However, blindly optimizing this objective will significantly hurt non-NDGC metrics.

To mitigate this issue, we propose a reweighting method to make the fine-tuning process aware of the importance of the ground truth answer. Specifically, we update the relevance label $\boldsymbol{y}$ by:

$$y_i' = \begin{cases} \frac{y_i+2}{3}, & i = index_{gt} \\ \frac{y_i}{3}, & otherwise \end{cases} \tag{13}$$

where $index_{gt}$ is the index of the ground truth answer.

4 Experiments

Using the VisDial v1.0 dataset, we experiment with 4 types of SeqDiaN: SeqIPN with GloVe Embedding (Pennington et al., 2014) (SeqIPN-GE), SeqIPN with DistilBert Embedding (Sanh et al., 2019) (SeqIPN-DE), SeqMRN with GloVe Embedding (SeqMRN-GE) and SeqMRN with DistilBert Embedding (SeqMRN-DE). For each type, we consider both discriminative and generative models. We trained Dense Symmetric Co-Attention Network (Nguyen and Okatani, 2018) from scratch. We use NDCG[1], MRR[2], recall (R@1, 5, 10), and mean rank to evaluate the models' performance.

In discriminative task, the model ranks the 100 candidate answers based on discriminative score, which is defined as the dot product similarity between the representation of dialogue and that of candidate answer.

In training and evaluation phases, to simplify the framework, the generative task is to rank the 100 candidate answers too. Given a candidate answer A, its generative score is defined as $\frac{lld_A}{\sqrt{|A|}}$, where lld_A is the answer's log-likelihood and $|A|$ is the answer's length. Based on generative score, the rank of 100 candidate answers is well defined, as well as the sparse metric MRR and Recall. However, in inference phase, we obtain the answer via distribution over vocabulary and beam search at every step as usual.

4.1 Quantitative Results

4.1.1 Model Comparison

We compare the performance between SeqDialN models of different configurations. We use Memory Network (MN) (Das et al., 2017), History-Conditioned Image Attentive Encoder (HCIAE)(Lu et al., 2017), Sequential Co-Attention Model (CoAtt)(Wu et al., 2018) and ReDAN (Gan et al., 2019) as baselines in this study because published work (Gan et al., 2019) reports the performance of these models with both discriminative and generative decoders.

Model	NDCG↑	MRR↑	R@1↑	R@5↑	R@10↑	Mean↓
MN-D(Das et al., 2017)	55.13	60.42	46.09	78.14	88.05	4.63
HCIAE-D(Lu et al., 2017)	57.65	62.96	48.94	80.50	89.66	4.24
CoAtt-D(Wu et al., 2018)	57.72	62.91	48.86	80.41	89.83	4.21
ReDAN-D(T=1)(Gan et al., 2019)	58.49	63.35	49.47	80.72	90.05	4.19
ReDAN-D(T=2)(Gan et al., 2019)	59.26	63.46	49.61	80.75	89.96	4.15
ReDAN-D(T=3)(Gan et al., 2019)	59.32	**64.21**	50.60	81.39	90.26	4.05
SeqIPN-GE-D	58.44	58.74	44.87	75.49	85.30	5.56
SeqIPN-DE-D	58.18	59.49	45.58	76.08	86.40	5.15
SeqMRN-GE-D	59.73	61.32	47.59	78.03	87.04	5.08
SeqMRN-DE-D	**60.17**	57.98	44.46	74.16	84.50	5.86
Model	**NDCG↑**	**MRR↑**	**R@1↑**	**R@5↑**	**R@10↑**	**Mean↓**
MN-G(Das et al., 2017)	56.99	47.83	38.01	57.49	64.08	18.76
HCIAE-G(Lu et al., 2017)	59.70	49.07	39.72	58.23	64.73	18.43
CoAtt-G(Wu et al., 2018)	59.24	49.64	40.09	59.37	65.92	17.86
ReDAN-G(T=1)(Gan et al., 2019)	59.41	49.60	39.95	59.32	65.97	17.79
ReDAN-G(T=2)(Gan et al., 2019)	60.11	49.96	40.36	59.72	66.57	17.53
ReDAN-G(T=3)(Gan et al., 2019)	60.47	**50.02**	40.27	59.93	66.78	17.40
SeqIPN-GE-G	63.30	48.77	38.36	59.29	68.24	13.36
SeqIPN-DE-G	60.72	47.86	38.16	57.08	64.89	15.27
SeqMRN-GE-G	63.01	49.22	38.75	59.62	68.47	13.00
SeqMRN-DE-G	**64.15**	49.72	39.33	60.17	69.73	12.37

Table 1: Performance of SeqDialN models on VisDial v1.0 validation set. Left: discriminative SeqDialN. Right: generative SeqDialN. ↑ indicates higher is better. ↓ indicates lower is better.

In Table 1, "-D" stands for discriminative model and "-G" for generative model. SeqMRN-DE-D and SeqMRN-DE-G outperform all baselines and other SeqDialN models on NDCG[1] for both discriminative and generative cases. Especially for the generative case, SeqMRN-DE-G outperforms the second place ReDAN-G(T=3) by $> 3.6\%$ NDCG. Meanwhile, the MRR difference between ReDAN-G(T=3) and SeqMRN-DE-G is merely 0.3, SeqMRN-DE-G still outperforms ReDAN-G(T=3) on average performance. We arrive at the conclusion that SeqMRN-DE-G is a new state-of-the-art **generative** visual dialog model.

SeqIPN with GloVe Embedding is the simplest SeqDialN. However, SeqIPN-GE-D achieves better NDCG than well-known discriminative baselines such as MN-D, HCIAE-D and CoAtt-D. In addition, SeqIPN-GE-G even outperforms all generative baselines on NDCG. The model simplicity and performance gain together validate the merit of considering visual dialog as a visual-linguistic vector sequence.

4.1.2 Ensemble SeqDialN Analysis

In this section, we add VisDial-BERT(Murahari et al., 2019) as a baseline. At this stage, the comparison is conducted between models trained **without** *dense annotation*[3].

As discriminative SeqDialN and generative SeqDialN rank the 100 candidate answers via discriminative score and generative score respectively, the uniform task definition facilitates the ensemble process. Given a set of SeqDialN models, we sim-

Model	NDCG↑	MRR↑	R@1↑	R@5↑	R@10↑	Mean↓
ReDAN: 4 Dis. + 4 Gen.(Gan et al., 2019)	65.13	54.19	42.92	66.25	74.88	8.74
ReDAN+ (Diverse Ens.)(Gan et al., 2019)	67.12	56.77	44.65	69.47	79.90	5.96
VisDial-BERT: w/L-only(Murahari et al., 2019)	62.64	67.86	54.54	84.34	92.36	3.44
VisDial-BERT: w/CC+VQA(Murahari et al., 2019)	64.94	**69.10**	55.88	85.50	93.29	3.25
SeqDialN: 4 Dis.	64.66	64.67	51.74	80.49	89.10	4.34
SeqDialN: 4 Gen.	65.55	50.69	40.61	60.50	69.35	12.94
SeqMRN-DE-D + SeqIPN-GE-G	67.26	56.41	44.44	69.67	79.51	7.44
SeqDialN: 4 Dis + 4 Gen	**68.61**	58.11	45.94	71.66	81.22	6.73

Table 2: Comparison of SeqDialN to state-of-the-art visual dialog models on VisDial v1.0 validation set.

ply average scores of all models to obtain the new score to rank the 100 candidate answers and evaluate the metrics based on the new rank.

In Table 2, "SeqDialN: 4 Dis." is an ensemble of the 4 types of discriminative SeqDialN models while "SeqDialN: 4 Gen." an ensemble of the 4 types of generative SeqDialN models. Our best model outperforms ReDAN and ReDAN+ by significant margin on both NDCG ($>$ 1.5%) and MRR ($>$ 1%). Our model also outperforms VisDial-BERT(Murahari et al., 2019) by $>$ 3.5% NDCG despite the latter being pretrained on several large-scale datasets.

VisDial-BERT(Murahari et al., 2019) has roughly 250M parameters, the configuration "w/L-only" is trained only on VisDial v1.0-train set, which is more suitable to compare with SeqDialN. SeqIPN-GE-G has less than 69M parameters but it can outperform "w/L-only" on NDCG ($>$ 0.5%). The ensemble configuration (SeqMRN-DE-D + SeqIPN-GE-G) has roughly the same parameters as "w/L-only" and it further outperforms "w/L-only" by $>$ 4% NDCG. Actually, it even outperforms "w/CC+VQA" by $>$ 2% NDCG. The advantage of VisDial-BERT (Murahari et al., 2019) is the high MRR score it achieves.

We also evaluate SeqDialN on VisDial v1.0 test-std set. Table 3 shows the comparison between our model and state-of-the-art visual dialog models trained **without** *dense annotations*[3]. SeqDialN achieves state-of-the-art performance on NDCG, even a single generative SeqDialN can outperform most previous work on that metric. At present, SeqDialN doesn't perform well on MRR, which is partly because it is hard for generative models to produce exactly the same answer as the ground truth, even when conditioned on the same semantic scenarios.

4.1.3 Fine-tuning with Dense Annotations

We fine-tune discriminative SeqDialN with *dense annotations*[3]. Table 4 shows the proposed reweighting method greatly mitigates performance drop in our fine-tuning experiment. We list the

Model	NDCG↑	MRR↑	R@1^	R@5↑	R@10↑	Mean↓
GNN(Zheng et al., 2019)	52.82	61.37	47.33	77.98	87.83	4.57
CorefNMN(Kottur et al., 2018)	54.70	61.50	47.55	78.10	88.80	4.40
RvA(Niu et al., 2019)	55.59	63.03	49.03	80.40	89.83	4.18
DualVD(Jiang et al., 2020)	56.32	63.23	49.25	80.23	89.70	4.11
HACAN(Yang et al., 2019)	57.17	64.22	50.88	80.63	89.45	4.20
SN(Guo et al., 2019)	57.32	62.20	47.90	80.43	89.95	4.17
SN†(Guo et al., 2019)	57.88	63.42	49.30	80.77	90.68	3.97
NMN(Kottur et al., 2018)	58.10	58.80	44.15	76.88	86.88	4.81
DAN(Kang et al., 2019)	57.59	63.20	49.63	79.75	89.35	4.30
DAN†(Kang et al., 2019)	59.36	64.92	51.28	81.60	90.88	3.92
ReDAN†(Gan et al., 2019)	61.86	53.13	41.38	66.07	74.50	8.91
VisDial-BERT: w/CC+VQA(Murahari et al., 2019)	63.87	**67.50**	53.85	84.68	93.25	3.32
ReDAN+ †(Gan et al., 2019)	64.47	53.74	42.45	64.68	75.68	6.64
SeqMRN-DE-G (single)	62.54	48.63	37.90	59.95	69.03	12.47
SeqDialN: 4 Gen.	63.78	49.98	39.50	60.48	69.27	12.97
SeqMRN-DE-D + SeqIPN-GE-G	65.56	55.66	43.23	69.15	79.93	7.44
SeqDialN: 4 Dis. + 4 Gen.	**66.91**	56.84	44.30	70.85	80.93	6.87

Table 3: Comparison of SeqDialN to state-of-the-art visual dialog models on VisDial v1.0 test-std set. ↑ indicates higher is better. ↓ indicates lower is better. † denotes ensembles. All models have been trained **without** *dense annotations*[3]

Model	NDCG↑	MRR↑	R@1↑	R@5↑	R@10↑	Mean↓
SeqMRN-DE-D	70.23	38.33	23.04	55.17	71.51	9.29
SeqMRN-DE-D*	**70.72**	**53.59**	**42.35**	**65.05**	**77.73**	**7.27**
SeqIPN-DE-D	69.12	37.93	23.10	53.83	69.84	9.70
SeqIPN-DE-D*	**69.68**	**52.2**	**41.13**	**62.94**	**75.54**	**7.78**

Table 4: Using reweighting method to lessen performance drop on VisDial v1.0 validate set. * denotes fine-tuning with reweighting method.

fine-tuning statistics for one SeqIPN and one SeqMRN as representatives.

Table 5 compares SeqDialN with state-of-the-art models trained **with** *dense annotations*. On VisDial v1.0 test-std set, our model achieves comparable NDCG as others while outperforming them on MRR. It is interesting to note that VisDial-BERT (Murahari et al., 2019) outperforms our model on MMR by $>$ 5% before fine-tuning. After fine-tuning however, our model outperforms it on MRR by nearly 5%. This observation validates the effectiveness of the reweighting method in preserving a model's overall performance when trained with *dense annotations*[3]. In addition, we find fine-tuning generative models don't improve NDCG as much as discriminative case.

4.2 Ablation Study

We note SeqMRN yeilds the best performance in the single model comparison, we conduct further experiments to analyze contribution of its components. For simplicity, We train discriminative SeqMRN in different configurations to 13 epochs without fine-tuning.

Model	NDCG↑	MRR↑	R@1^	R@5↑	R@10↑	Mean↓
MReal-BDAI†(Qi et al., 2019b)	74.02	52.62	40.03	68.85	79.15	6.76
P1P2†(Qi et al., 2019a)	**74.91**	49.13	36.68	62.96	78.55	7.03
VisDial-BERT: w/CC+VQA(Murahari et al., 2019)	74.47	50.74	37.95	64.13	80.00	6.28
SeqDialN: 4 Dis.	72.41	**55.11**	43.23	67.65	79.77	6.55

Table 5: Comparison of SeqDialN to state-of-the-art visual dialog models on VisDial v1.0 test-std set. All models have been trained **with** *dense annotations*[3]

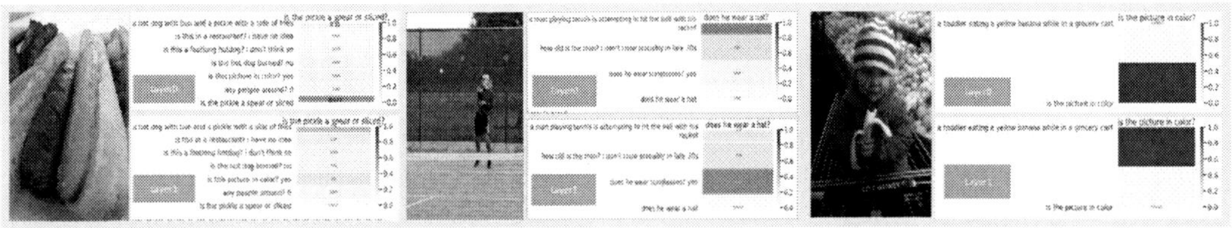

Figure 4: SeqMRN: learn to reason in attention stacks. Color strength indicates attention weight, the darker highlighting the higher attention paid.

4.2.1 Effectiveness of visual-linguistic joint representation

We close the modules in DCN (Nguyen and Okatani, 2018) which apply cross modality attention between vision and language features. Thus the two modalities are fused in a simple summation way in DCN.

In this configuration, the two modalities won't be aware of the existence of each other until the masked self-attention step in Transformer. Item named SeqMRN-DE-D-LateFusion in Table 6 shows its performance, which drops on all metrics. Especially on NDCG, it drops 3.14%.

This experiment demonstrates the positive impact of our early fusion, as we say, the visual-linguistic joint representation. Further analysis reveals early fusion helps enhance the model's capability to filter out irrelevant answers. We find that each image in *dense annotation*[3] of VisDial v1.0 has on average 12.68 answers with non-zero relevant-score. On average, We find SeqMRN-DE-D-LateFusion ranks 5.58 (44.00%) zero relevant-score answers into the top 12.68 predictions, while this number of SeqMRN-DE-D is 5.36 (42.27%).

Model	NDCG↑	MRR↑	R@1↑	R@5↑	R@10↑	Mean↓
SeqMRN-DE-D	**59.49**	**61.53**	**47.68**	**78.67**	**87.88**	**4.79**
SeqMRN-DE-D-NoQC	59.08	61.25	47.34	78.58	87.72	4.86
SeqMRN-DE-D-LateFusion	56.35	61.14	47.11	78.29	87.48	4.83

Table 6: Ablation Study on VisDial v1.0 validation set.

4.2.2 Effectiveness of Query Correction Layer

In Table 6, the item SeqMRN-DE-D-NoQC shows the performance of the configuration by closing the Query Correction Layer illustrated in section 3.3.2. We see that performance drops on all metrics as well.

We find Query Correction Layer enhances the model's capability to integrate history information based on the given query, thus it helps answer the query which requires dialog history. (Agarwal et al., 2020) points out that not all questions in VisDial v1.0 dataset need dialogue history to answer. They have proposed a dataset named VisDialConv(Agarwal et al., 2020), which is actually a subset of VisDial v1.0 validation dataset including 97 instances which answer needs the reference to dialog history.

We run both SeqMRN-DE-D and SeqMRN-DE-D-NoQC on VisDialConv dataset. SeqMRN-DE-D gets 51.11% NDCG and SeqMRN-DE-D-NoQC gets 50.22%, the former has 1.77% relative improvement. As illustrated in Figure 5, the score distribution of the two models are similar, which concentrates in range [0.2, 0.9]. However, SeqMRN-DE-D scores significantly more instances in range [0.6, 0.7] than the other. SeqMRN-DE-D also scores less instances in the low range [0.0, 0.2] but scores more instances in the high range [0.8, 1]. These observations support the conclusion that Query Correction Layer helps answer history related questions.

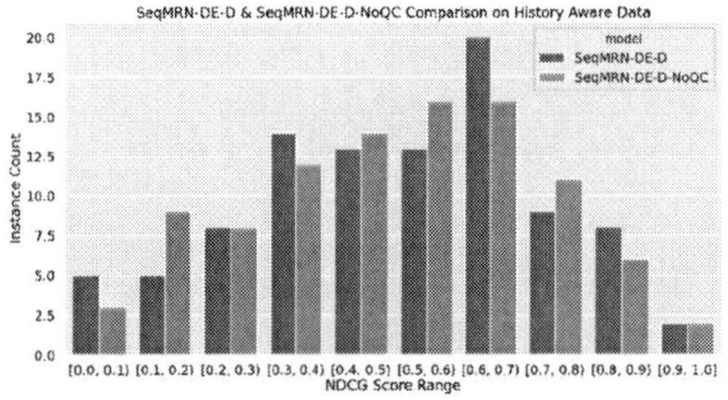

Figure 5: NDCG Distribution Comparison on VisDialConv

4.3 Qualitative Analysis

We use the 3 examples in Fig. 4 to illustrate SeqMRN's reasoning capability. On the left, the question asks: *"Is the pickle a spear or sliced?"*. In SeqMRN's first reasoning block (layer0), the question focus on preserving its own information (its self attention weight being 0.671). However, in the second reasoning block (layer1), the question pays more attention to the first round which has *"pickle"* related information. This example demonstrates the attention gets the right "correction" in Query Correction Layer.

In the middle, the question asks: *"Does he wear a hat?"* Due to the word *"he"*, in SeqMRN's first reasoning block (layer0), the attention is on the caption (0.69), which has words *"man"* and *"his"*. However, in the second reasoning block (layer1), the attention turns to the round *"does he wear sunglasses? yes"*. Note the semantic similarity between *"wear sunglasses"* and *"wear hat"* (they are both wearables on the head). This example shows the attention making decisions based upon refined knowledge about the context in a deeper stack.

On the right, the question asks: *"Is the picture in color?"* In SeqMRN's first reasoning block, the attention focuses on itself. However, in the second reasoning block, the attention switches to the caption. Most likely in deeper stack, it make the inference like: *only a color image makes a banana look "yellow"*.

5 Conclusion

We presented Sequential Visual Dialog Network (SeqDialN) based on a novel idea that treats dialog rounds as a visual-linguistic vector sequence. We explore both discriminative and generative models and set up a new state-of-the-art **generative** visual dialog model. Even though our model is trained only on VisDial v1.0 dataset, it achieves competitive performance against other models trained on much larger vision-language datasets, which facilitates its deployment in industrial environment.

References

Shubham Agarwal, Trung Bui, Joon-Young Lee, Ioannis Konstas, and Verena Rieser. 2020. History for visual dialog: Do we really need it? *arXiv preprint arXiv:2005.07493*.

Peter Anderson, Xiaodong He, Chris Buehler, Damien Teney, Mark Johnson, Stephen Gould, and Lei Zhang. 2018. Bottom-up and top-down attention for image captioning and visual question answering. In *Proceedings of the IEEE conference on computer vision and pattern recognition*, pages 6077–6086.

Abhishek Das, Satwik Kottur, Khushi Gupta, Avi Singh, Deshraj Yadav, José MF Moura, Devi Parikh, and Dhruv Batra. 2017. Visual dialog. In *Proceedings of the IEEE Conference on Computer Vision and Pattern Recognition*, pages 326–335.

Zhe Gan, Yu Cheng, Ahmed Kholy, Linjie Li, Jingjing Liu, and Jianfeng Gao. 2019. Multi-step reasoning via recurrent dual attention for visual dialog. In *Proceedings of the 57th Annual Meeting of the Association for Computational Linguistics*, pages 6463–6474.

Dalu Guo, Chang Xu, and Dacheng Tao. 2019. Image-question-answer synergistic network for visual dialog. In *Proceedings of the IEEE Conference on Computer Vision and Pattern Recognition*, pages 10434–10443.

Sepp Hochreiter and Jürgen Schmidhuber. 1997. Long short-term memory. *Neural computation*, 9(8):1735–1780.

X. Jiang, J. Yu, Z. Qin, Y. Zhuang, X. Zhang, Y. Hu, and Q. Wu. 2020. Dualvd: An adaptive dual encoding model for deep visual understanding in visual dialogue. *AAAI*.

Gi-Cheon Kang, Jaeseo Lim, and Byoung-Tak Zhang. 2019. Dual attention networks for visual reference resolution in visual dialog. In *Proceedings of the 2019 Conference on Empirical Methods in Natural Language Processing and the 9th International Joint Conference on Natural Language Processing (EMNLP-IJCNLP)*, pages 2024–2033.

Satwik Kottur, José MF Moura, Devi Parikh, Dhruv Batra, and Marcus Rohrbach. 2018. Visual coreference resolution in visual dialog using neural module networks. In *Proceedings of the European Conference on Computer Vision (ECCV)*, pages 153–169.

Jiasen Lu, Dhruv Batra, Devi Parikh, and Stefan Lee. 2019. Vilbert: Pretraining task-agnostic visiolinguistic representations for vision-and-language tasks. In *Advances in Neural Information Processing Systems*, pages 13–23.

Jiasen Lu, Anitha Kannan, Jianwei Yang, Devi Parikh, and Dhruv Batra. 2017. Best of both worlds: Transferring knowledge from discriminative learning to a generative visual dialog model. In *Advances in Neural Information Processing Systems*, pages 314–324.

Jiasen Lu, Jianwei Yang, Dhruv Batra, and Devi Parikh. 2016. Hierarchical question-image co-attention for visual question answering. In *Advances in neural information processing systems*, pages 289–297.

Minh-Thang Luong, Hieu Pham, and Christopher D Manning. 2015. Effective approaches to attention-based neural machine translation. In *Proceedings of the 2015 Conference on Empirical Methods in Natural Language Processing*, pages 1412–1421.

Vishvak Murahari, Dhruv Batra, Devi Parikh, and Abhishek Das. 2019. Large-scale pretraining for visual dialog: A simple state-of-the-art baseline. *arXiv preprint arXiv:1912.02379*.

Duy-Kien Nguyen and Takayuki Okatani. 2018. Improved fusion of visual and language representations by dense symmetric co-attention for visual question answering. In *Proceedings of the IEEE Conference on Computer Vision and Pattern Recognition*, pages 6087–6096.

Yulei Niu, Hanwang Zhang, Manli Zhang, Jianhong Zhang, Zhiwu Lu, and Ji-Rong Wen. 2019. Recursive visual attention in visual dialog. *Proceedings of the IEEE Conference on Computer Vision and Pattern Recognition*, pages 6679–6688.

Jeffrey Pennington, Richard Socher, and Christopher D Manning. 2014. Glove: Global vectors for word representation. In *Proceedings of the 2014 conference on empirical methods in natural language processing (EMNLP)*, pages 1532–1543.

Jiaxin Qi, Yulei Niu, Jianqiang Huang, and Hanwang Zhang. 2019a. Two causal principles for improving visual dialog.

Jiaxin Qi, Yulei Niu, Hanwang Zhang, Jianqiang Huang, Xian-Sheng Hua, and Ji-Rong Wen. 2019b. Learning to answer: Fine-tuning with generalized cross entropy for visual dialog challenge 2019. [Online; accessed November 12, 2019].

Shaoqing Ren, Kaiming He, Ross Girshick, and Jian Sun. 2015. Faster r-cnn: Towards real-time object detection with region proposal networks. In *Advances in neural information processing systems*, pages 91–99.

Victor Sanh, Lysandre Debut, Julien Chaumond, and Thomas Wolf. 2019. Distilbert, a distilled version of bert: smaller, faster, cheaper and lighter. In *NeurIPS EMC^2 Workshop*.

Kihyuk Sohn. 2016. Improved deep metric learning with multi-class n-pair loss objective. In *Advances in Neural Information Processing Systems*, pages 1857–1865.

Ashish Vaswani, Noam Shazeer, Niki Parmar, Jakob Uszkoreit, Llion Jones, Aidan N Gomez, Łukasz Kaiser, and Illia Polosukhin. 2017. Attention is all you need. In *Advances in neural information processing systems*, pages 5998–6008.

Qi Wu, Peng Wang, Chunhua Shen, Ian Reid, and Anton Van Den Hengel. 2018. Are you talking to me? reasoned visual dialog generation through adversarial learning. In *Proceedings of the IEEE Conference on Computer Vision and Pattern Recognition*, pages 6106–6115.

Tianhao Yang, Zheng-Jun Zha, and Hanwang Zhang. 2019. Making history matter: Gold-critic sequence training for visual dialog. *CoRR*, abs/1902.09326.

Zichao Yang, Xiaodong He, Jianfeng Gao, Li Deng, and Alex Smola. 2016. Stacked attention networks for image question answering. In *Proceedings of the IEEE conference on computer vision and pattern recognition*, pages 21–29.

Zhou Yu, Jun Yu, Jianping Fan, and Dacheng Tao. 2017. Multi-modal factorized bilinear pooling with co-attention learning for visual question answering. In *Proceedings of the IEEE international conference on computer vision*, pages 1821–1830.

Zilong Zheng, Wenguan Wang, Siyuan Qi, and Song-Chun Zhu. 2019. Reasoning visual dialogs with structural and partial observations. *Proceedings of the IEEE Conference on Computer Vision and Pattern Recognition*, pages 6669–6678.

A Template-guided Hybrid Pointer Network for Knowledge-based Task-oriented Dialogue Systems

Dingmin Wang[1], Ziyao Chen[2], Wanwei He[3], Li Zhong[4], Yunzhe Tao[5], Min Yang[3]
[1]Department of Computer Science, University of Oxford, UK
[2]Tencent, Guangzhou, China
[3]Shenzhen Institutes of Advanced Technology, Chinese Academy of Sciences, China
[4]ByteDance, Shenzhen, China, [5]Amazon Web Services, Seattle, USA
dingmin.wang@cs.ox.ac.uk yateschen@tencent.com yunzhet@amazon.com
{ww.he,min.yang}@siat.ac.cn zhongli.reginald@bytedance.com

Abstract

Most existing neural network based task-oriented dialogue systems follow *encoder-decoder* paradigm, where the decoder purely depends on the source texts to generate a sequence of words, usually suffering from instability and poor readability. Inspired by the traditional template-based generation approaches, we propose a template-guided hybrid pointer network for the knowledge-based task-oriented dialogue system, which retrieves several potentially relevant answers from a pre-constructed domain-specific conversational repository as guidance answers, and incorporates the guidance answers into both the encoding and decoding processes. Specifically, we design a memory pointer network model with a gating mechanism to fully exploit the semantic correlation between the retrieved answers and the ground-truth response. We evaluate our model on four widely used task-oriented datasets, including one simulated and three manually created datasets. The experimental results demonstrate that the proposed model achieves significantly better performance than the state-of-the-art methods over different automatic evaluation metrics [1].

1 Introduction

Task oriented dialogue systems have attracted increasing attention recently due to broad applications such as reserving restaurants and booking flights. Conventional task-oriented dialogue systems are mainly implemented by rule-based methods (Lemon et al., 2006; Wang and Lemon, 2013), which rely heavily on the hand-crafted features, establishing significant barriers for adapting the dialogue systems to new domains. Motivated by the great success of deep learning in various NLP tasks, the neural network based methods (Bordes et al., 2017; Eric and Manning, 2017; Madotto et al., 2018) have dominated the study since these methods can be trained in an end-to-end manner and scaled to different domains.

Despite the remarkable progress of previous studies, the performance of task-oriented dialogue systems is still far from satisfactory. On one hand, due to the exposure bias problem (Ranzato et al., 2016), the neural network based models, e.g., the sequence to sequence models (seq2seq), tend to accumulate errors with increasing length of the generation. Concretely, the first several generated words can be reasonable, while the quality of the generated sequence deteriorates quickly once the decoder produces a "bad" word. On the other hand, as shown in previous works (Cao et al., 2018; Madotto et al., 2018), the Seq2Seq models are likely to generate non-committal or similar responses that often involve high-frequency words or phrases. These responses are usually of low informativeness or readability. This may be because that arbitrary-length sequences can be generated, and it is not enough for the decoder to be purely based on the source input sentence to generate informative and fluent responses.

We demonstrate empirically that in task-oriented dialogue systems, the responses for the requests with similar types often follow the same sentence structure except that different named entities are used according to the specific dialogue context. Table 1 shows two conversations from real task-oriented dialogues about navigation and weather. From the navigation case, we can observe that although the two requests are for different destinations, the corresponding responses are similar in sentence structure, replacing "children's health" with "5677_springer_street". For the weather example, it requires the model to first detect the entity "carson" and then query the corresponding information from the knowledge base (KB). After obtaining

[1]https://github.com/wdimmy/THPN

Proceedings of the 1st Workshop on Document-grounded Dialogue and Conversational Question Answering, pages 18–28
August 5–6, 2021. ©2021 Association for Computational Linguistics

Table 1: Two example conversations from real dialogues about navigation and weather.

Navigation		Weather	
User	please give me directions to 5677_spring_street	**User**	what is the temperature of carson on tuesday
Retrieve	q1: direct me to stanford children's health a1: no problem, I will be navigating you to stanford children's health right now	Retrieve	q1: the temperature of new_york on wednesday a1: the temperature in new_york on wednesday will be low_of_80f and high_of_90f
KB		KB	carson: tuesday low_of_20f carson: tuesday high_of_40f
Gold	no problem, I will be navigating you to 5677_spring_street right now	**Gold**	the temperature in carson on tuesday will be low_of_20f and high_of_40f

the returned KB entries, we generate the response by replacing the corresponding entities in the retrieved candidate answer. Therefore, we argue that the golden responses of the requests with similar types can provide a reference point to guide the response generation process and enable to generate high-quality responses for the given requests.

In this paper, we propose a template-guided hybrid pointer network (THPN to generate the response given a user-issued query, in which the domain specific knowledge base (KB) and potentially relevant answers are leveraged as extra input to enrich the input representations of the decoder. Here, *knowledge base* refers to the database to store the relevant and necessary information for supporting the model in accomplishing the given tasks. We follow previous works and use a triple (subject, relation, object) representation. For example, the triple (Starbucks, address, 792 Bedoin St) is an example in KB representing the information related to the Starbucks. Specifically, given a query, we first retrieve top-n answer candidates from a pre-constructed conversational repository with question-answer pairs using BERT (Devlin et al., 2018). Then, we extend memory networks (Sukhbaatar et al., 2015) to incorporate the commonsense knowledge from KB to learn the knowledge-enhanced representations of the dialogue history. Finally, we introduce a gating mechanism to effectively utilize candidate answers and improve the decoding process. The main contributions of this paper can be summarized as follows:

- We propose a hybrid pointer network consisting of entity pointer network (EPN) and pattern pointer network (PPN) to generate informative and relevant responses. EPN copies entity words from dialogue history, and PPN extracts pattern words from retrieved answers.
- We introduce a gating mechanism to learn the semantic correlations between the user-issued query and the retrieved candidate answers, which reduces the "noise" brought by the retrieved answers.
- We evaluate the effectiveness of our model on four benchmark task-oriented dialogue datasets from different domains. Experimental results demonstrate the superiority of our proposed model.

2 Related Work

Task-oriented dialogue systems are mainly studied via two different approaches: pipeline based and end-to-end. Pipeline based models (Williams and Young, 2007; Young et al., 2013) achieve good stability but need domain-specific knowledge and handcrafted labels. End-to-end methods have shown promising results recently and attracted more attention since they are easily adapted to a new domain.

Neural network based dialogue systems can avoid the laborious feature engineering since the neural networks have great ability to learn the latent representations of the input text. However, as revealed by previous studies (Koehn and Knowles, 2017; Cao et al., 2018; He et al., 2019), the performance of the sequence to sequence model deteriorates quickly with the increase of the length of generation. Therefore, how to improve the stability and readability of the neural network models has attracted increasing attention. Eric et al. (2017) proposed a copy augmented Seq2Seq model by copying relevant information directly from the KB information. Madotto et al. (2018) proposed a generative model by employing the multi-hop attention over memories with the idea of pointer network. Wu et al. (2019) proposes a global-to-locally pointer mechanism to effectively utilize the knowledge base information, which improves the quality of the generated response.

Previous proposed neural approaches have shown the importance of external knowledge in the sequence generation (Chen et al., 2017; Zhu et al., 2018; Yang et al., 2019; Zhang et al., 2019; Ding et al., 2019), especially in the task-oriented dialogue systems where an appropriate response usually requires correctly extracting knowledge from the domain-specific or commonsense knowledge base (Madotto et al., 2018; Zhu et al., 2018; Qin et al., 2019). However, it is still under great exploration with regard with the inclusion of external knowledge into the model. Yan et al. (2016); Song et al. (2018) argue that retrieval and generative methods have their own demerits and merits, and they have achieved good performance in the chit-chat response generation by incorporating the retrieved results in the Seq2Seq based models. Zhu et al. (2018) proposed an adversarial training approach, which is enhanced by retrieving some related candidate answers in the neural response generation, and Ghazvininejad et al. (2018) also applies a similar method in the neural conversation model. In addition, in task-oriented dialogue tasks, the copy mechanism (Gulcehre et al., 2016) has also been widely utilized (Eric and Manning, 2017; Madotto et al., 2018), which shows the superiority of generation based methods with copy strategy.

3 Methodology

We build our model based on a seq2seq dialogue generation mode, and the overall architecture is exhibited in Figure 1. Each module will be elaborated in the following subsections.

3.1 Encoder Module

By checking if a word is in the given KB, we divide words into two types: entity words (EW) and non-entity words (NEW). Taking "what is the temperature of carson on tuesday" as an example, all words are NEW except for "carson" and "tuesday".

We represent a multi-turn dialogue as $D = \{(u_i, s_i)\}_{i=1}^{T}$, where T is the number of turns in the dialogue, and u_i and s_i denote the utterances of the user and the system at the ith turn, respectively. KB information is represented as $KB = \{k_1, k_2, \cdots, k_l\}$, where k_i is a tuple and l is the size of KB. Following Madotto et al. (2018), we concatenate the previous dialogue and KB as input. At first turn, input to the decoder is $[u_1; KB]$, the concatenation of first user request and KB. For $i > 1$, previous history dialog information is included, namely, input is supposed to be $[u_1, s_1, \cdots, u_i; KB]$. We define words in the concatenated input as a sequence of tokens $W = \{w_1, w_2, \cdots, w_n\}$, where $w_j \in \{u_1, s_1, \cdots, u_i, KB\}$, n is the number of tokens.

In this paper, we use the memory network (MemNN) proposed in Sukhbaatar et al. (2015) as the encoder module. The memories of MemNN are represented by a set of trainable embedding matrices $M = \{M^1, M^2, \cdots, M^K\}$, where K represents the number of hops and each M^k maps the input into vectors. Different from Sukhbaatar et al. (2015); Madotto et al. (2018), we initialize each M^k with the pre-trained embeddings[2], whose weights are set to be trainable. At hop k, W is mapped to a set of memory vectors, $\{m_1^k, m_2^k, \cdots, m_n^k\}$, where the memory vectors m_i^k of dimension d from M^k is computed by embedding each word in a continuous space, in the simplest case, using an embedding matrix A. A query vector q is used as a reading head, which will loop over K hops and compute the attention weights at hop k for each memory by taking the inner product followed by a softmax function,

$$p_i^k = softmax\left(\left(q^k\right)^T m_i^k\right) \tag{1}$$

where p_i^k is a soft memory selector that decides the memory relevance with respect to the query vector q. The model then gets the memory c^k by the weighted sum over m^{k+1},

$$c^k = \sum_i p_i^k m_i^{k+1} \tag{2}$$

In addition, the query vector is updated for the next hop by $q^{k+1} = q^k + c^k$. In total, we can achieve K hidden states encoded from MemNN, represented as $C = \{c^1, c^2, \cdots, c^K\}$.

Masking NEW in the history dialogue We observe that the ratio of non-entity words in both the history dialogue and the expected response is extremely low. Therefore, to prevent the model from copying non-entity words from the history dialogue, we introduce an array R_h[3] whose elements are zeros and ones, where 0 denotes NEW and 1 for EW. When w_i is pointed to, and if i is the sentinel location or $R_h[i] = 0$, then w_i will not be copied.

[2] https://s3-us-west-1.amazonaws.com/fasttext-vectors/wiki.en.vec.

[3] The length of R_h equals to that of W.

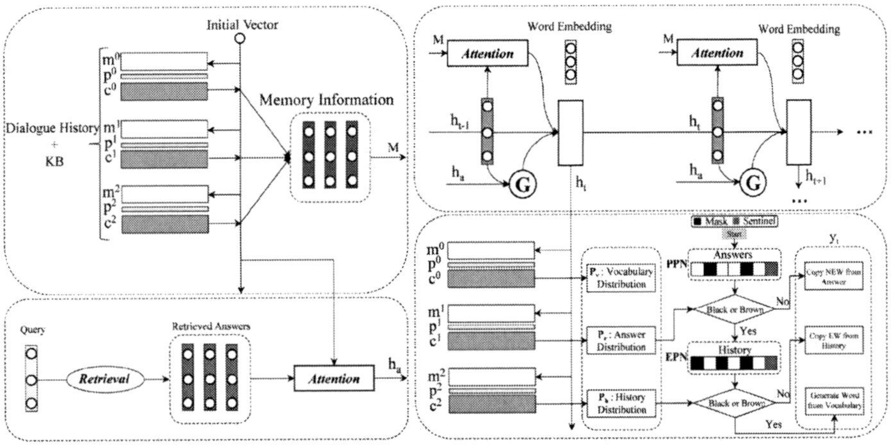

Figure 1: The overall structure of our model. During test time, given a user query q, we retrieve at most 3 similar questions to q using BERT from QA Paris repository, and the corresponding answers are used as our answer templates. The retrieved answers as well as the dialogue history and KB information are then utilized for the response generation. Especially, we utilize the gating mechanism to filter out noise from unrelated retrieval results. Finally, words are generated either from the vocabulary or directly copying from the multi-source information using a hybrid pointer network.

3.2 Retrieval Module

For each dataset, we use the corresponding training data to pre-construct a question-answer repository. In particular, we treat each post-response (u_i and s_i) in a dialogue as a pair of question-answer. To effectively retrieve potentially relevant answers, we adopt a sentence matching based approach, in which each sentence is represented as a dense vector, and the cosine similarity serves as the selection metrics. We have explored several unsupervised text matching methods, such as BM25 (Robertson et al., 2009), Word2Vec (Mikolov et al., 2013b), and BERT (Devlin et al., 2018), and revealed that BERT could achieve the best performance. In addition, based on our preliminary experiments, we observed that the number of retrieved answer candidates have an impact on the model performance, so we define a threshold θ for controlling the number of retrieval answer candidates.

Specifically, for each question in the pre-constructed database, we pre-compute the corresponding sentence embedding using BERT. Then, for each new user-issued query u_q, we embed u_q into u_q^e, and search in the pre-constructed database for the most similar requests based on cosine similarity. The corresponding answers are selected and serve as our answer candidates.

Masking EW in the retrieved answers In real dialogue scenes, the reply's sentence structure might be similar but the involved entities are usually different. To prevent the model from copying these entities, we introduce another array R_r similar to R_h mentioned before. Finally, the retrieved candidate answers are encoded into low-dimension distributed representations, denoted as $AN = \{a_1, a_2, \cdots, a_m\}$, where m is the total number of the words. Moreover, by an interaction between c^K and $AN = \{a_1, a_2, \cdots, a_m\}$, we obtain a dense vector h_a as the representation of the retrieved answers,

$$h_a = W_2 tanh\left(\sum_{i=1}^{m}\left(W_1\left[c^K; a_i\right]\right)\right) \quad (3)$$

3.3 Decoder Module

We first apply Gated Recurrent Unit (GRU) (Chung et al., 2014) to obtain the hidden state h_t,

$$h_t = \text{GRU}\left(\phi^{emb}(y_{t-1}), h_{t-1}^*\right) \quad (4)$$

where $\phi^{emb}(\cdot)$ is an embedding function that maps each token to a fixed-dimensional vector. At the first time step, we use the special symbol "SOS" as y_0 and the initial hidden state $h_0^* = h_a$. h_{t-1}^* consists of three parts, namely, the last hidden state h_{t-1}, the attention over $C = \{c^1, c^2, \cdots, c^K\}$ from the encoder module, denoted as H^c, and H^g, which is calculated by linearly transforming last state h_{t-1} and h_a with a multi-layer perceptron network. We formulate H^c and H^g as follows:

Attention over $\mathbf{C} = \{\mathbf{c}^1, \mathbf{c}^2, \cdots, \mathbf{c}^K\}$ Since MemNN consists of multiple hops, we believe that different hops are relatively independent and have their own semantic meanings over the history dialog. At different time steps, we need to use different semantic information to generate different tokens, so our aim is to get a context-aware representation. We can achieve it by applying attention mechanism to the hidden states achieved at different hops,

$$H^c = \sum_{i=1}^{K} \alpha_{i,t} c^i, \quad \alpha_{i,t} = \frac{e^{\eta(h_{t-1}, c^i)}}{\sum_{i=1}^{K} e^{\eta(h_{t-1}, c^i)}} \quad (5)$$

where η is the function that represents the correspondence for attention, usually approximated by a multi-layer neural network.

Template-guided gating mechanism As reported in Song et al. (2018), the top-ranked retrieved reply is not always the one that best match the query, and multiple retrieved replies may provide different reference information to guide the response generation. However, using multiple retrieved replies may increase the probability of introducing "noisy" information, which adversely reduces the quality of the response generation. To tackle this issue, we add a gating mechanism to the hidden state of candidate answers, aiming at extracting valuable "information" at different time steps. Mathematically,

$$H^g = sigmoid(h_a \odot h_{t-1}) \odot h_a \quad (6)$$

We use element-wise multiplication to model the interaction between candidate answers (h_a) and last hidden state of GRU. h^*_{t-1} is obtained by concatenating h_{t-1}, H^c, and H^g.

Hybrid pointer networks We use another MemNN with three hops for the response generation, where h_t of GRU serves as the initial reading head, as shown in Figure 1. The output of MemNN is denoted as $O = \{o^1, o^2, o^3\}$ and attention weights are $P_o = \{p_o^1, p_o^2, p_o^3\}$.

Other than a candidate softmax P_v used for generating a word from the vocabulary, we adopt the idea of Pointer Softmax in Gulcehre et al. (2016), and introduce an Entity Pointer Networks (EPN) and a Pattern Pointer Networks (PPN), where EPN is trained to learn to copy entity words from dialogue history (or KB), and PPN is responsible for extracting pattern words from retrieved answers. For EPN, we use a location softmax P_h, which is a pointer network where each of the output dimension corresponds to the location of a word in the context sequence. Likewise, we introduce a location softmax P_r for PPN. P_v is generated by concatenating the first hop attention read out and the current query vector,

$$P_v = \mathit{softmax}(W_v[o^1; h_t]) \quad (7)$$

For P_r and P_h, we take the attention weights at the second MemNN hop and the third hop of the decoder, respectively: $P_r = p_o^2$ and $P_h = p_o^3$. The output dimensions of P_h and P_v vary according to the length of the corresponding target sequence.

With the three distributions, the key issue is how to decide which distribution should be chosen to generate a word w_i for the current time step. Intuitively, entity words are relatively important, so we set the selection priority order as $P_r > P_h > P_v$. Instead of using a gate function for selection (Gulcehre et al., 2016), we adopt the sentinel mechanism proposed in Madotto et al. (2018). If the expected word is not appearing in the memories, then P_h and P_r are trained to produce a sentinel token[4]. When both P_h and P_r choose the sentinel token or the masked position, our model will generate the token from P_v. Otherwise, it takes the memory content using P_v or P_r.

4 Experimental Settings

4.1 Datasets

We use four public multi-turn task-oriented dialog datasets to evaluate our model, including bAbI (Weston et al., 2015), In-Car Assistant (Eric and Manning, 2017) , DSTC2 (Henderson et al., 2014) and CamRest (Wen et al., 2016). bAbI is automatically generated and the other three datasets are collected from real human dialogs.

bAbI We use tasks 1-5 from bAbI dialog corpus for restaurant reservation to verify the effectiveness of our model. For each task, there are 1000 dialogs for training, 1000 for development, and 1000 for testing. Tasks 1-2 verify dialog management to check if the model can track the dialog state implicitly. Tasks 3-4 verify if the model can leverage the KB tuples for the task-oriented dialog system. Tasks 5 combines Tasks 1-4 to produce full dialogs.

[4]We add a special symbol to the end of each sentence. For example, "good morning" is converted to "good morning $$$". Therefore, if the model predicts the location of "$$$", it means that the expected word is not appearing in the context sequence.

In-Car Assistant This dataset consists of 3,031 multi-turn dialogs in three distinct domains: calendar sheduling, weather information retrieval, and point-of-interest navigation. This dataset has an average of 2.6 conversation turns and the KB information is complicated. Following the data processing in Madotto et al. (2018), we obtain 2,425/302/304 dialogs for training/validation/testing respectively.

DSTC2 The dialogs were extracted from the Dialogue State Tracking Challenge 2 for restaurant reservation. Following Bordes et al. (2017), we use merely the raw text of the dialogs and ignore the dialog state labels. In total, there are 1618 dialogs for training, 500 dialogs for validation, and 1117 dialogs for testing. Each dialog is composed of user and system utterances, and API calls to the domain-specific KB for the user's queries.

CamRest This dataset consists of 676 human-to-human dialogs in the restaurant reservation domain. This dataset has much more conversation turns with 5.1 turns on average. Following the data processing in Wen et al. (2017), we divide the dataset into training/validation/testing sets with 406/135/135 dialogs respectively.

4.2 Implementation Detail

We use the 300-dimensional word2vec vectors to initialize the word embeddings. The size of the GRU hidden units is set to 256. The recurrent weight parameters are initialized as orthogonal matrices. We initialize the other weight parameters with the normal distribution $N(0, 0.01)$ and set the bias terms as zero. We train our model with Adam optimizer (Kingma and Ba, 2015) with an initial learning rate of $1e-4$. By tuning the hyper-parameters with the grid search over the validation sets, we find the other best settings in our model as follows. The number of hops for the memory network is set to 3, and gradients are clipped with a threshold of 10 to avoid explosion. In addition, we apply the dropout (Hinton et al., 2012) as a regularizer to the input and output of GRU, where the dropout rate is set to be 0.4.

4.3 Baseline Models

We compare our model with several existing end-to-end task-oriented dialogue systems[5]:

- **Retrieval method**: This approach directly uses the retrieved result as the answer of the given utterance. Specifically, we use BERT-Base as a feature extractor for the sentences, and we use the cosine distance of the features as our retrieve scores, and then select the one with the highest score.
- **Attn**: Vanilla sequence-to-sequence model with attention (Luong et al., 2015).
- **MemNN**: An extended Seq2Seq model where the recurrence read from a external memory multiple times before outputting the target word (Sukhbaatar et al., 2015).
- **PtrUnk**: An augmented sequence-to-sequence model with attention based copy mechanism to copy unknown words during generation (Gulcehre et al., 2016).
- **CASeq2Seq**: This is a copy-augmented Seq2Seq model that learns attention weights to dialogue history with copy mechanism (Eric and Manning, 2017).
- **Mem2Seq**: A memory network based approach with multi-hop attention for attending over dialogue history and KB tuples (Madotto et al., 2018).
- **BossNet**: A bag-of-sequences memory architecture is proposed for disentangling language model from KB incorporation in task-oriented dialogues (Raghu et al., 2019).
- **WMM2Seq**: This method adopts a working memory to interact with two separated memory networks for dialogue history and KB entities (Chen et al., 2019).
- **GLMP**: This is an augmented memory based model with a global memory pointer and a local memory pointer to strengthen the model's copy ability (Wu et al., 2019).

4.4 Automatic Evaluation Metrics

In bAbI dataset, we adopt a common metric per-response accuracy (Bordes et al., 2017) to evaluate the model performance. Following previous works (Madotto et al., 2018), for three real human dialog datasets, we employ bilingual evaluation understudy (BLEU) (Papineni et al., 2002) and Entity F1 scores to evaluate the model's ability to generate relevant entities from knowledge base and to

[5]Part of experimental results of baseline models are directly extracted from corresponding published papers.

capture the semantics of the user-initiated dialogue flow (Eric and Manning, 2017).

BLEU We use BLEU to measure the n-gram (i.e., 4-gram) matching between the generated responses and the reference responses. The higher BLEU score indicates a better performance of the conversation system. Formally, we compute the 4-gram precision for the generated response Y as:

$$P(Y, \hat{Y}) = \frac{\sum_{\tilde{Y}} \min(\eta(\tilde{Y}, Y), \eta(\tilde{Y}, \hat{Y}))}{\sum_{\tilde{Y}} \eta(\tilde{Y}, Y)} \quad (8)$$

where $\tilde{Y}$ traverses all candidate 4-grams, Y and $\hat{Y}$ are the ground-truth and predicted responses, $\eta(\tilde{Y}, Y)$ indicates the number of 4-grams in Y. After achieving the precision, the BLEU score is then calculated as:

$$BLEU = \nu(Y, \hat{Y}) \exp(\sum_{n=1}^{4} \beta_n \log P(Y, \hat{Y})) \quad (9)$$

where $\beta_n = 1/4$ is a weight score. $\nu(Y, \hat{Y})$ is a brevity penalty that penalizes short sentences. The higher BLEU score indicates better performance of the conversation system.

Per-response Accuracy We adopt the per-response accuracy metric to evaluate the dialog system's capability of generating an exact, correct responses. A generated response is considered right only if each word of the system output matches the corresponding word in the gold response. The final per-response accuracy score is calculated as the percentage of responses that are exactly the same as the corresponding gold dialogues. Per-response accuracy is a strict evaluation measure, which may only be suitable for the simulated dialog datasets.

Entity F1 Entity F1 metric is used measure the system's capability of generating relevant entities from the provided task-oriented knowledge base. Each utterance in the test set has a set of gold entities. An entity F1 is computed by micro-averaging over all the generated responses.

5 Experimental Results

5.1 Automatic Evaluation on Four Datasets

bAbI The dataset is automatically generated based on some rules, thus many requests and their corresponding replies are quite similar in terms of the syntactic structure and the wording usage. According to the results shown in Table 5, we can see that our model achieves the best per-response scores in all the five tasks. It is also believed that the retrieved results can contribute to guiding the response generation in this case, which can be inferred from the high threshold value ($\theta = 0.8$).

In-Car Assistant Dataset As shown in Table 6, our model achieves all best metrics (BLEU, Ent.F1, Sch.F1, Wea.F1 and Nav.F1) over other reported models. The possible reason is that the retrieved answers with high relevance to the gold answers provide valid sentence pattern information. By using this sentence pattern information, our model can better control the generation of responses. Additionally, our model improves the success rate of generation correct entities which appeared in the dialogue history.

Method	BLEU	Ent.F1	Sch.F1	Wea.F1	Nav.F1
R_h^+ & R_r^+	**12.8**	**37.8**	**50.0**	**37.9**	**27.5**
R_h^+ & R_r^-	12.5	36.1	49	34.6	26.7
R_h^- & R_r^+	12.3	36.8	49.8	36.6	26.1
R_h^- & R_r^-	11.6	34.8	48.3	31.8	26.5

Table 2: Masking comparison experiment on In-Car Assistant. $+$ means with masking and $-$ denotes without. R_h^+ & R_r^+ means that we simultaneously mask NEW and EW in the history dialogue and retrieved answers.

θ	# of RA	BLEU
0.3	2.48	56.1
0.4	2.16	56.2
0.5	1.90	**59.8**
0.6	1.75	56.6
1.0	1.00	56.5

Table 3: Experimental results in terms of BLEU on DSTC2 by using different θ. # of RA denotes the average number of retrieved answers.

Dataset	BM25	word2vec	BERT
Task1	68.7	63.1	74.8
Task2	80.6	83.2	93.7
Task3	83.4	77.3	80.3
Task4	87.5	87.5	87.5
Task5	82.9	66.6	83.8
DSTC2	45.3	37.3	47.1
CAMREST	27.7	29.0	30.9
KVR	33.5	33.7	35.3

Table 4: Comparison of different matching methods.

Task	Retrieval	Attn	MemNN	PtrUnk	Mem2Seq	BossNet	GLMP	WMM2Seq	THPN
Task1	74.8	100	99.9	100	100	100	100	100	**100**
Task2	93.7	100	100	100	100	100	100	100	**100**
Task3	80.3	74.8	74.9	85.1	94.5	95.2	**96.3**	94.9	95.8
Task4	87.5	57.2	59.5	100	100	100	100	100	**100**
Task5	83.8	98.4	96.1	99.4	98.2	97.3	99.2	97.9	**99.6**

Table 5: Per-response scores on the five tasks of the bAbI dataset with $\theta = 0.8$.

Method	BLEU	Ent.F1	Sch.F1	Wea.F1	Nav.F1
Retrieval	15.3	20.1	24.9	26.3	9.4
Attn	9.3	19.9	23.4	25.6	10.8
CASeq2Seq	8.7	13.3	13.4	15.6	11.0
MemNN	8.3	22.7	26.9	26.7	14.9
PtrUnk	8.3	22.7	26.9	26.7	14.9
Mem2Seq	12.6	33.4	49.3	32.8	20.0
BossNet	8.3	35.9	50.2	34.5	21.6
THPN	**12.8**	**37.8**	**50.0**	**37.9**	**27.5**

Table 6: Evaluation results on the In-Car Assistant dataset with $\theta = 0.3$.

DSTC2 and CamRest Datasets We also present the evaluation on DSTC2 and CamRest datasets in Table 8 and Table 9, respectively. By comparing the results, we can notice that our model performs better than the compared methods. On the DSTC2, our model achieves the state-of-the-art performance in terms of both Entity F1 score and BLEU metrics, and has a comparable per-response accuracy with compared methods. On the CamRest, our model obtains the best Entity F1 score but has a drop in BLEU in comparison to Mem2Seq model.

5.2 Ablation Study

An ablation study typically refers to removing some components or parts of the model, and seeing how that affects performance. To measure the influence of the individual components, we evaluate the proposed THPN model with each of them removed separately, and then measure the degradation of the overall performance. Table 7 reports ablation study results of THPN on bAbI and DSTC2 datasets by removing retrieved answers (w/o IR), removing EPN and PPN in decoding (w/o Ptr), removing answer-guided gating mechanism (w/o Gate), respectively. For example, "w/o Gate" means we do not use the answer-guided gating mechanism while keeping other components intact.

If the retrieved answer is not used, the performance reduces dramatically, which can be interpreted that without the guiding information from the retrieved answer, the decoder may deteriorate quickly once it produce a "bad" word since it solely relies on the input query.

If no copy mechanism is used, we can see that Entity F1 score is the lowest, which indicates that many entities are not generated since these entity words may not be included in the vocabulary. Therefore, the best way to generate some unseen words is to directly copy from the input query, which is consistent with the findings of previous work (Eric et al., 2017; Madotto et al., 2018).

If the gate is excluded, we can see around 2% drop for DSTC2. A possible reason is that some useless retrieved answers introduce "noise" to the system, which deteriorates the response generation.

5.3 Effect of Masking Operation

To validate the effectiveness of the masking operation, we carry out a comparison experiment on In-Car Assistant, and present the results in Table 2. From Table 2, we can see that R_h^+ & R_r^+ achieves the best performance while R_h^- & R_r^- has the lowest scores. By diving into the experimental results, we find that if we do not mask EW in the retrieved answers, the model copies many incorrect entities from the retrieved answers, which reduces the Entity F1 scores. If we do not mask NEW in the history dialogue, the percentage of NEW copied from the history dialogue is high, most of which are unrelated to the gold answer, thus bringing down the BLEU score.

5.4 Analysis on Retrieved Results

Comparison of Different Retrieval Methods According to our preliminary experimental results, we observed that better retrieved candidate answers could further improve the overall model performance in response generation. Therefore, we also conduct experiments to evaluate the effectiveness of three popular text matching methods, including BM25 (Robertson et al., 2009), word2vec (Mikolov et al., 2013a) and BERT (Devlin et al., 2018).

Task	Task1 (BLEU)	Task2 (BLEU)	Task3 (BLEU)	Task4 (BLEU)	Task5 (BLEU)	DSTC2 (BLEU)	DSTC2 (F1)	DSTC2 (Per-Res)
THPN	100	100	98.9	100	99.9	59.8	76.8	47.7
W/O IR	100	100	96.5	100	99.2	57.8	73.2	45.9
W/O Ptr	100	100	97.7	89.9	98.5	58.1	72.6	46.1
W/O Gate	100	100	95.9	94.4	99.2	57.7	74.1	45.8

Table 7: Ablation test results of our THPN model on bAbI and DSTC2 datasets.

Method	Ent.F1	BLEU
Retrieval	21.1	47.1
Attn	67.1	56.6
KV Net	71.6	55.4
Mem2Seq	75.3	55.3
GLMP	67.4	58.1
THPN	**76.8**	**59.8**

Table 8: Evaluation on DSTC2($\theta = 0.5$).

Method	Ent.F1	BLEU
Retrieval	7.9	**21.2**
Attn	21.4	5.9
PtrUnk	16.4	2.1
KV Net	9.1	4.3
Mem2Seq	27.7	12.6
THPN	**30.9**	12.9

Table 9: Evaluation on CamRest($\theta = 0.4$).

Here, BLEU is utilized as our evaluation criterion. From the experimental results shown in Table 4, we can see that using BERT (Devlin et al., 2018), a transformer-based pre-trained language model, achieves the highest BLEU scores. A possible reason is that the size of each training dataset is limited, the word co-occurrence based algorithms (e.g., BM25) may not capture the semantic information, thus result in poor retrieving performance.

One vs. Multiple Retrieved Answers Cosine similarity is not an absolute criterion and there is no guarantee that a candidate with higher cosine value will always provide more reference information to the response generation. Therefore, we conduct an experiment to investigate the effect of the number of retrieved answers. By setting different cosine threshold values θ, we retrieve different numbers of answer candidates. In particular, if no answer candidate satisfies the given threshold, we choose one with the highest cosine value. To limit the number of retrieved answers, we only select the top-3 results if there are more than three answer candidates that have higher consine values than the given threshold θ.

Table 3 gives the experimental results of DSTC2 dataset under different threshold θ values. When θ is set to be 1.0, it is considered as a special case where only one answer is retrieved. We can observe that using multiple answer candidates obtains higher performance than only using one result. It is intuitive that the model will be misguided if the retrieved single answer has no relation to the given request, and using multiple candidate answers can ameliorate this issue.

Setting of θ Although using more retrieved answers might improve the chance of including the relevant information, it may also bring more "noise" and adversely affect the quality of retrieved answers. From Table 3, we can see that with the reduced value of θ, the average number of retrieved candidate answers increase, but the model performance does not improve accordingly. Experimental results on the other datasets demonstrate that the θ is not fixed and needs to be adjusted according to the experimental data.

6 Conclusion

In task-oriented dialog systems, the words and sentence structures are relatively limited and fixed, thus it is intuitive that the retrieved results can provide valuable information in guiding the response generation. In this paper, we retrieve several potentially relevant answers from a pre-constructed domain-specific conversation repository as guidance answers, and incorporate the guidance answers into both the encoding and decoding processes. We copy the words from the previous context and the retrieved answers directly, and generate words from the vocabulary. Experimental results over four datasets have demonstrated the effectiveness of our model in generating informative responses. In the future, we plan to leverage the dialogue context information to retrieve candidate answers turn by turn in multi-turn scenarios.

References

Antoine Bordes, Y-Lan Boureau, and Jason Weston. 2017. Learning End-to-end Goal-oriented Dialog. *International Conference on Learning Representations*.

Ziqiang Cao, Wenjie Li, Sujian Li, and Furu Wei. 2018. Retrieve, Rerank and Rewrite: Soft Template Based Neural Summarization. In *Proceedings of the 56th Annual Meeting of the Association for Computational Linguistics (Volume 1: Long Papers)*, volume 1, pages 152–161.

Qian Chen, Xiaodan Zhu, Zhen-Hua Ling, Diana Inkpen, and Si Wei. 2017. Neural natural language inference models enhanced with external knowledge. *arXiv preprint arXiv:1711.04289*.

Xiuyi Chen, Jiaming Xu, and Bo Xu. 2019. A working memory model for task-oriented dialog response generation. In *Proceedings of the 57th Annual Meeting of the Association for Computational Linguistics*, pages 2687–2693.

Junyoung Chung, Caglar Gulcehre, KyungHyun Cho, and Yoshua Bengio. 2014. Empirical Evaluation of Gated Recurrent Neural Networks on Sequence Modeling. *arXiv preprint arXiv:1412.3555*.

Jacob Devlin, Ming-Wei Chang, Kenton Lee, and Kristina Toutanova. 2018. Bert: Pre-training of Deep Bidirectional Transformers for Language Understanding. *North American Chapter of the Association for Computational Linguistics*.

Xiao Ding, Kuo Liao, Ting Liu, Zhongyang Li, and Junwen Duan. 2019. Event representation learning enhanced with external commonsense knowledge. *arXiv preprint arXiv:1909.05190*.

Mihail Eric, Lakshmi Krishnan, Francois Charette, and Christopher D Manning. 2017. Key-value retrieval networks for task-oriented dialogue. In *Proceedings of the 18th Annual SIGdial Meeting on Discourse and Dialogue*, pages 37–49.

Mihail Eric and Christopher D Manning. 2017. A Copy-augmented Sequence-to-sequence Architecture Gives Good Performance on Task-oriented Dialogue. *European Association of Computational Linguistics*, page 468.

Marjan Ghazvininejad, Chris Brockett, Ming-Wei Chang, Bill Dolan, Jianfeng Gao, Wen-tau Yih, and Michel Galley. 2018. A Knowledge-grounded Neural Conversation Model. In *Thirty-Second AAAI Conference on Artificial Intelligence*.

Caglar Gulcehre, Sungjin Ahn, Ramesh Nallapati, Bowen Zhou, and Yoshua Bengio. 2016. Pointing the unknown words. In *Proceedings of the 54th Annual Meeting of the Association for Computational Linguistics (Volume 1: Long Papers)*, volume 1, pages 140–149.

Tianxing He, Jingzhao Zhang, Zhiming Zhou, and James Glass. 2019. Quantifying exposure bias for neural language generation. *arXiv preprint arXiv:1905.10617*.

Matthew Henderson, Blaise Thomson, and Jason D Williams. 2014. The Second Dialog State Tracking Challenge. In *Proceedings of the 15th Annual Meeting of the Special Interest Group on Discourse and Dialogue*, pages 263–272.

Geoffrey E Hinton, Nitish Srivastava, Alex Krizhevsky, Ilya Sutskever, and Ruslan R Salakhutdinov. 2012. Improving Neural Networks by Preventing Co-adaptation of Feature Detectors. *arXiv preprint arXiv:1207.0580*.

Diederik P Kingma and Lei Ba. 2015. ADAM: A Method for Stochastic Optimization. In *Proceedings of the 3rd International Conference on Learning Representations*.

Philipp Koehn and Rebecca Knowles. 2017. Six Challenges for Neural Machine Translation. *arXiv preprint arXiv:1706.03872*.

Oliver Lemon, Kallirroi Georgila, James Henderson, and Matthew Stuttle. 2006. An isu dialogue system exhibiting reinforcement learning of dialogue policies: generic slot-filling in the talk in-car system. In *Proceedings of the Eleventh Conference of the European Chapter of the Association for Computational Linguistics: Posters & Demonstrations*, pages 119–122. Association for Computational Linguistics.

Thang Luong, Hieu Pham, and Christopher D Manning. 2015. Effective Approaches to Attention-based Neural Machine Translation. *Proceedings of the 2015 Conference on Empirical Methods in Natural Language Processing*, pages 1412–1421.

Andrea Madotto, Chien-Sheng Wu, and Pascale Fung. 2018. Mem2seq: Effectively incorporating knowledge bases into end-to-end task-oriented dialog systems. In *Proceedings of the 56th Annual Meeting of the Association for Computational Linguistics (Volume 1: Long Papers)*, pages 1468–1478.

Tomas Mikolov, Kai Chen, Greg Corrado, and Jeffrey Dean. 2013a. Efficient estimation of word representations in vector space. *arXiv preprint arXiv:1301.3781*.

Tomas Mikolov, Ilya Sutskever, Kai Chen, Greg S Corrado, and Jeff Dean. 2013b. Distributed representations of words and phrases and their compositionality. In *Advances in neural information processing systems*, pages 3111–3119.

Kishore Papineni, Salim Roukos, Todd Ward, and Wei-Jing Zhu. 2002. BLEU: a method for automatic evaluation of machine translation. In *Proceedings of the 40th annual meeting on association for computational linguistics*, pages 311–318.

Libo Qin, Yijia Liu, Wanxiang Che, Haoyang Wen, Yangming Li, and Ting Liu. 2019. Entity-consistent end-to-end task-oriented dialogue system with kb retriever. *arXiv preprint arXiv:1909.06762*.

Dinesh Raghu, Nikhil Gupta, et al. 2019. Disentangling language and knowledge in task-oriented dialogs. In *Proceedings of the 2019 Conference of the North American Chapter of the Association for Computational Linguistics: Human Language Technologies, Volume 1 (Long and Short Papers)*, pages 1239–1255.

Marc'Aurelio Ranzato, Sumit Chopra, Michael Auli, and Wojciech Zaremba. 2016. Sequence level training with recurrent neural networks. *International Conference on Learning Representations*.

Stephen Robertson, Hugo Zaragoza, et al. 2009. The probabilistic relevance framework: Bm25 and beyond. *Foundations and Trends® in Information Retrieval*, 3(4):333–389.

Yiping Song, Rui Yan, Cheng-Te Li, Jian-Yun Nie, Ming Zhang, and Dongyan Zhao. 2018. An Ensemble of Retrieval-Based and Generation-Based Human-Computer Conversation Systems.

Sainbayar Sukhbaatar, Jason Weston, Rob Fergus, et al. 2015. End-to-end memory networks. In *Advances in neural information processing systems*, pages 2440–2448.

Zhuoran Wang and Oliver Lemon. 2013. A simple and generic belief tracking mechanism for the dialog state tracking challenge: On the believability of observed information. In *Proceedings of the SIGDIAL 2013 Conference*, pages 423–432.

Tsung-Hsien Wen, Milica Gasic, Nikola Mrkšić, Lina M Rojas Barahona, Pei-Hao Su, Stefan Ultes, David Vandyke, and Steve Young. 2016. Conditional generation and snapshot learning in neural dialogue systems. In *Proceedings of the 2016 Conference on Empirical Methods in Natural Language Processing*, pages 2153–2162.

Tsung-Hsien Wen, David Vandyke, Nikola Mrksic, Milica Gasic, Lina Maria Rojas-Barahona, Pei-Hao Su, Stefan Ultes, and Steve J. Young. 2017. A network-based end-to-end trainable task-oriented dialogue system. In *Proceedings of the 15th Conference of the European Chapter of the Association for Computational Linguistics, EACL 2017, Valencia, Spain, April 3-7, 2017, Volume 1: Long Papers*, pages 438–449. Association for Computational Linguistics.

Jason Weston, Antoine Bordes, Sumit Chopra, Alexander M Rush, Bart van Merriënboer, Armand Joulin, and Tomas Mikolov. 2015. Towards ai-complete question answering: A set of prerequisite toy tasks. *arXiv preprint arXiv:1502.05698*.

Jason D Williams and Steve Young. 2007. Partially observable markov decision processes for spoken dialog systems. *Computer Speech & Language*, 21(2):393–422.

Chien-Sheng Wu, Richard Socher, and Caiming Xiong. 2019. Global-to-local memory pointer networks for task-oriented dialogue. In *7th International Conference on Learning Representations, ICLR 2019, New Orleans, LA, USA, May 6-9, 2019*. OpenReview.net.

Rui Yan, Yiping Song, and Hua Wu. 2016. Learning to Respond with Deep Neural Networks for Retrieval-based Human-computer Conversation System. In *Proceedings of the 39th International ACM SIGIR conference on Research and Development in Information Retrieval*, pages 55–64.

Pengcheng Yang, Lei Li, Fuli Luo, Tianyu Liu, and Xu Sun. 2019. Enhancing topic-to-essay generation with external commonsense knowledge. In *Proceedings of the 57th Annual Meeting of the Association for Computational Linguistics*, pages 2002–2012.

Steve Young, Milica Gašić, Blaise Thomson, and Jason D Williams. 2013. Pomdp-based statistical spoken dialog systems: A review. *Proceedings of the IEEE*, 101(5):1160–1179.

Yue Zhang, Rui Wang, and Luo Si. 2019. Syntax-enhanced self-attention-based semantic role labeling. *arXiv preprint arXiv:1910.11204*.

Qingfu Zhu, Lei Cui, Weinan Zhang, Furu Wei, Yining Chen, and Ting Liu. 2018. Retrieval-Enhanced Adversarial Training for Neural Response Generation. *arXiv preprint arXiv:1809.04276*.

Automatic Learning Assistant in Telugu

Meghana Bommadi, Shreya Terupally, Radhika Mamidi
Language Technologies Research Centre
International Institute of Information Technology Hyderabad, India
meghana.bommadi@research.iiit.ac.in , shreya.reddy@students.iiit.ac.in,
radhika.mamidi@iiit.ac.in

Abstract

This paper presents a learning assistant that tests one's knowledge and gives feedback that helps a person learn at a faster pace. A learning assistant (based on an automated question generation) has extensive uses in education, information websites, self-assessment, FAQs, testing ML agents, research, etc. Multiple researchers, and companies have worked on Virtual Assistance, but majorly in English. We built our learning assistant for Telugu language to help with teaching in the mother tongue, which is the most efficient way of learning[1]. Our system is built primarily based on Question Generation in Telugu.

Many experiments were conducted on Question Generation in English in multiple ways. We have built the first hybrid machine learning and rule-based solution in Telugu, which proves efficient for short stories or short passages in children's books. Our work covers the fundamental question forms with question types: adjective, yes/no, adverb, verb, when, where, whose, quotative, and quantitative (how many/how much). We constructed rules for question generation using Part of Speech (POS) tags and Universal Dependency (UD) tags along with linguistic information of the surrounding relevant context of the word. Our system is primarily built on question generation in Telugu, and is also capable of evaluating the user's answers to the generated questions.

1 Introduction

Research on Virtual Assistants is renowned since they being widely used in recent times for numerous tasks. These assistants are generated using large datasets and high-end Natural Language Understanding (NLU) and Natural Language Generation (NLG) tools. NLU and NLG are used in interactive NLP applications such as AI-based dialogue systems/voice assistants like SIRI, Google Assistant, Alexa, and similar personal assistants. Research is still going on to make these assistants work in major Indian languages as well.

An automated learning assistant like our system is not only useful for the learning process for humans but also for machines in the process of testing ML systems[2]. Research has been done for Question Answer generating system in English[3], concentrating on basic Wh-questions with a rule-based approach[4], question template based approaches[5] etc. For a low-resourced language like Telugu, a complete AI-based solution can be non-viable. There are hardly any datasets available for the system to produce significant accuracy. A completely rule-based system might leave out principle parts of the abstract. There is a chance that all the questions cannot be captured inclusively by completely handwritten rules. Hence, we want to introduce a mixed rule-based and AI-based solution to this problem.

Our system works on the following three crucial steps:

1. Summarization
2. Question Generation
3. Answer Evaluation

We implemented summarization using two techniques viz. Word Frequency (see 4.1), and TextRank (see 4.2) which are explained further in section 4. Summarization

We attempted to produce questions, concentrating on the critical points of a text that are generally

[1](Roshni, 2020) (Nishanthi, 2020)

[2](Hidenobu Kunichika, 2004)
[3](Maria Chinkina, 2017)
[4](Payal Khullar)
[5](Hafedh Hussein, 2014)

Proceedings of the 1st Workshop on Document-grounded Dialogue and Conversational Question Answering, pages 29–37
August 5–6, 2021.

asked in assessment tests. Questions posed to an individual challenge their knowledge and understanding of specific topics, so we formed questions in each sentence in as many ways as possible. We based this model on children's stories, so the questions we wanted to produce aim to be simpler and more objective.

Based on the observation of the data chosen and analysis of all the possible causes, we developed a set of rules for each part of speech that can be formed into a question word in Telugu. We maximized the possible number of questions in each sentence with all the keywords. We built rules for question generation based on POS tags, UD tags and information surrounding the word, which is comparable with *Vibhaktis* (case markers) in Telugu grammar.

The Question Generation in manually evaluated and the detailed error analysis is given in section 8.1. Our Learning Assistant evaluates using string matching, keyword matching for Telugu answers, and a pre-trained sentence transformer model using XLM-R.(Nils Reimers, 2019)

2 Related Work

Previously, Holy Lovenia, Felix Limanta et al.[2018] (Holy Lovenia, 2018) experimented on Q&A pair Generation in English where they succeeded in forming What, Who, and Where questions. Rami Reddy et al.[2006] (Rami Reddy Nandi Reddy, 2006) worked on Dialogue based Question Answering System in Telugu for Railway inquiries, which majorly concentrated on Answer Generation for a given query. Similar work has done by (Hoojung Chung) on dealing with practical question answering system in restricted domain. Shudipta Sharma et al.[2018](Shudipta Sharma) worked on automatic Q&A pair generation for English and Bengali texts using NLP tasks like verb decomposition, subject auxiliary inversion for a question tag.

3 Dataset

We have used a Telugu stories dataset taken from a website called kathalu wordpress".[6] This dataset was chosen because of a variety in the themes of the stories, wide vocabulary and sentences of varying lengths.

1. Number of stories : 21
2. Average number of sentences : 56
3. Average number of words : 281
4. Genre of the stories : Moral Stories for Children

For testing we used stories by Prof. N. Lakshmi Aiyar:

1. Number of stories : 5
2. Average number of sentences : 190
3. Average number of words : 1060
4. Genre of the stories : Realistic Fiction

4 Summarization

Since Telugu is a low resource language, we used statistical and unsupervised methods for this task. Summarization also ensures the portability of our system to other similar low resource languages.

For summarization, we did a basic data preprocessing (spaces, special characters, etc.) in addition to root-word extraction using Shiva Reddy's POS tagger[7].

We used two types of existing summarization techniques:

1. Word Frequency-based summarization
2. TextRank based frequency

4.1 Word Frequency-based Summarization

WFBS (Word Frequency-based Summarization) is calculated using the word frequency in the passage.[8] This process is based on the idea that the keywords or the main words will frequently appear in the text, and those words with lower frequency have a high probability of being less related to the story.

All the sentences that carry crucial information are produced successfully by this method because the keywords are used repeatedly in children's stories, subsequently causing the highest frequency.

We used a dynamic ratio (a ratio that can be changed or chosen by the user as an input) for getting the desirable amount of summary (short summary or a longer summary, for example: k% of

[6] `https://kathalu.wordpress.com/`

[7] `http://sivareddy.in/downloads`

[8] (Ani Nenkova) (Mr. Shubham Bhosale)

the sentences, the system will output k% of sentences with the highest frequent words from the dictionary) This ratio, when dynamically changed, performed better than the fixed ratio of word selection.

Steps followed in WFBS are:

1. Sentences are extracted from the input file.
2. The file is prepossessed and the words are tokenized.
3. Stop words are removed.
4. Frequency of each word is calculated and stored in dictionaries.
5. The sentences with least frequent word are removed.
6. Calculated the ratio of words that occur in highest to lowest frequency order.

4.2 TextRank based Frequency

TextRank is a graph-based ranking model[9] that prioritizes each element based on the values in the graph. This process is done in the following steps:

1. A graph is constructed using each sentence as a node
2. Similarity between the two nodes is marked as the edge weight between the nodes
3. Each sentence is ranked based on the similarity with the whole text
4. The page-rank algorithm is run until convergence
5. The sentences with top N ranking as summarized text is given as the output

The TextRank algorithm is a graph based method that updates the sentence score WS iteratively using the following equation (1).

$$WS(V_i) = (1-d) + d * \sum_{V_j \varepsilon In(V_i)} \frac{w_{ij}}{\sum_{V_k \varepsilon Out(V_j)} w_{jk}} WS(V_j) \quad (1)$$

Where d = damping factor (0.85), w_{ij} is the similarity measure between ith and jth sentences.

This method has the advantage of using the similarity between the two sentences to rank them instead of high-frequency words.

We used two kinds of **similarity** measures for the TextRank based summarization:

1. **Common words**: A measure of similarity based on the number of common words in two sentences after removing stop words. We used root word extraction of the common words for better results since Telugu is a fusional and agglutinative language and has repeated words with a different suffix each time.
2. **Best Match 25**: A measure of the similarity between two passages, based on term frequencies in the passage.[10]

The results observed by this method captures crucial information of the story, but lesser readability and fluency was observed. Within the similarity measures, BM25 has shown slightly better results since the BM25 algorithm ranks sentences based on the importance of particular words (inverse document frequency - IDF) instead of just using the frequency of words.

5 Answer Phrase Selection

Candidate answers are words/phrases that depict some vital information in a sentence. Adjectives, adverbs, and the subject of a sentence are some examples of such candidates.

The answer selection module utilizes two main NLP components - POS Tagging (Part of Speech tagging) and UD parsing (Universal Dependency parsing), along with language-specific rules to determine the answer words in an input sentence.

5.1 POS Tagging

We followed state-of-the-art method by Siva Reddy et al. (2011) (Siva Reddy, 2011), Cross-Language POS Taggers" an implementation of a TnT-based Telugu POS Tagger [11] to parse our data.

The tagger learns morphological analysis and POS tags at the same time, and outputs the lemma (root word), POS tag, suffix, gender, number and case marker for each word.

The model was pre-trained on a Telugu corpus containing approximately 3.5 million tokens and

[9](Joshi, 2018)(Liang, 2019)

[10](Federico Barrios, 2016)

[11]`https://bitbucket.org/sivareddyg/telugu-part-of-speech-tagger/src/master/`

had an evaluation accuracy of 90.73% for the main POS tag.

5.2 UD Tagging

A Bi-LSTM model using Keras is structured and trained using Telugu UD tags dataset UD_Telugu-MTG". [12]

The Bi-LSTM model outputs the UD tags for each word in a sentence using Keras. We considered the subject, which is marked subj" by UD tagger, as the selected answer phrase for a sentence based on the condition that it marked root and punctuation correctly.

This model gave 85% accurate results, including the PAD tags(padding tags), which might not be an adequate result, but based on the conditions and given that the tags subj" is labeled in a sentence scarcely, the results have been considered to be acceptable.

5.3 Rules

The outputs of the POS Tagging and UD Parsing modules are used as the crucial markers in our language-specific rules. In addition to conditions based on word surroundings, these tags select one or more answer phrases in each sentence.

We classify the rules into different categories, typically based on their usage and interrogative forms.

1. **Quantifiers, Adjectives, Adverbs**: Words with the QC, RB, and JJ POS tag, respectively. For words with JJ tags, the word and the corresponding determiners (if present) are selected as the answer candidate.

2. **Possession based**: Words with PRP and NN tags that have suffixes as "టి"," యొక్క", "కి" and "కు" (Ti",yokka",ki" and ku"). The suffix "టి" (Ti") is used for words like "అతని", "వాళ్ళ", "కంటి", "విద్యార్థుల" (atani"-his, vAlla"-their's, kanTi"-eyes', vidyArthula"-students')

3. **Time-Place based** : Noun words with a "లో" (lO") suffix, along with other words present in custom list of time-related words ("మార్నింగ్", "ఇయర్")(morning", year") come under this category.

4. **Direct and Reported Speech**: The word "అని" is generally used to denote direct speech in Telugu. Phrases before the word "అని", along with phrases in quotation marks, are chosen as answer phrases.

5. **Verbs**: Telugu follows the SOV (Subject Object Verb) structure, in general. If the last word has a V" POS tag in a sentence, then we selected the verb and adjacent adverbs as an answer candidate.

6. **Subject**: We use the UD tags to determine the subject of a sentence. As an additional check, we only select the candidate subjects in those sentences whose last word is tagged as the root verb, and the subject is a noun.

6 Question Formation

Questions are formed according to the chosen phrases chosen previously, and the question words are replaced using further conditions if required.

1. **Quantifiers, Adjectives, Adverbs**: The words that are marked JJ POS are replaced with "ఎటువంటి" (eTuvanti"- what kind of) RB POS tagged that are followed by verbs with "గా" (gA") suffix are replaced by "ఎలా" (elA"-how) and the QC tagged words that are not articles ("ఒక" (oka"- one/once) were chosen and changed based on the following word. If the quantifier is followed by "శాతం", "మంది" ,"వరకు" (shAtam",maMdi",varaku") then the word is replaced with "ఎంత" (eMta"-how much), if the quantifier has a suffix it is added to the question word.

   For example: "1700కు" - "ఎంతకు" (eMtaku) and the rest of the quantifiers like ఐదు పిచ్చుకలు (meaning five sparrows) are replaced with "ఎన్ని"(enni"-how many) ("ఎన్ని పిచ్చుకలు" (how many sparrows) in this case).

2. **Possession based**: The nouns and pronouns that satisfied the rules are replaced with "ఎవరి" (evari"-whose) and the dative cases are replaced with "ఎవరికి" (evariki"-to whom). This could be an exception for non-human nouns and pronouns. In the children's stories, most of the nouns are personified, so there were fewer errors than we presumed.

   For example: A sentence with a phrase

[12] https://github.com/UniversalDependencies/UD_Telugu-MTG (Bogdani, 2018)

like "రాముడి ఇల్లు..." (ram's house...) would form a question like "ఎవరి ఇల్లు.." (whose house..)

3. **Time-Place based**: We made a list of words that are used to convey time. If the lemma of the word matched the word in the dictionary, then we marked it time" and was replaced with "ఎప్పుడు" (eppuDu"-when) or else it was marked as a place and replaced with "ఎక్కడ" (ekkaDa"-where).

   For example: A sentence with the phrase "రేపు వస్తాడు" (he will come tomorrow) will form a question "ఎప్పుడు వస్తాడు?"(when will he come).

4. **Direct and Reported Speech** : The whole speech phrase or the phrase that is quoted is replaced with "ఏమని" (Emani") in the sentence.

   For example: A phrase in quotes in a sentence like దుర్యోధనుడు "ఏమంటివి ఏమంటివి..!" అని అన్నాడు. (Duryodhan said,"what did you say..!".) would form a question like దుర్యోధనుడు ఏమని అన్నాడు? (what did Duryodhan say?)

5. **Verbs** : The verb is replaced with "ఏమి చేస్తూ" Emi cEstu"-doing what) + <suffix>". The appropriate suffix is chosen from the information lost in the lemmatized word.

   Additionally, the verb tags were used to form polar questions. The interrogative form of a sentence in Telugu can be constructed by adding intonation to the verb, so we added "ఆ" (A") vowel at the end of the verb to make a yes or no question. The answer phrase to this question would be "అవును" (avunu"-yes), followed by the original phrase.

   For example: A sentence with a verbal phrase like "సీత వెళుతూ ఉంది"(Sita is going) will form a question like "సీత ఏమి చేస్తూ ఉంది? "(What is Sita doing?).

6. **Subject** : Based on the suffix of the verb the subject is replaced with "ఏది", "ఏవి" or "దేని", "వేటికి" (meaning what, which simultaneously) or "ఎవరు" (evaru"-who) if the subject has a gender and marked a human in POS tags, and the root suffix is changed accordingly for "ఎవరు" (evaru"-who (honorific)).

   For example: "గంగ అక్కడి నుంచి వెళ్లిపోయింది." (Ganga left from that place) forms a question like "ఎవరు అక్కడి నుంచి వెళ్లిపోయారు?" (Who left from there?).

7 Answer Evaluation

User's answer for the question generated is evaluated in two ways depending on the form of input.

1. Telugu Answer Evaluation
2. Multilingual Answer Evaluation

7.1 Telugu Answer Evaluation

A string input in Telugu is taken from the user and string matching is done for the whole sentence to the answer phrase stored from Question and Answer Pair Generation. Answer could be either in the sentence form or in a phrasal form that has the keywords which the question was formed on.

7.2 Multilingual Answer Evaluation

7.2.1 Sentence Transformers

Similar to word embedding, where the learned representation of same words have similar representation, sentence embedding (Nikhil, 2017) maps semantic information of sentences into vectors. Multilingual Sentence Embedding deals with sentences in multiple languages that are mapped in a closer vector space if they have similar meanings.

Sentence Transformers are Multilingual Sentence Embedding (Ivana Kvapilíková, 2020; Mikel Artetxe, 2019) formed using BERT / RoBERTa / XLM-RoBERTa & Co. with PyTorch[13]. This framework provides an easy way of computing dense vector representation of sentences in multiple languages. They are called sentence transformers since the models are based on transformer networks like BERT / RoBERTa / XLM-RoBERTa etc.

We use a pre-trained sentence transformer (Nils Reimers, 2019) based cross-lingual sentence embedding system which can take a sentence in a language and create an embedding in a multilingual space. The answer phrases and sentences are stored in a dictionary. The answers in a different language are taken as an input and are pro-

[13](Reimers, 2021)(Horev, 2018) (Ferreira, 2020)

jected into multilingual space and the similarity is checked using cosine similarity with the stored answer phrase in Telugu.

In the final system we used syntax matching to mark the user's answer if the input is in Telugu and used sentence transformers if the input is in any other lanuage.

8 Results

We obtained results that resemble commonly used questions covering nine POS and UD tags. The questions generated by this system are successful and are most similar to academic questions we see in textbooks. We did manual error analysis for the question and answer pair generated. In most cases, it has produced legible results that resemble human-made questions, but there were errors in a few complex sentences. Out of the 916 questions formed, only 34 were either completely erroneous or illegible. The rest were both grammatically correct and significant for the context of the story. The system successfully obtained all possible questions for each simple sentence, not requiring further linguistic analysis.

Table 1 lists the number of times each question word occurred and the number of times it appeared wrong in the experiment with five stories. Table 2 in section 9 shows the sample question and answers generated by the system for children stories.

8.1 Question Generation Error Analysis

The Question Generation by the system is manually annotated by two human evaluators with Computational Linguistics background. Guidelines given to the evaluators are:

- Question with grammatical mistakes are marked as errors.
- Semantic errors in question are marked as errors.
- Questions that are highly irrelevant to the story are marked as errors.

Errors are equally influenced by the word tags, the context of the word, and the word's position in a sentence. We analysed each and every way the errors occurred and could occur.

Errors in elA" ('how') questions are often caused due to spaces between the words and suffixes in the dataset we chose.

Question word	Occurrences	Errors
ఎలా (elA)	64	2
ఎన్ని (enni)	76	5
ఎంతకు (eMtaku)	4	0
ఎంత (eMta)	3	0
ఎవరి (evari)	187	0
ఎవరికి (evariki)	1	0
ఏమి (Emi)	69	3
దేని (dEni)	45	10
ఎవరు (evaru)	20	0
ఎప్పుడు(eppuDu)	7	0
ఎక్కడ (ekkaDa)	21	5
ఏమి చేస్తూ (Emi cEstU)	148	2
ఏమని (Emani)	10	0
ఆ (A)	148	0
ఎటువంటి (eTuvaMTi)	103	6
వేటికి (vETiki)	10	1

Table 1: Question Types

enni" (quantifier - based) questions are built from diverse quantifiers (for example: time, age, number of people - these quantifiers are often written as sandhi with the word, which causes the POS tagger to give ambiguous tags) and numerous ways of writing quantifiers in Telugu. Few quantifier question word errors occurred due to wrong POS tagging of cross-coded words (words that are actually in English but written in Telugu script). In Telugu, two numbers are used together when representing non-specific quantities between the two numbers (x y means from x to y), for example, reMDu (two) mUDu(three) nimishAlu (minutes)" meaning two to three minutes. This kind of representation makes the system assume there are two quantifiers, and the sentence is eligible for two questions based on the same.

dEni" (subject-based) questions have errors because of ambiguous suffixes and inaccuracies in UD tagging. The lack of human identification in the system made human subjects also replaceable with dEnini" instead of evarini". Another error was due to subjects that were nominal (names) with end syllables similar to common suffixes (which are included as word context in the rule formation). These names were split and formed incorrect question words. For example, the name

Shalini" was converted to interrogative form as dEnini". The rest of the errors are due to wrong POS tags, cross-codes, and initials/abbreviations.

Emi" ('what') question forms also have similar POS tags and cross-codes issues. Few of these errors occurred due to punctuation marks between the same sentence, breaking it up into multiple sentences.

eTuvaMTi" ('what-kind-of') question forms run into issues where there is personification. General questions based on adjectives for humans are based on a person's subtle qualities; however, in a few cases, the adjective that was chosen is inapt to be formed into a question (less similar to human made question). The question that was formed was still grammatically correct in both human and non-human subjects; nevertheless, it is more suitable and precise for a non-human noun. For example (ఎలాంటి శాలిని/what kind of Shalini- పరిచయమైన శాలిని/ the Shalini, that I know)

ekkaDa" ('where') based question forms show errors when an abstract word is used as a place, for example - In thoughts", In that age". Certain quantitative words in Telugu can be appended with -lO to convey meanings like in youth", in hundreds". They tend to pass the rules in question generation. Our list of time-related words is not exhaustive, so a few time-related words are also tagged under ekkaDa" (place) because of the same suffix.

Most of the tags are error free except for a few ambiguous errors since the rules select answer phrases precisely or do not consider it. Some of the examples of the questions that are produced by the system are listed below in Table-2 in the appendix. The results can be improved to make the question formation more precise by increasing the number of rules by observing further data.

The anaphora resolution is a limitation in this system; thus, most of the in-appropriation in the answer section was caused due to this.

For example:

Q: ఎవరి చదువంతా సిటీలో, దర్జాగా ... సాగింది?
Q: Whose studies got completed in the city luxuriously?
A: నీ చదువంతా సిటీలో, దర్జాగా ... సాగింది.
A: Your studies got completed in the city luxuriously.

In this case the question is aptly formed but the answer is slightly ill-formed.

There were few errors due to the POS tagger we used. It marked wrong POS tags for cross coded text.

For example:

Q: నీలం కుమావత్, ఎన్ని?
Q: Neelam Kumawath, how many?
A: నీలం కుమావత్, ఐ.
A: Neelam Kumawath, I.

The error in this question and answer pair is the "ఐ" 'I' which is an initial (Neelam Kumavat, I) is marked as a number.

9 Conclusions

We have built a mixed rule-based and AI-based question and answer generating system with 96.28% accuracy.

We used two methods for summarization and two similarity measures. We constructed observation-based rules for the dataset in a particular domain. There is a chance of varying results if we test this system for data in a different domain, but it gives accuracies above 95% for any data in the domain chosen.

We tested question generation in the news article domain, which gave grammatically correct questions. The error rate may increase if we use complex words and phrases that need tags beyond the proposed set of rules.

We plan to extend our work to be able to include:

1. Anaphora Resolution
2. Extending to other domains

3. Cover more types of questions
4. Improving the UD tagging model

For testing the meticulousness of the user, as a future task, we wish to use:

1. Questions on minor details
2. NE (Named Entities) and CN (Common Nouns)

Q: ఎటువంటి మోట తో వంగడం కష్టంగా వుంది?
A: అంత పెద్ద మోట తో వంగడం కష్టంగా వుంది

Q: చెప్పులు , బట్టలు , గాజులు , పళ్ళు, గిన్నెలు బజారులో ఎలా కొని , ఊళ్ళో ఇంటింటికి వెళ్లి అమ్ముకునే వాడు?
A: చెప్పులు , బట్టలు , గాజులు , పళ్ళు , గిన్నెలు బజారులో చవకగా కొని , ఊళ్ళో ఇంటింటికి వెళ్లి అమ్ముకునే వాడు

Q: సామాన్లన్నీ మోట కట్టి , గాడిద మీద వేసి , బజారు నుంచి ఊళ్ళో , ఊళ్లోనుంచి తిరిగి ఎవరి ఇంటికి తిప్పేవాడు?
A: సామాన్లన్నీ మోట కట్టి , గాడిద మీద వేసి , బజారు నుంచి ఊళ్ళో , ఊళ్లోనుంచి తిరిగి అతని ఇంటికి తిప్పేవాడు

Q: అమాయక పిచుక ఎక్కడకి, ఎందుకు అని అడగకుండా, ఆ కాకులను గుడ్డిగా నమ్మి ఏమి చేసింది?
A: అమాయక పిచుక ఎక్కడకి, ఎందుకు అని అడగకుండా, ఆ కాకులను గుడ్డిగా నమ్మి వాటితో వెళ్ళింది.

Q: పిచుక మాట నమ్మలేదు కదా , దాని వెప్పు అసహ్యంగా చూసి మరో ఎన్ని దెబ్బలు వేసారు?
A: పిచుక మాట నమ్మలేదు కదా , దాని వెప్పు అసహ్యంగా చూసి మరో రెండు దెబ్బలు వేసారు

Q: ఆ కాకులతో పిచుకకి స్నేహం అయ్యిందా?
A: అవును, ఆ కాకులతో పిచుకకి స్నేహం అయ్యింది.

Q: ఒకానొకప్పుడు ఎక్కడ ఒక అమాయకపు పిచుక వుండేది?
A: ఒకానొకప్పుడు ఒక ఊరిలో ఒక అమాయకపు పిచుక వుండేది.

Q: ఏమని పిచుక ప్రాధేయ పడింది?
A: బాబోయ్! బాబోయ్! నా తప్పేమీ లేదు, నేను అమాయకురాలిని, నేనేమీ చేయలేదు, నన్ను వదిలేయండి! అని పిచుక ప్రాధేయ పడింది.

Table 2: Sample questions generated by the system

References

Lucy Vanderwende Ani Nenkova. The impact of frequency on summarization.

Bogdani. 2018. Parts of speech tagging using lstm (long short term memory) neural networks.

Luis Argerich Rosita Wachenchauzer Federico Barrios, Federico Lt'opez. 2016. Variations of the similarity function of textrank for automated summarization.

Diogo Ferreira. 2020. What are sentence embeddings and why are they useful?

Shawkat Guirguis Hafedh Hussein, Mohammed Elmogy. 2014. Automatic english question generation system based on template driven scheme.

Tsukasa Hirashima Akira Takeuchi Hidenobu Kunichika, Tomoki Katayama*. 2004. Automated question generation methodsfor intelligent english learning systems and its evaluation.

Agus Gunawan Holy Lovenia, Felix Limanta. 2018. Automatic question-answer pairs generation from text.

Kyoung-Soo Han Do-Sang Yoon Joo-Young Lee Hae-Chang Rim Hoojung Chung, Young-In Song. A practical qa system in restricted domains.

Rani Horev. 2018. Bert explained: State of the art language model for nlp.

Gorka Labaka-Eneko Agirre Ondej Bojar Ivana Kvapilíková, Mikel Artetxe. 2020. Unsupervised multilingual sentence embeddings for parallel corpus mining.

Prateek Joshi. 2018. An introduction to text summarization using the textrank algorithm (with python implementation).

Xu Liang. 2019. Understand textrank for keyword extraction by python: A scratch implementation by python and spacy to help you understand pagerank and textrank for keyword extraction.

Detmar Meurers Maria Chinkina. 2017. Question generation for language learning: From ensuring texts are read to supporting learning.

Holger Schwenk Mikel Artetxe. 2019. Massively multilingual sentence embeddings for zero-shot cross-lingual transfer and beyond.

Ms. Vrushali Bhise Rushali A. Deshmukh Mr. Shubham Bhosale, Ms. Diksha Joshi. Automatic text summarization based on frequency count for marathi e-newspaper.

Nishant Nikhil. 2017. Sentence embedding: A literature review - towards data science.

Iryna Gurevych Nils Reimers. 2019. Sentence-bert: Sentence embeddings using siamese bert-networks.

Rajathurai Nishanthi. 2020. Understanding of the importance of mother tongue learning.

Mukul Hase Manish Shrivastava Payal Khullar, Konigari Rachna. Automatic question generation using relative pronouns and adverbs.

Sivaji Bandyopadhyay Rami Reddy Nandi Reddy. 2006. Dialogue based question answering system in telugu.

Nils Reimers. 2021. Sentencetransformers documentation - sentence-bert: Sentence embeddings using siamese bert-networks.

Roshni. 2020. 8 reasons why the nep's move to teaching in mother tongue could transform teaching and learning in india.

Md. Sajjatul Islam Md. Shahnur Azad Chowdhury-Md. Jiabul Hoque Shudipta Sharma, Muhammad Kamal Hossen. Automatic question and answer generation from bengali and english texts.

Serge Sharoff Siva Reddy. 2011. Cross language pos taggers (and other tools) for indian languages: An experiment with kannada using telugu resources.

10 Appendix

List of words related to time:
'అప్పుడు', 'రోజు' , 'కాలం', 'సాయంకాలం', 'ఉదయం', 'మధ్యాహ్నం', 'రాత్రి', 'పగలు', 'నెల', 'వారం', 'సంవత్సరం', 'సూర్యాస్తమయం', 'శుభోదయం', 'దినం', 'సమయం', 'వర్తమానం' , 'పూర్వం', 'భవిష్యత్తు', 'సోమవారం', 'మంగళవారం', 'బుధవారం', 'గురువారం', 'శుక్రవారం', 'శనివారం', 'ఆదివారం', 'మాసం'

Translations Then, day, time period, evening, morning, afternoon, night, morning(synonym), month, week, year, sunset, sunrise, day(synonym), time, present, past, future, Monday, Tuesday, Wednesday, Thursday, Friday, Saturday, Sunday, month(synonym).

Table 3: This set comprises of the time-related words that have a high chance of being used in a storybook.

Q:What kind of sack was hard to carry?
A:That much of a heavy sack was hard to carry.

Q:In the market how was he buying sandals, clothes, bangles, fruits, utensils - and sold them in the village?
A:In the market how was buying sandals, clothes, bangles, fruits, utensils for cheap rates and sold them in the village.

Q:Packing all the things, putting them on the donkey, from market to village, from village to whose house was he taking them?
A:Packing all the things, putting them on the donkey, from market to village, from village to his own house he was taking them.

Q:How did the innocent sparrow believed the crows without even asking why and where?
A:The innocent sparrow believed the crows blindly without even asking why and where.

Q:Instead of believing the sparrow, looking at it with disgust how many times did they beat it?
A:Instead of believing the sparrow, looking at it with disgust they beat it 2 times.

Q:Did the sparrow made friends with the crows?
A:Yes, the sparrow made friends with the crows.

Q:Once upon a time where was the innocent sparrow living?
A:Once upon a time the innocent sparrow was living in a village.

Q:What did the sparrow say pleadingly?
A:The sparrow said pleadingly, "No! no! I didn't do any mistake, I'm innocent, I did nothing, please leave me."

Table 4: Translations of the results in Table 2 in section 9

Combining Open Domain Question Answering with a Task-Oriented Dialog System

Jan Nehring, Nils Feldhus, Akhyar Ahmed, Harleen Kaur
German Research Centre for Artificial Intelligence (DFKI)
Berlin, Germany
`firstname.lastname@dfki.de`

Abstract

We apply the modular dialog system framework to combine open-domain question answering with a task-oriented dialog system. This meta dialog system can answer questions from Wikipedia and at the same time act as a personal assistant. The aim of this system is to combine the strength of an open-domain question answering system with the conversational power of task-oriented dialog systems. After explaining the technical details of the system, we combined a new dataset out of standard datasets to evaluate the system. We further introduce an evaluation method for this system. Using this method, we compare the performance of the non-modular system with the performance of the modular system and show that the modular dialog system framework is very suitable for this combination of conversational agents and that the performance of each agent decreases only marginally through the modular setting.

1 Introduction

Nehring and Ahmed (2021) defined a modular dialog system (MDS) as a dialog system that consists of multiple modules. In this paper, we want to use this framework to combine a task-oriented dialog system (TODS) with an open-domain question answering system (ODQA). For our experiments, we construct the TODS using the Frankenbot framework trained on the CLINC150 dataset (Larson et al., 2019) to build a dialog system from the personal assistant domain. For the ODQA system, we use DrQA (Chen et al., 2017) which uses Wikipedia among other corpora as knowledge sources.

The resulting meta dialog system combines the strengths and evens out the weaknesses of both approaches. ODQA can answer a wide range of questions. Furthermore, one can easily extend the system with new information as it only requires unstructured text as a knowledge base. It is not trivial to fix the mistakes of ODQA, so we have little control over the system.

Creating the TODS on the other hand requires a lot of manual work. It is not feasible to cover the amount of questions an ODQA system can answer. Therefore, the amount of topics that the TODS can talk about is rather limited. The strength of the TODS approach is its fine-grained control. Errors can easily be corrected by adding a small amount of training data and retraining the model. A TODS cannot only answer questions, but it can also understand other user queries. For example, the TODS can understand greetings and respond with a greeting, a task that is not possible for ODQA systems. Another strength of TODS is the possibility to create complex dialogs spanning multiple turns using a dialog manager.

Question answering has been augmented with TODS before (Banchs et al., 2013; D'Haro et al., 2015; Coronado et al., 2015; Podgorny et al., 2019). In this work, we apply the MDS framework to the combination of an ODQA system and a TODS. The other works mentioned here usually performed a user-based evaluation showing that the meta dialog system works. We present a method to evaluate such a system automatically. The method inspects module selection, ODQA and TODS individually and measures the performance change of those from the non-modular to the modular scenario. We show that the performance drop is very low because the module selection performs very well in our setup with an f1-measure of 0.964.

The remainder of this paper is structured as follows: Section 2 gives an overview over the background related to conversational agents, DrQA, Frankenbot, the MDS framework, evaluation measures and datasets. Next, section 3 explains how we created our dataset out of existing datasets. The setup of our MDS and implementation details are

Proceedings of the 1st Workshop on Document-grounded Dialogue and Conversational Question Answering, pages 38–45
August 5–6, 2021.

covered in section 4. Section 5 introduces our evaluation methodology, followed by the results and their discussion in 6. The following sections discuss conclusions (7) and future work (8).

2 Background

2.1 Conversational Agents

Zhu et al. (2021) define ODQA as the task of identifying answers to natural questions from a large corpus of documents. A typical system works in two steps: First, it selects a document from the corpus that contains the answer. Second, they generate the answer from this document, either in natural language (generative QA) or as the span of text containing the answer (extractive QA) (Zhu et al., 2021). Examples of such systems are DrQA (Chen et al., 2017), QuASE (Sun et al., 2015), YodaQA (Baudiš and Šedivý, 2015) and DeepQA (Ferrucci et al., 2010).

There are many ways to create a TODS. In this paper, we limit ourselves to TODS that build on the GUS architecture (Bobrow et al., 1977). Many modern chatbot frameworks like Amazon Alexa[1], Google Dialogflow[2] and others build on this surprisingly old architecture (Jurafsky and Martin, 2020). In GUS, each user utterance is processed by the Natural Language Understanding (NLU) unit. The NLU first performs intent classification which is the task of assigning one of many pre-defined user intents to the utterance. An important concept of GUS is the semantic frame which defines a set of slots. These slots represent information that the dialog system needs to understand and fill in from the user utterances in order to fulfill a task. For example, the semantic frame "restaurant reservation" consists of the slots "number of persons", "date and time". When a user utters "I want to book a table for three persons" the TODS can detect the intent "table reservation" and fill the slot "number of persons". The output of the NLU is fed into the Dialog Manager (DM). The DM keeps track of the dialog state and can be either rule-based or machine-learned. The dialog manager can, for example, decide to ask about the date and time of the reservation if the intent "table reservation" is detected, the slot "number of persons" is filled out but the slot "date and time" is still missing. Answers are usually based on the dialog state. In this paper, we limit ourselves to rule-based DMs and answers written manually by the chatbot designers. For a more detailed discussion of TODS, we refer to Jurafsky and Martin (2020).

A MDS, as defined by Nehring and Ahmed (2021), combines multiple dialog systems to form a meta dialog system. Each of these dialog systems is called a module. For each incoming user utterance, the module selection component chooses the module that produces the answer. The MDS framework does not define how to implement the module selection component, the actual implementation can vary from MDS to MDS. Another characteristic of the MDS is that modules are independent from each other, do not share a common state and do not share models or parameters. The MDS architecture consists of multiple subsequent models, in contrast to a joint architecture that uses one joint module for all tasks. This allows the combination of different, usually incompatible technologies under one framework.

2.2 DrQA

Chen et al. (2017) introduced the extractive question answering system DrQA. To answer a question, DrQA starts with an information retrieval step to detect the relevant article from the Wikipedia corpus. The information retrieval is based on bigram hashing and TF-IDF metrics. In the second step DrQA uses a recurrent neural network to identify the answer span in the retrieved document used as context. DrQA is trained on multiple datasets, including the Stanford Question Answering Dataset (Rajpurkar et al., 2016).

2.3 Frankenbot

Frankenbot is a framework for TODS that is capable of holding longer conversations spanning multiple turns by mapping the conversation onto pre-defined dialog trees. It consists of a set of nodes, each containing a possible answer. Furthermore, each node contains a pre-defined condition. Conditions can be e.g. "The detected intent is X", "The detected intent is Y and the slot Z is not filled out" and similar.

Frankenbot uses the Dual Intent and Entity Transformer (Bunk et al., 2020) as NLU for intent classification and slot filling. First, each utterance is processed by the NLU. Next, the dialog manager determines which nodes are active, meaning that they are candidates for the answer generation. Top-level nodes are always active. Nested nodes are

[1] https://developer.amazon.com/en-US/alexa

[2] https://cloud.google.com/dialogflow

only active if their parent node produced the answer in the previous turn. After the active nodes have been determined, the DM evaluates the conditions of all active nodes in a certain order (depth-first). The first node whose condition matches produces the answer.

2.4 Evaluation measures

In extractive QA, F1 is the standard measure (Chen et al., 2019). It is computed over tokens in the candidate and the reference. Automatic evaluation measures in QA are flawed because they rely on a gold standard of correct answers (Chen et al., 2019). When the tested QA system gives a correct answer which is not defined in the gold standard, the correct answer will be counted as an error. We note that there is still no consensus about an automated metric for question answering that correlates well with human judgment (Chen et al., 2019).

Evaluating a TODS in an automated manner suffers from similar problems but we can evaluate individual components of the TODS. Intent classification is the task of labeling a user utterance with one of a set of predefined intents. F1 scores are usually used to evaluate the performance of intent classification of the NLU component (Deriu et al., 2019; Liu et al., 2019).

2.5 Datasets

The CLINC150 dataset (Larson et al., 2019) is a dataset to evaluate the intent classification performance of a TODS for the personal assistant domain. Crowd workers wrote 22,500 user utterances for 150 intents. It contains the same amount of utterances for each intent. The dataset contains 1,200 out-of-scope utterances that belong to none of the intents which we did not use.

The Stanford Question Answering Dataset (SQuAD) (Rajpurkar et al., 2016) is a standard dataset for question answering which contains over 100.000+ questions. It contains a list of contexts, and each of them is a paragraph of text. The questions are always related to a context. Furthermore, it contains answers to the questions that are annotated as a span of text from the context. It is split into a training (80%), a development (10%), and a test (10%) dataset.

2.6 Hybrid Dialog Systems

There are many approaches how to combine several dialog tasks in one dialog system. One approach is a hierarchical architecture composed of several agents. They use a classifier to select the right agent for each utterance (Coronado et al., 2015; Banchs et al., 2013; Planells et al., 2013; Pichl et al., 2018) or a ranking approach that generates answers by each DS and then selects the best answer (Song et al., 2018; Tanaka et al., 2019; Paranjape et al., 2020). Other approaches use a joint architecture to solve multiple dialog tasks (Lewis et al., 2020; Shuster et al., 2020).

3 Creating a combined dataset for question answering and intent recognition

To our knowledge, no dataset exists to evaluate a TODS and a QA system at the same time. Therefore, we combined the SQuAD and CLINC150 datasets to form a single dataset for the evaluation of the combined system. Beyond the original labels from CLINC150 (intents) and SQuAD (answers), each sample has an additional label for the module selection which we call the true module. One must note that due to the nature of the MDS, we need to train each module on its own. DrQA is already pre-trained on the SQuAD training dataset and we did not retrain it. We kept 50% of the CLINC150 samples to train the Frankenbot and call this dataset $train_F$. We then train the module selection on the $train_M S$ part of the dataset. For parameter selection, we reserve $valid_M S$ samples. Finally, we use the dataset $test_{full}$ for the evaluation of the full system.

dataset	number of samples
all	32,390
$\text{all}_{\text{CLINC150}}$	21,820
$\text{all}_{\text{SQuAD}}$	10,570
train_{F}	11,250
train_{MS}	7,900
test_{MS}	2,634
$\text{test}_{\text{full}}$	10,606

Table 1: Dataset statistics

Table 1 shows statistics about this dataset. We used 11,250 samples to train the Frankenbot TODS ($train_F$). We do not need a training set for DrQA in our dataset and use the development subset of SQuAD only for $train_F$, $valid_M S$, and $test_{full}$.

We reserved 10,534 samples to train and validate the module selection. With a 75-25 split, it results in 7,900 samples for training ($train_{MS}$) and 2,634 samples for testing ($valid_{MS}$). For the evaluation of the full system, we reserved 10,606 samples ($test_{full}$). We aimed for an equal amount of samples from CLINC150 and SQuAD in the train_{MS}, test_{MS}, and $\text{test}_{\text{full}}$ sections of the dataset and therefore randomly subsampled the CLINC150 dataset.

The SQuAD dataset contains multiple questions for each context, e.g. it contains 810 questions related to a short paragraph about a Super Bowl game. If we split the SQuAD dataset randomly, the module selection might overfit on such statistical cues, learning that the word Super Bowl is a hint that this utterance is aimed at the ODQA system. Therefore, we did not assign the SQuAD questions to the datasets at random, but split it along those contexts so that each context appears in either $train_{MS}$ or $test_{full}$, but not in both.

While the input questions of SQuAD use correct casing, the user utterances of CLINC150 use a mix of correct casing and lower casing. Furthermore, CLINC150 uses punctuation marks only sometimes while SQuAD always uses punctuation marks, mostly question marks. This makes our dataset unrealistic because it leads to distinguishing criteria which will not occur in real world data. We removed these differences to make the utterances more uniform and therefore more realistic by lowercasing all user utterances and removing all punctuation marks.

Many questions from SQuAD can be answered only when the context of the question is known. For example the question "Who approved of this plan?" is only answerable with the context paragraph at hand. DrQA retrieves the context from Wikipedia and therefore cannot answer this question. To get a more realistic impression of the performance of the DrQA module, we manually annotated 100 questions from $test_{full}$ that can be answered in the ODQA scenario.

We published the dataset under the Creative Commons Attribution Share Alike license CC-BY-SA 4.0 under this link[3].

4 Modular Dialog System

Figure 1 shows the architecture of the MDS that we used in our experiments. It contains two modules: The ODQA system DrQA and the TODS Frankenbot.

The module selection component decides for each user utterance which module will answer the utterance. We formulate this as a text classification task with the candidate modules as target classes, i.e., the module selection predicts each incoming user utterance as either DrQA or Frankenbot. We used BERT with a sequence classification head (Devlin et al., 2019) for this classification task. It is trained on dataset train_{MS} and evaluated on test_{MS}.

[3]link will be available in camera ready version

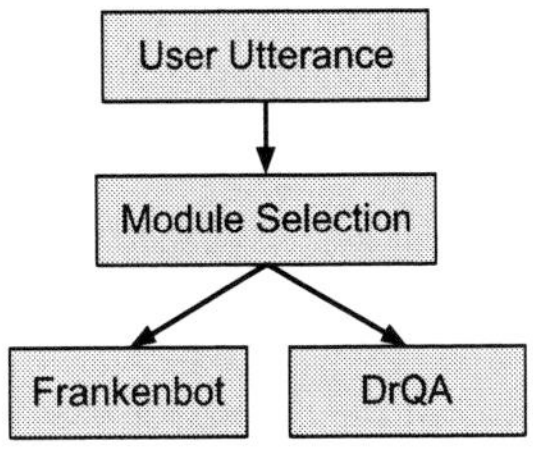

Figure 1: Architecture of the MDS

4.1 Modules

Our MDS consists of the two modules DrQA and Frankenbot. The DrQA module uses the implementation published by its authors[4] without further modification.

The Frankenbot module uses the Frankenbot framework as the technical backend for a TODS. We used the CLINC150 dataset to train the NLU. The CLINC150 dataset contains single turn utterances only so our dialog system does not use a deep dialog management either. The user makes his query, for example "Put the lights on". Using this dataset the dialog system cannot ask back, for example "In which room?".

Frankenbot can also predict samples as out of scope (oos) when the confidence of the intent classification is below a certain manually defined threshold. The oos class indicates that Frankenbot cannot answer this utterance.

5 Evaluation

5.1 Evaluation of the single modules

Following the approach of the SQuAD dataset (Rajpurkar et al., 2016), we measure the quality of the DrQA module using token-based F1 scores. Following the approach of the CoQA challenge (Reddy et al., 2019), we did not take the exact match measure into account.

Next we want to evaluate the quality of Frankenbot in the MDS. One can evaluate many aspects of

[4]https://github.com/facebookresearch/DrQA

Frankenbot. Since Frankenbot's answers are manually predefined, we make the assumption that they are çorrect and we do not want to evaluate them here. Another factor in the evaluation of dialog systems is the dialog management. In this work, we do not want to evaluate the quality of the dialog management but the quality of the modular dialog system. We argue that Frankenbot can produces the correct answer as long when the intent classification produced the correct intent. Therefore, we evaluate the quality of the intent classification to estimate the quality of the TODS. We evaluate the intent classification using F1 scores. It is a multi-class classification setting and we use the micro-average to calculate a weighted final score out of the F1 scores for each intent.

5.2 Evaluation of module selection

Module selection is a classification task and therefore its evaluation is straightforward. We use F1 scores to calculate the performance of the module selection. We use the $test_{full}$ dataset to calculate the scores of module selection. We repeated this evaluation ten times and averaged the results.

5.3 Evaluation of the full system

Here, we present a framework that can evaluate both systems jointly. The evaluation framework can then compare the performance change from a non-modular dialog system to a modular system. We also repeated this evaluation ten times and averaged the results.

For a fine-grained evaluation of the full system, we calculate scores for the non-modular and for the modular scenario. The *non-modular* scenario evaluates how the system would perform if it was not modular. Bypassing the module selection, it evaluates each module on its own data. In our case, it uses the CLINC150 part of the test dataset to evaluate the Frankenbot and the SQuAD part of the test dataset to evaluate the SQuAD.

The *modular scenario* evaluates the MDS. In this scenario, we evaluate each module on its own data again, but this time including the module selection. In this setting, it is possible that the module selection makes a mistake and incorrectly assigns a sample to the other module.

In case we are evaluating Frankenbot and a Frankenbot sample gets confused as DrQA, we label it with the intent class "oos" for out-of-scope. This will lower the F1 score of Frankenbot, but it will not affect the score of DrQA.

In case we misclassify a sample during DrQA's evaluation as Frankenbot, we assume that the dialog system answered with an empty string and continue the evaluation. We could use the actual answer of the dialog system instead of this arbitrary string, but we believe that the empty string provides a more stable error because it does not produce random matches on the token basis and has the same length always. Again, this misclassified sample only produces an error in the DrQA module and not in the Frankenbot module.

To get a joint score for the whole system, we take the macro-average between the F1 scores of intent recognition and QA and name it *joint F1*. This makes sense for the modular scenario only.

5.4 Questions that are answerable in ODQA

As stated earlier, we found that many questions from SQuAD are not answerable in the ODQA scenario. Therefore, we calculate the evaluation once for the full dataset and once only for questions that are answerable in the ODQA scenario. This evaluation includes all samples from CLINC150 and 100 questions from SQuAD that we manually annotated for being answerable without knowledge of the context document.

This is an additional error analysis of our specific system and not part of the evaluation method that we suggest for this kind of MDS.

6 Results and Discussion

Table 2 shows the results of the non-modular and modular evaluation across the evaluation using the full dataset and the subset of the dataset containing only questions that DrQA can answer.

	F1 Franken-bot	F1 DrQA	joint F1
Full evaluation data			
non-modular	0.897	0.340	-
modular	0.895	0.326	0.611
Questions that DrQA can answer			
non-modular	0.897	0.451	-
modular	0.892	0.442	0.670

Table 2: Results

6.1 Results of module evaluation

The evaluation of Frankenbot's NLU reports an F1 score of 0.897. The numbers are the same for the evaluation on the full data and on questions that

DrQA can answer, because it is an evaluation on the same data.

The evaluation of DrQA reports an F1 score of 0.36 in the non-modular setting which is comparable to the results reported in the original paper (Chen et al., 2017). The F1 score rises to 0.451 in the subset of SQuAD questions that DrQA can answer.

6.2 Results of Module Selection

The F1 score of the module selection is 0.964. This shows that the module selection does not introduce a large error source. This is different from the findings of Nehring and Ahmed (2021) where the modular setting introduced a large error. We believe that the high quality of module selection is partly a result of the different natures of the datasets. CLINC150 mostly contains commands like "Switch on the light" or "Play the next song in the radio" while SQuAD contains only questions. Our BERT-based classifier can easily distinguish between the two. We conclude from this result that the MDS framework is suitable for the combination of ODQA and TODS.

6.3 Results of the full system evaluation

The very high performance of module selection reflects itself in the results of the evaluation of the modular setting. Since the module selection is almost always correct, it does not introduce a significant additional error.

It is obvious that the quality is lower in the modular scenario compared to the non-modular scenario: The module selection is an additional source of error only and the performance of a module cannot improve through the module selection. This low performance drop is an indicator that the MDS framework is very suitable for this combination of dialog systems.

6.4 Error analysis of module selection

Table 3 shows the confusion matrix of the module selection over dataset $test_{full}$. In the former results sections, we repeated each experiment 10 times and averaged the results. In this section we show the results of one of these 10 module selections.

The amount of DrQA samples being misclassified as Frankenbot is 26x higher than the amount of Frankenbot samples being misclassified as DrQA. We assume that this is due to the nature of the datasets. Each of the intents from the CLINC150 dataset describe a narrow topic and therefore more suitable for the text classification of the module selection. The questions of DrQA do not share a common topic and are therefore harder to detect.

	Frankenbot	**DrQA**
Frankenbot	5,268	16
DrQA	421	4,903

Table 3: Confusion Matrix of module selection with the predicted module in the rows and true label in the columns and the true module in the columns.

7 Conclusion

We used the MDS framework to combine TODS and ODQA using the example of DrQA and Frankenbot. Using this framework, one can extend the capabilities of ODQA with the conversational capabilities of a TODS. Further, we introduced an evaluation method that a) evaluates the performance of module selection and b) compares the performance of the underlying ODQA and TODS systems in the modular and in the non-modular setting.

The evaluation showed that DrQA and Frankenbot work very well together as a MDS. The MDS introduces only a minimal additional error.

We believe that the MDS framework is especially suitable for practical applications because one can extend an existing TODS with a ODQA system or vice versa easier using MDS compared to a framework that performs TODS and ODQA together in a joint model. Although we did not prove it, we expect that when we exchange one of the modules, e.g. the Frankenbot system with Rasa[5], Google Dialogflow or IBM Watson Assistant[6], the performance of the MDS will change only in that module.

We present this evaluation framework for our specific use case, but we expect it to generalize to other settings as well such as using more than two modules. It can also work with other performance measures than F1 scores, although one needs to think about how to calculate a joint score out of different scores and how to deal with errors of the module selection in the modular scenario.

[5]https://rasa.com

[6]https://www.ibm.com/cloud/watson-assistant

8 Future Work

The module selection showed very good results. In future work, we want to try the module selection with other or smaller datasets to find out if this high performance is stable across datasets.

We showed that the combination of a single-turn ODQA with a single-turn TODS works very well. An interesting extension of this paper would be to use a multi-turn ODQA as in the CoQA challenge and a multi-turn TODS and find a way to automatically evaluate both together.

9 Acknowledgment

This research was partially supported by the German Federal Ministry of Education and Research (BMBF) through the project SIM3S (19F2058A).

References

Rafael E. Banchs, Ridong Jiang, Seokhwan Kim, Arthur Niswar, and Kheng Hui Yeo. 2013. AIDA: Artificial Intelligent Dialogue Agent. In *Proceedings of the SIGDIAL 2013 Conference*, pages 145–147, Metz, France. Association for Computational Linguistics.

Petr Baudiš and Jan Šedivý. 2015. Modeling of the Question Answering Task in the YodaQA System. In *Proceedings of the 6th International Conference on Experimental IR Meets Multilinguality, Multimodality, and Interaction - Volume 9283*, CLEF'15, page 222–228, Berlin, Heidelberg. Springer-Verlag.

Daniel G. Bobrow, Ronald M. Kaplan, Martin Kay, Donald A. Norman, Henry Thompson, and Terry Winograd. 1977. GUS, a Frame-Driven Dialog System. *Artif. Intell.*, 8(2):155–173.

Tanja Bunk, Daksh Varshneya, Vladimir Vlasov, and Alan Nichol. 2020. DIET: Lightweight Language Understanding for Dialogue Systems.

Anthony Chen, Gabriel Stanovsky, Sameer Singh, and Matt Gardner. 2019. Evaluating Question Answering Evaluation. In *MRQA@EMNLP*.

Danqi Chen, Adam Fisch, Jason Weston, and Antoine Bordes. 2017. Reading Wikipedia to answer open-domain questions. In *Proceedings of the 55th Annual Meeting of the Association for Computational Linguistics (Volume 1: Long Papers)*, pages 1870–1879, Vancouver, Canada. Association for Computational Linguistics.

Miguel Coronado, Carlos A. Iglesias, and Alberto Mardomingo. 2015. A Personal Agents hybrid architecture for question answering featuring social dialog. In *2015 International Symposium on Innovations in Intelligent SysTems and Applications (INISTA)*, pages 1–8.

Jan Deriu, Alvaro Rodrigo, Arantxa Otegi, Guillermo Echegoyen, Sophie Rosset, Eneko Agirre, and Mark Cieliebak. 2019. Survey on Evaluation Methods for Dialogue Systems. *Artificial Intelligence Review*, 54(1):755–810.

Jacob Devlin, Ming-Wei Chang, Kenton Lee, and Kristina Toutanova. 2019. BERT: Pre-training of deep bidirectional transformers for language understanding. In *Proceedings of the 2019 Conference of the North American Chapter of the Association for Computational Linguistics: Human Language Technologies, Volume 1 (Long and Short Papers)*, pages 4171–4186, Minneapolis, Minnesota. Association for Computational Linguistics.

Luis Fernando D'Haro, Seokhwan Kim, Kheng Hui Yeo, Ridong Jiang, Andreea I. Niculescu, Rafael E. Banchs, and Haizhou Li. 2015. CLARA: A Multifunctional Virtual Agent for Conference Support and Touristic Information. In *Natural Language Dialog Systems and Intelligent Assistants*, pages 233–239. Springer International Publishing.

David Ferrucci, Eric Brown, Jennifer Chu-Carroll, James Fan, David Gondek, Aditya A. Kalyanpur, Adam Lally, J. William Murdock, Eric Nyberg, John Prager, Nico Schlaefer, and Chris Welty. 2010. Building Watson: An Overview of the DeepQA Project. *AI Magazine*, 31(3):59–79.

Dan Jurafsky and James H. Martin. 2020. *Speech and Language Processing : An Introduction to Natural Language Processing, Computational Linguistics, and Speech Recognition.* Pearson Prentice Hall, Upper Saddle River, N.J.

Stefan Larson, Anish Mahendran, Joseph J. Peper, Christopher Clarke, Andrew Lee, Parker Hill, Jonathan K. Kummerfeld, Kevin Leach, Michael A. Laurenzano, Lingjia Tang, and Jason Mars. 2019. An Evaluation Dataset for Intent Classification and Out-of-Scope Prediction. In *Proceedings of the 2019 Conference on Empirical Methods in Natural Language Processing and the 9th International Joint Conference on Natural Language Processing (EMNLP-IJCNLP)*, pages 1311–1316, Hong Kong, China. Association for Computational Linguistics.

Mike Lewis, Yinhan Liu, Naman Goyal, Marjan Ghazvininejad, Abdelrahman Mohamed, Omer Levy, Veselin Stoyanov, and Luke Zettlemoyer. 2020. BART: Denoising sequence-to-sequence pre-training for natural language generation, translation, and comprehension. In *Proceedings of the 58th Annual Meeting of the Association for Computational Linguistics*, pages 7871–7880, Online. Association for Computational Linguistics.

Jiao Liu, Yanling Li, and Min Lin. 2019. Review of Intent Detection Methods in the Human-Machine Dialogue System. *Journal of Physics: Conference Series*, 1267:12059.

Jan Nehring and Akhyar Ahmed. 2021. Normalisierungsmethoden für Intent Erkennung Modularer Dialogsysteme. In *Tagungsband der 32. Konferenz. Elektronische Sprachsignalverarbeitung (ESSV-2021), March 3-5, Berlin, Germany*. TUDpress.

Ashwin Paranjape, Abigail See, Kathleen Kenealy, Haojun Li, Amelia Hardy, Peng Qi, Kaushik Ram Sadagopan, Nguyet Minh Phu, Dilara Soylu, and Christopher D. Manning. 2020. Neural generation meets real people: Towards emotionally engaging mixed-initiative conversations.

Jan Pichl, Petr Marek, Jakub Konrád, Martin Matulík, Hoang Long Nguyen, and Jan Šedivý. 2018. Alquist: The alexa prize socialbot.

Joaquin Planells, Lluís F. Hurtado, Encarna Segarra, and Emilio Sanchis. 2013. A multi-domain dialog system to integrate heterogeneous spoken dialog systems. In *INTERSPEECH 2013, 14th Annual Conference of the International Speech Communication Association, Lyon, France, August 25-29, 2013*, pages 1891–1895. ISCA.

Igor Podgorny, Yason Khaburzaniya, and Jeff Geisler. 2019. Conversational Agents and Community Question Answering. In *Extended Abstracts of the 2019 CHI Conference on Human Factors in Computing Systems, CHI 2019, Glasgow, Scotland, UK, May 04-09, 2019*. ACM.

Pranav Rajpurkar, Jian Zhang, Konstantin Lopyrev, and Percy Liang. 2016. SQuAD: 100,000+ questions for machine comprehension of text. In *Proceedings of the 2016 Conference on Empirical Methods in Natural Language Processing*, pages 2383–2392, Austin, Texas. Association for Computational Linguistics.

Siva Reddy, Danqi Chen, and Christopher D. Manning. 2019. CoQA: A Conversational Question Answering Challenge. *Transactions of the Association for Computational Linguistics*, 7:249–266.

Kurt Shuster, Da Ju, Stephen Roller, Emily Dinan, Y-Lan Boureau, and Jason Weston. 2020. The dialogue dodecathlon: Open-domain knowledge and image grounded conversational agents. In *Proceedings of the 58th Annual Meeting of the Association for Computational Linguistics*, pages 2453–2470, Online. Association for Computational Linguistics.

Yiping Song, Cheng-Te Li, Jian-Yun Nie, Ming Zhang, Dongyan Zhao, and Rui Yan. 2018. An Ensemble of Retrieval-Based and Generation-Based Human-Computer Conversation Systems. In *Proceedings of the Twenty-Seventh International Joint Conference on Artificial Intelligence, {IJCAI-18}*, pages 4382–4388. International Joint Conferences on Artificial Intelligence Organization.

Huan Sun, Hao Ma, Wen-tau Yih, Chen-Tse Tsai, Jingjing Liu, and Ming-Wei Chang. 2015. Open Domain Question Answering via Semantic Enrichment. In *Proceedings of the 24th International Conference on World Wide Web*, WWW '15, page 1045–1055, Republic and Canton of Geneva, CHE. International World Wide Web Conferences Steering Committee.

Ryota Tanaka, Akihide Ozeki, Shugo Kato, and Akinobu Lee. 2019. An Ensemble Dialogue System for Facts-Based Sentence Generation. *CoRR*, abs/1902.01529.

Fengbin Zhu, Wenqiang Lei, Chao Wang, Jianming Zheng, Soujanya Poria, and Tat-Seng Chua. 2021. Retrieving and Reading: A Comprehensive Survey on Open-domain Question Answering.

CAiRE in DialDoc21: Data Augmentation for Information-Seeking Dialogue System

Yan Xu*, Etsuko Ishii*, Genta Indra Winata, Zhaojiang Lin, Andrea Madotto, Zihan Liu, Peng Xu and Pascale Fung
Center for Artificial Intelligence Research (CAiRE)
The Hong Kong University of Science and Technology, Clear Water Bay, Hong Kong
{yxucb,eishii,giwinata}@connect.ust.hk, pascale@ece.ust.hk

Abstract

Information-seeking dialogue systems, including knowledge identification and response generation, aim to respond to users with fluent, coherent, and informative responses based on users' needs, which. To tackle this challenge, we utilize data augmentation methods and several training techniques with the pre-trained language models to learn a general pattern of the task and thus achieve promising performance. In DialDoc21 competition, our system achieved 74.95 F1 score and 60.74 Exact Match score in subtask 1, and 37.72 SacreBLEU score in subtask 2. Empirical analysis is provided to explain the effectiveness of our approaches.

1 Introduction

Recent progress in research has opened up real-life applications of dialogue systems (Winata et al., 2021; Ishii et al., 2021), of which information-seeking dialogue systems are one of the major types. The goal of such dialogue systems is to provide fluent and coherent responses with sufficient information to users based on their needs, retrieving information using the dialogue history. The performance of an information-seeking dialogue system can be evaluated from three aspects: (1) user utterance understanding, (2) relevant knowledge retrieval, and (3) agent response generation (Feng et al., 2020).

This paper presents work on the DialDoc-21 Shared Task, which is to teach a dialogue system to identify the most relevant knowledge in the associated document for generating agent responses in natural language. It is composed of two subtasks: Knowledge Identification (KI) to retrieve the knowledge from the document, and Response Generation (RG) to generate an agent utterance utilizing the retrieved knowledge.

To tackle this problem, we leverage the pre-trained language models from Liu et al. (2019a) and Lewis et al. (2020) and explore data augmentation methods with several training techniques so as to avoid over-fitting to the DialDoc datasets and to teach the model the general pattern of the task. Ensemble and post-processing are conducted to further improve the model performance. Experimental results show that data augmentation is a simple but effective approach for knowledge identification in information-seeking dialogue systems (Madotto et al., 2020a), while bringing improvement to response generation at the same time. In the DialDoc-21 competition, our system achieved 74.95 of F1 score and 60.74 of Exact Match in subtask 1, and 37.72 SacreBLEU score (Post, 2018) in subtask 2[1].

2 Datasets

Doc2Dial dataset In this shared task, we mainly focus on the Doc2Dial dataset (Feng et al., 2020). Doc2Dial addresses the challenge of modeling different dialogue scenes with documents and providing free-form responses while allowing follow-up questions from the agent. The shared task evaluation is divided into a testdev phase and a test phase. The main difference between these is that in the test phase, out-of-domain (OOD) data samples are included by selecting documents from the domain which is unseen in the training process. The testdev phase only covers 30% of the data samples in the final test phase.

Besides Doc2Dial, several other datasets are leveraged for augmentation, as follows:

MRQA 2019 Shared Task dataset is a collection of multiple reading comprehension datasets for evaluating the generalization ability of QA models. Six datasets are assigned to the training split,

* These two authors contributed equally.

[1]The code is available at: https://github.com/HLTCHKUST/CAiRE_in_DialDoc21.

Proceedings of the 1st Workshop on Document-grounded Dialogue and Conversational Question Answering, pages 46–51
August 5–6, 2021. ©2021 Association for Computational Linguistics

Model	Initialization	Training	
		Data	Method
$\texttt{RoBERTa}_{\mathrm{mrqa}}$	$\texttt{RoBERTa}_{\mathrm{large}}$	MRQA	PT
$\texttt{RoBERTa}_{\mathrm{mrqa_s}}$	$\texttt{RoBERTa}_{\mathrm{large}}$	MRQA_{small}	PT
$\texttt{RoBERTa}_{\mathrm{cqa}}$	$\texttt{RoBERTa}_{\mathrm{large}}$	Doc2Dial, CQA	FT
$\texttt{RoBERTa}_{\mathrm{f(cqa)}}$	$\texttt{RoBERTa}_{\mathrm{cqa}}$	Doc2Dial	FT
$\texttt{RoBERTa}_{\mathrm{f(mrqa)}}$	$\texttt{RoBERTa}_{\mathrm{mrqa}}$	Doc2Dial	FT
$\texttt{RoBERTa}_{\mathrm{cqa(mrqa)}}$	$\texttt{RoBERTa}_{\mathrm{mrqa}}$	Doc2Dial, CQA	FT
$\texttt{RoBERTa}_{\mathrm{cqa(mrqa_s)}}$	$\texttt{RoBERTa}_{\mathrm{mrqa_s}}$	Doc2Dial, CQA	FT
$\texttt{RoBERTa}_{\mathrm{f(cqa(mrqa_s))}}$	$\texttt{RoBERTa}_{\mathrm{cqa(mrqa_s)}}$	Doc2Dial	FT
$\texttt{RoBERTa}_{\mathrm{all}}$	$\texttt{RoBERTa}_{\mathrm{large}}$	Doc2Dial, CQA, and MRQA	FT

Table 1: The combinations of the experimental settings for the KI subtask. Two-stage training consists of two stages: pre-training (PT) and fine-tuning (FT).

which is not included in the evaluation. Among them, SearchQA (Dunn et al., 2017) and TriviaQA (Joshi et al., 2017) differ from the others by the data resource and have the least generalization ability compared to the other four datasets as reported in (Su et al., 2019). In this shared task, we consider two settings when leveraging the MRQA dataset: MRQA and $\mathrm{MRQA}_{\mathrm{small}}$ which excludes SearchQA and TriviaQA.

Conversational QA (CQA) datasets We also introduce three CQA datasets, CoQA (Reddy et al., 2019), QuAC (Choi et al., 2018), and DoQA (Campos et al., 2020), in the shared task because of their similar settings to the KI process.

Wizard-of-Wikipedia (WoW) is a commonly-used knowledge-grounded dialogue dataset (Dinan et al., 2018). It aims at providing content-full responses to user utterances based on Wikipedia documents.

3 Methodology

We utilize a series of data-augmentation approaches to enable the model to obtain better representations on both dialogue context and document context and learn a general pattern of the task with less domain bias. Namely, we have a two-stage training paradigm, the first step is pretraining (PT) to have a better model initialization, and the second step is fine-tuning (FT) to adapt to DialDoc task. For each step, we can apply the multi-task learning (MTL) strategy if we have multiple datasets by making the datasets format uniform and treat samples equally. As reported in Fisch et al. (2019), a model trained on multiple dataset under similar tasks, is supposed to provide a better initialization for further fine-tuning and is capable of generalizing to the data samples in other domains. Thus, we expect a model trained with MTL in the first step to offer a better initialization and in the second step to reduce the domain bias and avoid overfitting.

3.1 Knowledge Identification

In the KI task, we conduct experiments on a large pre-trained model, RoBERTa-large (Liu et al., 2019a), which has shown its effectiveness on many QA datasets (Ju et al., 2019). The MRQA dataset and three CQA above datasets are leveraged for data augmentation. The combinations of the experimental settings are considered as follows:

We consider using CQA datasets to enrich the data source. $\textbf{RoBERTa}_{\mathrm{cqa}}$ is fine-tuned on Doc2Dial and three CQA datasets using MTL method. $\textbf{RoBERTa}_{\mathrm{f(cqa)}}$ leverages the pre-trained $\texttt{RoBERTa}_{\mathrm{cqa}}$ model and is fine-tuned on Doc2Dial dataset for better performance.

We train the RoBERTa model on MRQA daztaset and $\mathrm{MRQA}_{\mathrm{small}}$ dataset described in § 2 using MTL respectively (denoted as $\texttt{RoBERTa}_{\mathrm{mrqa}}$ and $\texttt{RoBERTa}_{\mathrm{mrqa_s}}$). These models could be further fine-tuned while providing a better initialization (Fisch et al., 2019). $\textbf{RoBERTa}_{\mathrm{f(mrqa)}}$ is to further fine-tune $\texttt{RoBERTa}_{\mathrm{mrqa}}$ on Doc2Dial dataset. The corresponding settings are also applied to $\textbf{RoBERTa}_{\mathrm{f(mrqa_s)}}$ model. While $\textbf{RoBERTa}_{\mathrm{cqa(mrqa)}}$ is initialized with $\texttt{RoBERTa}_{\mathrm{mrqa}}$ and fine-tuned on Doc2Dial and three CQA datasets using MTL. $\textbf{RoBERTa}_{\mathrm{cqa(mrqa_s)}}$ follows the same setting as the former model, but use $\texttt{RoBERTa}_{\mathrm{mrqa_s}}$ model for initialization instead. $\textbf{RoBERTa}_{\mathrm{f(cqa(mrqa_s))}}$ is to further fine-tune $\texttt{RoBERTa}_{\mathrm{cqa(mrqa_s)}}$ on Doc2Dial dataset.

$\textbf{RoBERTa}_{\mathrm{all}}$ is trained on Doc2Dial, MRQA dataset and CQA datasets using MTL method.

For better readability, we summarize the model settings in Table 1. We also explore more combinations of the experimental settings, such as other combinations of the datasets and other pre-trained language models. However, those fail to bring the improvements as much as those we mentioned above.

Post-processing We further conduct post-processing on the model predictions based on our observation that the ground truths of the data samples are annotated by document splits which are provided together with the dataset. We consider including the whole split of the document once the prediction covers λ percent of it, where λ is set as 0.1. In addition, for better performance in the shared task, we also slightly extend the predictions when there is a "Yes" or "No" shown right in front of the predicted spans.

Ensemble To further boost the model performance, we build an ensemble of our existing models. We consider one prediction containing the start position and the end position of the document as a unit and conduct voting over all the predictions of each data sample. The most frequent one will be selected as the final prediction. We denote the ensemble result as $\texttt{RoBERTa}_{\text{ensemble}}$.

Knowledge Identification		Response Generation	
max input length	512	max input length	300
max answer length	50	max target length	200
batch size	120	batch size	60
document stride	128	beam size	4
learning rate	3e-5	learning rate	3e-5

Table 2: The hyper-parameter settings in the shared task.

Model	# of ckpt	EM	F1
Testdev Phase			
$\texttt{RoBERTa}_{\text{large}}$ (baseline)	-	58.08	72.17
$\texttt{RoBERTa}_{\text{cqa}}$	2	59.09(±1.01)	72.90(±0.25)
$\texttt{RoBERTa}_{\text{f(cqa)}}$	2	58.08(±1.01)	72.23(±0.18)
$\texttt{RoBERTa}_{\text{f(mrqa)}}$	1	58.08	72.30
$\texttt{RoBERTa}_{\text{f(mrqa}_s)}$	16	59.37(±1.89)	73.51(±1.60)
$\texttt{RoBERTa}_{\text{cqa(mrqa)}}$	1	58.08	72.59
$\texttt{RoBERTa}_{\text{cqa(mrqa}_s)}$	6	59.60(±1.35)	73.76(±1.57)
$\texttt{RoBERTa}_{\text{f(cqa(mrqa}_s))}$	1	60.10	75.02
$\texttt{RoBERTa}_{\text{all}}$	1	58.08	74.63
$\texttt{RoBERTa}_{\text{ensemble}}$	-	63.13	77.31
$\texttt{RoBERTa}_{\text{all}}$-postproc	-	57.07(-1.01)	74.15(-0.47)
$\texttt{RoBERTa}_{\text{ensemble}}$-postproc	-	63.13(-0.00)	76.73(-0.58)
Test Phase			
$\texttt{RoBERTa}^{*}_{\text{ensemble}}$	-	60.74	74.95

Table 3: The results of the selected models on the testdev and test phase of subtask 1 are listed. All the results are calculated with the corresponding predictions after post-processing except those with specific notations. For the models that are trained with multiple random seeds, the average scores and the standard deviations are presented. $\texttt{RoBERTa}^{*}_{\text{ensemble}}$ denotes the results of the ensemble model on the test set.

3.2 Response Generation

To obtain natural and relevant responses, we take advantage of the evidence to the query identified from § 3.1 and focusing on paraphrasing the corresponding knowledge sentences based on the dialogue context. We leverage the large pre-trained model $\text{BART}_{\text{large}}$ (Lewis et al., 2020). The process of training and inference can be summarized as three steps:

Pre-training on WoW dataset. We first pretrain the BART model on the WoW dataset for better initialization because of its similarity with the RG task. In the training process, the gold grounded knowledge sentences are concatenated with the dialogue context and fed into the model as the inputs.

Fine-tuning on Doc2Dial dataset. In the Doc2Dial dataset, the labels of the gold document splits are also provided in the training and validation set. The model is further fine-tuned on the Doc2Dial dataset using the same components for the input sequences in the first step. The model could be evaluated under two scenarios: (1) **Gold mode** ($\texttt{BART}_{\text{gold}}$), leveraging the gold labels of the knowledge evidence in the dataset as the knowledge inputs; (2) **Prediction mode** ($\texttt{BART}_{\text{pred}}$), leveraging the prediction of the KI process as the inputs.

Inference with Knowledge Evidence. During the testdev and test phase, we leverage the predictions from the KI process as the knowledge evidence components for the dialogue queries. The model generates responses based on a concatenation of the knowledge evidence and the dialogue context.

Post-processing To avoid serious information loss in the generations compared to the knowledge evidence for the OOD data samples, we compare the lengths of the knowledge evidence and the responses (denoted as L_{kn} and L_{resp}). The generated response will be replaced by the raw knowledge evidence as the final output if $L_{\text{resp}} \leq \alpha L_{\text{kn}}$, where α is set as 0.4.

4 Experiments

4.1 Training Details

Hyper-parameter Settings We apply different settings to utilize the dialogue history for the two subtasks. For subtask 1, we leverage all previous turns and build the input sequence in a reverse order to them. For subtask 2, we leverage one extra last turn in the time order and differentiate the speakers with special tokens. In Table 2, we list the selected hyper-parameters utilized in the shared task.

Model	SacreBLEU		
	val	testdev	test
$\texttt{BART}_{large}$ (baseline)	-	16.73	-
$\texttt{Gold}$	45.67	-	-
$\texttt{RoBERTa}_{ensemble}$	38.78	37.45	38.68
$\texttt{BART}_{gold}$	20.17	-	-
+WoW pre-traning	48.24	-	-
$\texttt{BART}_{pred}$	16.67	16.72	16.45
+WoW pre-traning	39.87	38.26	37.31
+WoW pre-training+postproc*	-	-	37.72

Table 4: The results of selected models on subtask 2 are listed. Gold denotes the gold knowledge evidence labels provided in the dataset. The model denoted with * is the final submission to the test phase.

Ensemble Settings In subtask 1, we make an ensemble of all the checkpoints of the models listed in Table 1 except $\texttt{RoBERTa}_{mrqa}$ and $\texttt{RoBERTa}_{mrqa_s}$. The details of the checkpoints can be found in Tabel 3.

Metrics and Model Selection In subtask 1, the Exact Match (EM) and uni-gram F1 score are utilized as the criteria, while in subtask 2, we evaluate the generation by SacreBLEU. We select the models with the best EM and SacreBLEU scores on the validation set respectively, for the two subtasks. Specifically for subtask 2, the model is selected under the gold mode.

4.2 Results and Discussion

4.2.1 Results

The results are shown in Table 3 and Table 4. For both subtasks, we observe gaps between the testdev phase and the test phase. For some of the models in subtask 1, multiple random seeds are applied in the training process. The performance gap may result from the domain difference of the partial data samples in the test phase, where the corresponding documents are unseen in the training set. In Table 3, without post-processing on the predictions, the model performance consistently drops to a certain extent, which indicates that post-processing is suitable for the Doc2Dial scenario. Ensemble, which is a common strategy to improve performance, shows its effectiveness in this task.

For subtask 2, the pre-training on WoW dataset brings huge improvement to the model. Interestingly, by just using the knowledge evidence predicted from the subtask 1 $\texttt{RoBERTa}_{ensemble}$ model or the gold knowledge evidence labels, the performance can even exceed that of the generative model on SacreBLEU scores, while the responses from $\texttt{BART}_{pred}$ are more fluent and natural. This may be caused by the information loss when paraphrasing the knowledge evidence to dialogue responses.

4.2.2 Discussion

In this task, we explore data augmentation methods and conduct two-stage training as auxiliary training strategy for improvement. Although resource- and time-consuming, this approach is easy to implement and effective at enabling the model to learn more general ability on the task.

4.2.3 Post-Challenge Improvements

From our findings, the hyper-parameter, the maximum answer length, is left untuned, which hurts the QA model performance to some degree. With a maximum answer length of 100, the EM and F1 score on the testdev set improve by 2.53 and 1.08, respectively, while a 64.42 EM and 77.27 F1 score are achieved on the test set. With the improved prediction from subtask 1, we achieve a 39.88 SacreBLEU score in subtask 2.

5 Related Work

Conversational QA is a type of reading comprehension task that requires understanding not only the question but also the previous conversation turns. Various datasets have been introduced in recent years, and many of them restrict answers to be extraction of a span from the reference document, while the others allow free-form responses (Choi et al., 2018; Reddy et al., 2019; Campos et al., 2020).

In addition to the works to enrich the contents of open-domain conversations by controllable generation (Lin et al., 2020; Madotto et al., 2020b), the knowledge grounded dialogue task aims to offer more informative conversation by leveraging an external knowledge source (Dinan et al., 2018; Xu et al., 2020). Relevant knowledge selection is the key to improving the whole system, and very recently, latent variable models have been attracting more attention for this purpose (Lian et al., 2019; Liu et al., 2019b; Kim et al., 2020; Chen et al., 2020; Xu et al., 2021).

6 Conclusion

In this paper, we utilize data augmentation methods and several training techniques with pre-trained language models to tackle the challenge of the information-seeking dialogue task. The results have indicated the effectiveness of our approaches. Moreover, data augmentation methods are easy to implement, which is promising for practical use.

References

Jon Ander Campos, Arantxa Otegi, Aitor Soroa, Jan Milan Deriu, Mark Cieliebak, and Eneko Agirre. 2020. Doqa: accessing domain-specific faqs via conversational qa. In *Proceedings of the ACL*, pages 7302–7314.

Xiuyi Chen, Fandong Meng, Peng Li, Feilong Chen, Shuang Xu, Bo Xu, and Jie Zhou. 2020. Bridging the gap between prior and posterior knowledge selection for knowledge-grounded dialogue generation. In *Proceedings of the EMNLP*, pages 3426–3437.

Eunsol Choi, He He, Mohit Iyyer, Mark Yatskar, Wentau Yih, Yejin Choi, Percy Liang, and Luke Zettlemoyer. 2018. Quac: Question answering in context. In *Proceedings of the EMNLP*, pages 2174–2184.

Emily Dinan, Stephen Roller, Kurt Shuster, Angela Fan, Michael Auli, and Jason Weston. 2018. Wizard of wikipedia: Knowledge-powered conversational agents. In *ICLR*.

Matthew Dunn, Levent Sagun, Mike Higgins, V Ugur Guney, Volkan Cirik, and Kyunghyun Cho. 2017. Searchqa: A new q&a dataset augmented with context from a search engine. *arXiv preprint arXiv:1704.05179*.

Song Feng, Kshitij Fadnis, Q Vera Liao, and Luis A Lastras. 2020. Doc2dial: a framework for dialogue composition grounded in documents. In *Proceedings of the AAAI*, volume 34, pages 13604–13605.

Adam Fisch, Alon Talmor, Robin Jia, Minjoon Seo, Eunsol Choi, and Danqi Chen. 2019. Mrqa 2019 shared task: Evaluating generalization in reading comprehension. In *Proceedings of the 2nd Workshop on Machine Reading for Question Answering*, pages 1–13.

Etsuko Ishii, Genta Indra Winata, Samuel Cahyawijaya, Divesh Lala, Tatsuya Kawahara, and Pascale Fung. 2021. Erica: An empathetic android companion for covid-19 quarantine.

Mandar Joshi, Eunsol Choi, Daniel S Weld, and Luke Zettlemoyer. 2017. Triviaqa: A large scale distantly supervised challenge dataset for reading comprehension. In *Proceedings of the ACL*, pages 1601–1611.

Ying Ju, Fubang Zhao, Shijie Chen, Bowen Zheng, Xuefeng Yang, and Yunfeng Liu. 2019. Technical report on conversational question answering. *arXiv preprint arXiv:1909.10772*.

Byeongchang Kim, Jaewoo Ahn, and Gunhee Kim. 2020. Sequential latent knowledge selection for knowledge-grounded dialogue. In *ICLR*.

Mike Lewis, Yinhan Liu, Naman Goyal, Marjan Ghazvininejad, Abdelrahman Mohamed, Omer Levy, Veselin Stoyanov, and Luke Zettlemoyer. 2020. Bart: Denoising sequence-to-sequence pretraining for natural language generation, translation, and comprehension. In *Proceedings of the ACL*, pages 7871–7880.

Rongzhong Lian, Min Xie, Fan Wang, Jinhua Peng, and Hua Wu. 2019. Learning to select knowledge for response generation in dialog systems. In *IJCAI International Joint Conference on Artificial Intelligence*, page 5081.

Zhaojiang Lin, Zihan Liu, Genta Indra Winata, Samuel Cahyawijaya, Andrea Madotto, Yejin Bang, Etsuko Ishii, and Pascale Fung. 2020. Xpersona: Evaluating multilingual personalized chatbot. *arXiv preprint arXiv:2003.07568*.

Yinhan Liu, Myle Ott, Naman Goyal, Jingfei Du, Mandar Joshi, Danqi Chen, Omer Levy, Mike Lewis, Luke Zettlemoyer, and Veselin Stoyanov. 2019a. Roberta: A robustly optimized bert pretraining approach. *arXiv preprint arXiv:1907.11692*.

Zihan Liu, Jamin Shin, Yan Xu, Genta Indra Winata, Peng Xu, Andrea Madotto, and Pascale Fung. 2019b. Zero-shot cross-lingual dialogue systems with transferable latent variables. In *Proceedings of the 2019 Conference on Empirical Methods in Natural Language Processing and the 9th International Joint Conference on Natural Language Processing (EMNLP-IJCNLP)*, pages 1297–1303.

Andrea Madotto, Samuel Cahyawijaya, Genta Indra Winata, Yan Xu, Zihan Liu, Zhaojiang Lin, and Pascale Fung. 2020a. Learning knowledge bases with parameters for task-oriented dialogue systems. In *Proceedings of the 2020 Conference on Empirical Methods in Natural Language Processing: Findings*, pages 2372–2394.

Andrea Madotto, Etsuko Ishii, Zhaojiang Lin, Sumanth Dathathri, and Pascale Fung. 2020b. Plug-and-play conversational models. In *Proceedings of the 2020 Conference on Empirical Methods in Natural Language Processing: Findings*, pages 2422–2433.

Matt Post. 2018. A call for clarity in reporting BLEU scores. In *Proceedings of the Third Conference on Machine Translation: Research Papers*, pages 186–191, Brussels, Belgium.

Siva Reddy, Danqi Chen, and Christopher D Manning. 2019. Coqa: A conversational question answering challenge. *Transactions of the Association for Computational Linguistics*, 7:249–266.

Dan Su, Yan Xu, Genta Indra Winata, Peng Xu, Hyeondey Kim, Zihan Liu, and Pascale Fung. 2019.

Generalizing question answering system with pre-trained language model fine-tuning. In *Proceedings of the 2nd Workshop on Machine Reading for Question Answering*, pages 203–211.

Genta Indra Winata, Holy Lovenia, Etsuko Ishii, Farhad Bin Siddique, Yongsheng Yang, and Pascale Fung. 2021. Nora: The well-being coach. *arXiv preprint arXiv:2106.00410*.

Peng Xu, Mostofa Patwary, Mohammad Shoeybi, Raul Puri, Pascale Fung, Animashree Anandkumar, and Bryan Catanzaro. 2020. Controllable story generation with external knowledge using large-scale language models. In *Proceedings of the 2020 Conference on Empirical Methods in Natural Language Processing (EMNLP)*, pages 2831–2845.

Yan Xu, Etsuko Ishii, Zihan Liu, Genta Indra Winata, Dan Su, Andrea Madotto, and Pascale Fung. 2021. Retrieval-free knowledge-grounded dialogue response generation with adapters. *arXiv preprint arXiv:2105.06232*.

Technical Report on Shared Task in DialDoc21

Jiapeng Li[*] **Mingda Li**[*] **Longxuan Ma**[*] **Weinan Zhang**[†] **Ting Liu**
Research Center for Social Computing and Information Retrieval
Harbin Institute of Technology, Harbin, Heilongjiang, China
{jpli,mdli,lxma,wnzhang,tliu}@ir.hit.edu.cn

Abstract

We participate in the DialDoc Shared Task sub-task 1 (Knowledge Identification). The task requires identifying the grounding knowledge in form of a document span for the next dialogue turn. We employ two well-known pre-trained language models (RoBERTa and ELECTRA) to identify candidate document spans and propose a metric-based ensemble method for span selection. Our methods include data augmentation, model pre-training/fine-tuning, post-processing, and ensemble. On the submission page, we rank 2nd based on the average of normalized F1 and EM scores used for the final evaluation. Specifically, we rank 2nd on EM and 3rd on F1.

1 Introduction

Our team SCIR-DT participates in the DialDoc shared task in the Document-grounded Dialogue and Conversational QA Workshop at the ACL-IJCNLP 2021. There are two sub-tasks based on the Doc2Dial dataset (Feng et al., 2020). The dataset contains goal-oriented conversations between a user and an assistive agent. Each dialogue turn is annotated with a dialogue scene, which includes role, dialogue act, and grounding in a document (or irrelevant to domain documents). The documents are from different domains, such as Social Security and Veterans Affairs. Sub-task1 is **Knowledge Identification** which requires identifying the grounding knowledge in form of document span for the next agent turn. The input is dialogue history, current user utterance, and associated document. The output should be a text span. The evaluation metrics are Exact Match (EM) and F1 (Rajpurkar et al., 2016). Sub-task2 is text generation which requires generating the next agent response in natural language. The input is dialogue history and associated document. The output is agent utterance. The evaluation metrics are SacreBLEU (Post, 2018) and human evaluations. We only participate in sub-task 1.

[*]These three authors contributed equally.
[†]Corresponding author.

2 Related Work

2.1 Document-grounded Dialogue (DGD) & Conversational QA (CQA)

The DGD maintains a dialogue pattern where external knowledge used in dialogues can be obtained from the given document. Recently, some DGD datasets (Moghe et al., 2018; Dinan et al., 2019) have been released to exploiting unstructured document information in open-domain dialogues. The Doc2Dial dataset is also document-grounded dialogue. However, the dialogue in Doc2Dial is goal-oriented which guides users to access various forms of information according to their needs.

The CQA (such as CoQA (Reddy et al., 2019), QuAC (Choi et al., 2018) and DoQA (Campos et al., 2020)) task is also based on background document, which aims to understand a text passage and answering a series of interconnected questions that appear in a conversation. The difference between DGD and CQA is the dialogue of DGD is more diversified (including chit-chat or recommendation) and not limited to QA. The Doc2Dial task is closely related to the CQA tasks. It shares the challenges and additionally introduces the dialogue scenes where the agent asks questions when the user query is identified as under-specified or additional verification required for a resolute solution.

2.2 Pre-trained Language Model (PLM)

The traditional word embeddings (Pennington et al., 2014) are fixed and context-independent, they could not resolve the out-of-vocabulary (OOV) problem and the ambiguity of words in different contexts. To address these problems, Pre-trained

Proceedings of the 1st Workshop on Document-grounded Dialogue and Conversational Question Answering, pages 52–56
August 5–6, 2021. ©2021 Association for Computational Linguistics

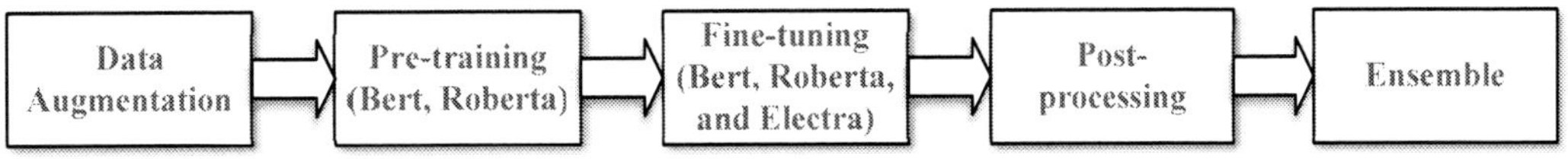

Figure 1: The pipeline methods we used in the competition.

Language Models (PLMs) such as BERT (Devlin et al., 2019) were introduced. BERT employed a Masked language modeling (MLM) method that first masked out some tokens from the input sentences and then trained the model to predict the masked tokens by the rest of the tokens. Concurrently, there was research proposing different enhanced versions of MLM to further improve on BERT. Instead of static masking, RoBERTa (Liu et al., 2019) improved BERT by dynamic masking and abandoned the Next Sentence Prediction (NSP) loss. Instead of masking the input, ELECTRA (Clark et al., 2020) replaced some input tokens with plausible alternatives sampled from a small generator network and trained a discriminative model that predicted whether each token in the corrupted input was replaced by the generator or not. When used for downstream tasks, these PLMs were first trained on a large corpus, then fine-tuned on specific tasks. The contextualized embedding has been proven to be better for the downstream NLP tasks (Qiu et al., 2020) than traditional word embedding. We adopt the BERT, RoBERTa, and ELECTRA in this competition.

3 Our Method

We first use two data augmentation methods to obtain a 5-times larger augmented dataset. We use the augmented data to re-train BERT and RoBERTa with the whole word masking technique and fine-tune BERT, RoBERTa, and ELECTRA models. We test several span post-processing methods and then propose an ensemble method with trainable parameters for final text span selection. The pipeline we used in this competition is illustrated in Figure 1.

3.1 Problem Statement

In sub-task 1, we focus on selecting the correct text span as knowledge from a document. For each example, the model is given a conversational context $\mathbf{C} = [C_1, C_2, ..., C_{|C|}]$ with $|C|$ turns from different speakers and a document $\mathbf{K} = [K_1, K_2, ..., K_{|K|}]$ with $|K|$ spans as external knowledge. Each span is labeled with start and end positions in $\mathbf{K}$. The model learns to select a document span K_i for the response with probability $P(K_i|\mathbf{K}, \mathbf{C}; \Theta)$, Θ is the model's parameters. Specifically, our model adopts the BERT-QA (Chadha and Sood, 2019) method and predicts the start and end positions of a span, if the predicted positions are not the boundaries of an existing span, we use some post-processing methods to modify them to the nearest K_i. The selected span K_i is used for sub-task 2 to generate a response. The model structure is shown in Figure 2. The input of the model is the sum of positional/segment/word embedding of dialogue and document. The output is a document span.

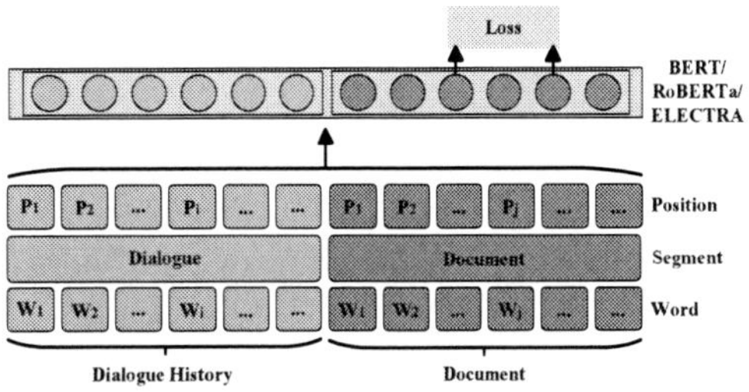

Figure 2: The models we used in the competition.

Table 1: Doc2Dial dataset statistics.

dataset	documents	dialogues	turns
Train	488	3474	44149
Validation	488	661	8539
dev-test	488	198	1353
final-test	573	787	5264

3.2 Data augmentation

The statistics of the Doc2Dial dataset are shown in Table 1. The final test set has an unseen domain that is not included in the training set. Besides the final test page, the organizers provide a dev-test page that uses a small set for additional testing. We use back-translation and Synonym substitution as data augmentation methods. We adopt the google translation service[1] to translate English into other languages (such as Spanish/German/Japanese/French),

[1] https://translate.google.com

then back-translated them into English[2]. Finally, we obtain 5-times document+dialogue data to pre-train the PLMs. Then we pair the 5-times dialogue data with documents translated from different languages, which gives 25 times data for fine-tuning.

3.3 Pre-training and Fine-tuning

We use the augmented data to pre-train two models: BERT and RoBERTa. We follow the Masked Language Model method with the whole word masking technique. We do not pre-train the ELECTRA model because we hope our ensemble method could leverage the prediction results from RoBERTa and ELECTRA to achieve a good performance on both seen and unseen domains. We pre-train RoBERTa on the augmented data to get a good performance on the seen domains. Meanwhile, we hope that ELECTRA can get a good prediction on the unseen domain. The unseen domain in the final-test set requires the knowledge packed in the parameters of the pre-trained model. Pre-training ELECTRA will lose this knowledge.

When fine-tuning these models (BERT, RoBERTa, and ELECTRA), the model structure and training objective is the same as the common method used in the span-extraction Reading Comprehension task. The training objective is defined as the sum of negative log probabilities of the true start and end positions by the predicted distributions, averaged over all N examples:

$$L = -\frac{1}{N}\sum_{n=1}^{N}[\log P(S_n^{start}) + \log P(S_n^{end})], \quad (1)$$

where S_n^{start} and S_n^{end} are the ground-truth span start and end positions of the n-th example .

3.4 Post Processing

Since the document is divided into consecutive spans and the task requires identifying a single span, we propose two different post-processing methods to fix the wrong predictions. The goal of these methods is to process the predicted incomplete span into a complete one. The first method is to expand the predicted start/end to the boundary of one standard span when the predicted positions are within it. The second is to move the predicted start/end to the boundary of the nearest span when the predicted positions are across two spans.

[2]When the back-translation sentence is the same as the original sentence, we employ synonym substitution with Wordnet (https://wordnet.princeton.edu/) to increase diversity.

3.5 Ensemble Method

Algorithm 1: Metric-based ensemble method.

During training: **Metric** = F1 or EM;
Input: S^R, S^E, S, $\tilde{W}^R$, $\tilde{W}^E$, S_{gt}.
Output: Weight for each model.
for $p \in$ range(start=0, stop=1, step=0.1) **do**
    Score = 0
    for $k \in \{\text{validation set}\}$ **do**
        Initialize W: $\{W_i = 0, i = 1, 2, ..., T\}$
        for i $\in$ [1, T]; **do**
            $W_i = p \cdot \tilde{W}_i^R + (1-p) \cdot \tilde{W}_i^E$
        end for
        Score += **Metric**($S_{argmax(W)}$, S_{gt})
    end for
    Record weight p^* for the Best Score.
end for

During test:
for $k \in \{\text{test set}\}$ **do**
    Initialize W: $\{W_i = 0, i = 1, 2, ..., T\}$
    for i $\in$ [1, T]; **do**
        $W_i = p^* \cdot \tilde{W}_i^R + (1-p^*) \cdot \tilde{W}_i^E$
    end for
    $S_k = S_{argmax(W)}$
end for

We propose a simple but efficient ensemble method (**Algorithm 1** shows the details) to utilize the advantages of different models. For each example, we calculate top N span candidates from each model and sort them in descending order with respect to model confidence. Each span is given a weight which is the reciprocal of its ranking number plus one. For example, candidates from RoBERTa are S_j^R, $(j = 1, 2, ..., N)$, and the corresponding weight is $W_j^R = \frac{1}{j+1}$. Similarly, S_j^E and W_j^E for ELECTRA. Then we use these candidates to form a final candidate dictionary S_i, $(i = 1, 2, ..., T)$, $N \leq T \leq 2N$, and the ensemble weight W_i of S_i, is calculated by $W_i = p \cdot \tilde{W}_i^R + (1-p) \cdot \tilde{W}_i^E$, $(i = 1, 2, ..., T)$. p is a hyperparameter and $\tilde{W}_i^R = W_j^R$ if there is a j such that $S_j^R \cong S_i$, 0 otherwise. $\cong$ means exact match here and $\tilde{W}_i^E$ follows the same definition. Then we use a specific metric, such as F1 or EM, to learn the optimal p^* with all examples in the validation set. When testing, we select one candidate as our final prediction using the learned weight[3].

[3]For example, a text span ranks 3rd in RoBERTa and ranks 4th in ELECTRA, p*=0.2, then the final weight to re-rank this span in S is 0.2*0.25+0.8*0.2 = 0.21.

Table 2: Experimental results. "DA/FT/PT/PP" means "data augmentation/fine-tuned/pre-trained/post-processing", respectively.

Models	On dev-test set		On final-test set	
	F1%	EM%	F1%	EM%
BERT (baseline - w/o DA)	66.84	48.48	66.45	48.67
BERT (FT)	67.62	50.01	67.29	49.82
RoBERTa (FT)	71.86	56.77	70.46	54.23
ELECTRA (FT)	72.51	57.58	70.91	54.64
RoBERTa (PT/FT)	72.08	60.10	71.55	58.70
ELECTRA (FT/PP)	72.79	58.08	71.27	55.65
RoBERTa (PT/FT/PP)	72.37	60.61	71.57	59.09
RoBERTa (PT/FT/PP) + ELECTRA (FT/PP)	**74.09**	**63.13**	**75.64**	**63.91**

4 Experiments and Analysis

4.1 Experimental Settings

Our implementations of BERT, RoBERTa, and ELECTRA are based on the public Pytorch implementation from Transformers[4]. All models are in large size. During pre-training, we follow the hyper-parameters setting of the original implementation. During fine-tuning, we truncated the length of the dialogue context to 60 tokens and maximum input length to 512 tokens. The maximum predicted span length is set to 90 words. Candidate span size N is set to 20. We use EM as the **Metric** in the ensemble method. We use a single Tesla v100s GPU with 32gb memory, the pre-training time is around 48 hours and fine-tuning time is around 24 hours for each model.

4.2 Experimental Results and Analysis

In this competition, each team has five submission opportunities on the final test page[5]. Table 2 shows the experimental results on dev-test/final-test sets of different models. The baseline given by the organizer is a BERT-large model without pre-trained on Doc2Dial data, we fine-tune the baseline on the training set of Doc2Dial data and get the F1 of 66.84 and EM of 48.48 on the dev-test set. When using augmented data to fine-tune the BERT-large model, we get 67.62 F1 and 50.01 EM. The results prove the effectiveness of dialogue data augmentation. We fine-tune RoBERTa and ELECTRA with the augmented data and they both outperform BERT. We use augmented data to pre-train the RoBERTa model before we fine-tune it. The F1 and EM increase to 72.08 and 60.10, respectively. It proves that pre-training on task data can further improve performance. Then we find Post-processing helps ELECTRA on both F1 and EM. We employ the PT/FT/PP on RoBERTa and get 72.37 F1 and 60.61 EM. At last, we employ our ensemble method on the best performance RoBERTa and ELECTRA models and achieve 74.09 F1 and 63.13 EM on the dev-test set. The last method also achieves our best F1 and EM on the final-test set, the ensemble results outperform the best single model (RoBERTa) more than 4% on both F1 and EM. For EM, the contribution ranks from big to small are Ensemble>Pre-training>Data Augmentation>Post Processing.

The ensemble method uses both PLM (RoBERTa) that is pre-trained with augmented data and PLM (ELECTRA) that is not pre-trained with augmented data. In this way, we can leverage the knowledge packed in the parameters of ELECTRA for the unseen domain of the final-test data. The ELECTRA(FT/PP) got an EM of 55.65 on the final-test set and the RoBERTa(PT/FT/PP) got an EM of 59.09. The ensemble method increased the EM to 63.91, indicating that the two models have a great difference of choice in spans and our ensemble method leverages the difference between the two models to achieve a better result.

5 Conclusion

We introduced our submission for Doc2Dial Shared Task. In sub-task 1, our model is based on RoBERTa and ELECTRA. We propose a simple but efficient ensemble method for knowledge selection in multi-turn dialogue. Our team SCIR-DT ranks 2nd on the final submission page. Apart from the methods we introduced, there are other methods that could further improve the performance of

[4]https://github.com/huggingface/transformers

[5]Each team has 20 more submission opportunities after the competition to help finish their technical report.

our model. For example, Feng et al. (2020) proved the dialogue act information was useful for subtask 1; there are some noisy data such as empty responses in the dialogue data could be filtered out during training; employing machine reading comprehension dataset such as SQuAD (Rajpurkar et al., 2016) or CQA dataset such as CoQA (Reddy et al., 2019) for pre-training and fine-tuning may also be helpful. However, due to the time limitation, we did not try all these methods during the competition. We hope these methods and experiences would be helpful for future contestants.

Acknowledgments

We thank the thoughtful suggestions from the reviewers. This paper is supported by the National Natural Science Foundation of China (No. 62076081, No. 61772153, and No. 61936010) and the Science and Technology Innovation 2030 Major Project of China (No. 2020AAA0108605).

References

Jon Ander Campos, Arantxa Otegi, Aitor Soroa, Jan Deriu, Mark Cieliebak, and Eneko Agirre. 2020. Doqa - accessing domain-specific faqs via conversational QA. In *Proceedings of the 58th Annual Meeting of the Association for Computational Linguistics, ACL 2020, Online, July 5-10, 2020*, pages 7302–7314. Association for Computational Linguistics.

Ankit Chadha and Rewa Sood. 2019. BERTQA - attention on steroids. *CoRR*, abs/1912.10435.

Eunsol Choi, He He, Mohit Iyyer, Mark Yatskar, Wentau Yih, Yejin Choi, Percy Liang, and Luke Zettlemoyer. 2018. Quac: Question answering in context. In *Proceedings of the 2018 Conference on Empirical Methods in Natural Language Processing, Brussels, Belgium, October 31 - November 4, 2018*, pages 2174–2184. Association for Computational Linguistics.

Kevin Clark, Minh-Thang Luong, Quoc V. Le, and Christopher D. Manning. 2020. ELECTRA: pretraining text encoders as discriminators rather than generators. In *8th International Conference on Learning Representations, ICLR 2020, Addis Ababa, Ethiopia, April 26-30, 2020*. OpenReview.net.

Jacob Devlin, Ming-Wei Chang, Kenton Lee, and Kristina Toutanova. 2019. BERT: pre-training of deep bidirectional transformers for language understanding. In *Proceedings of the 2019 Conference of the North American Chapter of the Association for Computational Linguistics: Human Language Technologies, NAACL-HLT 2019, Minneapolis, MN, USA, June 2-7, 2019, Volume 1 (Long and Short Papers)*, pages 4171–4186. Association for Computational Linguistics.

Emily Dinan, Stephen Roller, Kurt Shuster, Angela Fan, Michael Auli, and Jason Weston. 2019. Wizard of wikipedia: Knowledge-powered conversational agents. In *7th International Conference on Learning Representations, ICLR 2019, New Orleans, LA, USA, May 6-9, 2019*. OpenReview.net.

Song Feng, Hui Wan, R. Chulaka Gunasekara, Siva Sankalp Patel, Sachindra Joshi, and Luis A. Lastras. 2020. doc2dial: A goal-oriented document-grounded dialogue dataset. In *Proceedings of the 2020 Conference on Empirical Methods in Natural Language Processing, EMNLP 2020, Online, November 16-20, 2020*, pages 8118–8128. Association for Computational Linguistics.

Yinhan Liu, Myle Ott, Naman Goyal, Jingfei Du, Mandar Joshi, Danqi Chen, Omer Levy, Mike Lewis, Luke Zettlemoyer, and Veselin Stoyanov. 2019. Roberta: A robustly optimized BERT pretraining approach. *CoRR*, abs/1907.11692.

Nikita Moghe, Siddhartha Arora, Suman Banerjee, and Mitesh M. Khapra. 2018. Towards exploiting background knowledge for building conversation systems. In *Proceedings of the 2018 Conference on Empirical Methods in Natural Language Processing, Brussels, Belgium, October 31 - November 4, 2018*, pages 2322–2332. Association for Computational Linguistics.

Jeffrey Pennington, Richard Socher, and Christopher D. Manning. 2014. Glove: Global vectors for word representation. In *Proceedings of the 2014 Conference on Empirical Methods in Natural Language Processing, EMNLP 2014, October 25-29, 2014, Doha, Qatar, A meeting of SIGDAT, a Special Interest Group of the ACL*, pages 1532–1543. ACL.

Matt Post. 2018. A call for clarity in reporting BLEU scores. In *Proceedings of the Third Conference on Machine Translation: Research Papers, WMT 2018, Belgium, Brussels, October 31 - November 1, 2018*, pages 186–191. Association for Computational Linguistics.

Xipeng Qiu, Tianxiang Sun, Yige Xu, Yunfan Shao, Ning Dai, and Xuanjing Huang. 2020. Pre-trained models for natural language processing: A survey. *CoRR*, abs/2003.08271.

Pranav Rajpurkar, Jian Zhang, Konstantin Lopyrev, and Percy Liang. 2016. Squad: 100, 000+ questions for machine comprehension of text. In *Proceedings of the 2016 Conference on Empirical Methods in Natural Language Processing, EMNLP 2016, Austin, Texas, USA, November 1-4, 2016*, pages 2383–2392. The Association for Computational Linguistics.

Siva Reddy, Danqi Chen, and Christopher D. Manning. 2019. Coqa: A conversational question answering challenge. *Trans. Assoc. Comput. Linguistics*, 7:249–266.

Cascaded Span Extraction and Response Generation for Document-Grounded Dialog

Nico Daheim,[1] David Thulke,[1,2] Christian Dugast,[1,2] Hermann Ney[1,2]
[1] Human Language Technology and Pattern Recognition Group, RWTH Aachen University, Germany
[2] AppTek GmbH, Aachen, Germany
{daheim, thulke, dugast, ney}@i6.informatik.rwth-aachen.de

Abstract

This paper summarizes our entries to both subtasks of the first DialDoc shared task which focuses on the agent response prediction task in goal-oriented document-grounded dialogs. The task is split into two subtasks: predicting a span in a document that grounds an agent turn and generating an agent response based on a dialog and grounding document. In the first subtask, we restrict the set of valid spans to the ones defined in the dataset, use a biaffine classifier to model spans, and finally use an ensemble of different models. For the second subtask, we use a cascaded model which grounds the response prediction on the predicted span instead of the full document. With these approaches, we obtain significant improvements in both subtasks compared to the baseline.

1 Introduction

Unstructured documents contain a vast amount of knowledge that can be useful information for responding to users in goal-oriented dialog systems. The shared task at the first DialDoc Workshop focuses on grounding and generating agent responses in such systems. Therefore, two subtasks are proposed: given a dialog extract the relevant information for the next agent turn from a document and generate a natural language agent response based on dialog context and grounding document. In this paper, we present our submissions to both subtasks.

In the first subtask, we focus on modeling spans directly using a biaffine classifier and restricting the model's output to valid spans. We notice that replacing BERT with alternative language models results in significant improvements. For the second subtask, we notice that providing a generation model with an entire, possibly long, grounding document often leads to models struggling to generate factually correct output. Hence, we split the task into two subsequent stages, where first a grounding span is selected according to our method for the first subtask which is then provided for generation. With these approaches, we report strong improvements over the baseline in both subtasks. Additionally, we experimented with marginalizing over all spans in order to be able to account for the uncertainty of the span selection model during generation.

2 Related Work

Recently, multiple datasets and challenges concerning conversational question answering have been proposed. For example, Saeidi et al. (2018) introduced ShARC, a dataset containing ca. 32k utterances which include follow-up questions on user requests which can not be answered directly based on the given dialog and grounding. Similarly, the CoQA dataset (Reddy et al., 2019) provides 127k questions with answers and grounding obtained from human conversations. Closer related to the DialDoc shared task, the task in the first track of DSTC 9 (Kim et al., 2020) was to generate agent responses based on relevant knowledge in task-oriented dialog. However, the considered knowledge has the form of FAQ documents, where snippets are much shorter than those considered in this work.

Pre-trained trained language models such as BART (Lewis et al., 2020a) or RoBERTa (Liu et al., 2019) have recently become a successful tool for different kinds of natural language understanding tasks, such as question answering (QA), where they obtain state-of-the-art results (Liu et al., 2019; Clark et al., 2020). Naturally, they have recently also found their way into task-oriented dialog systems (Lewis et al., 2020a), where they are either used as end-to-end systems (Budzianowski and Vulić, 2019; Ham et al., 2020) or as components for a specific subtask (He et al., 2021).

Proceedings of the 1st Workshop on Document-grounded Dialogue and Conversational Question Answering, pages 57–62
August 5–6, 2021. ©2021 Association for Computational Linguistics

3 Task Description

The task of dialog systems is to generate an appropriate systems response u_{T+1} to a user turn u_T and preceding dialog context $u_1^{T-1} := u_1, ..., u_{T-1}$. In a document-grounded setting, u_{T+1} is based on knowledge from a set of relevant documents $D' \subseteq D$, where D denotes all knowledge documents. Feng et al. (2020) identify three tasks relevant to such systems, namely 1) user utterance understanding; 2) agent response prediction; 3) relevant document identification. The shared task deals with the second task and assumes the result of the third task to be known. They further split this task into *agent response grounding prediction* and *agent response generation*. More specifically, one subtask focuses on identifying the grounding of u_{T+1} and the second subtask on generating u_{T+1}. In both subtasks exactly one document $d \in D$ is given. Each document consists of multiple sections, whereby each section consists of a title and the content. In the doc2dial dataset, the latter is split into multiple subspans. In the following, we refer to these given subspans as *phrases* in order to avoid confusing them with arbitrary spans in the document.

Agent Response Grounding Prediction The first subtask is to identify a span in a given document that grounds the agent response u_{T+1}. It is formulated as a span selection task where the aim is to return a tuple (a_s, a_e) of start and end position of the relevant span within the grounding document d based on the dialog history u_1^T. In the context of the challenge, these spans always correspond to one of the given phrases in the documents.

Agent Response Generation The goal of response generation is to provide the user with a system response u_{T+1} that is based on the dialog context u_1^T and document d and fits naturally into the preceding dialog.

4 Methods

4.1 Baselines

Agent Response Grounding Prediction For the first subtask, Feng et al. (2020) fine-tune BERT for question answering as proposed by Devlin et al. (2019). Therefore, a start and end score for each token is calculated by a linear projection from the last hidden states of the model. These scores are normalized using a softmax over all tokens to obtain probabilities for the start and end positions. In order to obtain the probability of a specific span, the probabilities of the start and end positions are multiplied. If the length of the documents exceeds the maximum length supported by the model, a sliding window with stride over the document is used and each window is passed to the model. In training, if the correct span is not included in the window, the span only consisting of the begin of sequence token is used as target. In decoding the scores of all windows are combined to find the best span.

Agent Response Generation The baseline provided for the shared task uses a pre-trained BART model (Lewis et al., 2020a) to generate agent responses. The model is fine-tuned on the tasks training data by minimizing the cross-entropy of the reference tokens. As input, it is provided with the dialog context, title of the document, and the grounding document separated by special tokens. Inputs longer than the maximum sequence length supported by the model (1,024 tokens for BART) are truncated. Effectively, this means that parts of the document are removed that may include the information relevant to the response. An alternative to truncating the document would be to truncate the dialog context (i.e. removing the oldest turns which may be less relevant than the document). We did not do experiments with this approach in this work and always included the full dialog context in the input. For decoding beam search with a beam size of 4 is used.

4.2 Agent Response Grounding Prediction

Phrase restriction In contrast to standard QA tasks, in this task, possible start and end positions of spans are restricted to phrases in the document. This motivated us to also restrict the possible outputs of the model to these positions. That is, instead of applying the softmax over all tokens, it is only applied over tokens corresponding to the start or end positions of a phrase and thus only consider these positions in training and decoding.

Span-based objective The training objective for QA assumes that the probability of the start and end position are conditionally independent. Previous work (Fajcik et al., 2020) indicates that directly modeling the joint probability of start and end position can improve performance. Hence, to model this joint probability, we use a biaffine classifier as proposed by Dozat and Manning (2017) for dependency parsing.

Ensembling In our submission, we use an ensemble of multiple models for the prediction of spans to capture their uncertainty. More precisely, we use Bayesian Model Averaging (Hoeting et al., 1999), where the probability of a span $a = (a_s, a_e)$ is obtained by marginalizing the joint probability of span and model over all models H as:

$$p\left(a \mid u_1^T, d\right) = \sum_{h \in H} p_h\left(a \mid u_1^T, d\right) \cdot p(h) \quad (1)$$

The model prior $p(h)$ is obtained by applying a softmax function over the logarithm of the F1 scores obtained on a validation set. Furthermore, we approximate the span posterior distribution $p_h\left(a \mid u_1^T, d\right)$ by an n-best list of size 20.

4.3 Agent Response Generation

Cascaded Response Generation One main issue with the baseline approach is that the model appears to be unable to identify the relevant knowledge when provided with long documents. Additionally, due to the truncation, the input of the model may not even contain the relevant parts of the document. To solve this issue, we propose to model the problem by cascading span selection and response generation. This way, we only have to provide the comparatively short grounding span to the model instead of the full document. This allows the model to focus on generating an appropriate utterance and less on identifying relevant grounding information.

Similar to the baseline, we fine-tune BART (Lewis et al., 2020a). In training, we provide the model with the dialog context u_1^T concatenated with the document title and reference span, each separated by a special token. In decoding, the reference span is not available and we use the span predicted by our span selection model as input.

Marginalization over Spans Conditioning on only the ground truth span creates a mismatch between training and inference time since the ground truth span is not available at test time but has to be predicted. This leads to errors occurring in span selection being propagated in response generation. Further, the generation model is unable to take the uncertainty of the span selection model into account. Similar to Lewis et al. (2020b) and Thulke et al. (2021) we propose to marginalize over all spans S. We model the response generation as:

$$p\left(\hat{u} = u_{T+1} \mid u_1^T; d\right) = \prod_{i}^{N} \sum_{s \in S} p\left(\hat{u}_i, s \mid \hat{u}_1^{i-1}; u_1^T; d\right)$$

where the joint probability may be factorized into a span selection model $p\left(s \mid u_1^T; d\right)$ and a generation model $p\left(u_{T+1} \mid u_1^T, s; d\right)$ corresponding to our models for each subtask. For efficiency, we approximate S by the top 5 spans which we renormalize to maintain a probability distribution. The generation model is then trained with cross-entropy using an n-best list obtained from the separately trained selection model. A potential extension which we did not yet try is to train both models jointly.

5 Data

The shared task uses the doc2dial dataset (Feng et al., 2020) which contains 4,793 annotated dialogs based on a total of 487 documents. All documents were obtained from public government service websites and stem from the four domains *Social Security Administration (ssa)*, *Department of Motor Vehicles (dmv)*, *United States Department of Veterans Affairs (va)*, and *Federal Student Aid (studentaid)*. In the shared task, each document is associated with exactly one domain and is annotated with sections and phrases. The latter is described by a start and end index within the document and associated with a specific section that has a title and text. Each dialog is based on one document and contains a set of turns. Turns are taken either by a *user* or an *agent* and described by a dialog act and a list of grounding reference phrases in the document.

The training set of the shared task contains 3,474 dialogs with in total 44,149 turns. In addition to the training set, the shared task organizers provide a validation set with 661 dialogs and a testdev set with 198 dialogs which include around 30% of the dialogs from the final test set. The final test set includes an additional domain of unseen documents and comprises a total of 787 dialogs. Documents are rather long, have a median length of 817.5, and an average length of 991 tokens (using the BART subword vocabulary). Thus, in many cases, truncation of the input is required.

Subtask 1					Subtask 2		
		test		val		test	val
model	F1	EM	F1	EM	model	BLEU	
baseline	67.9	51.5	70.8	56.3	baseline (ours)	28.1	32.9
RoBERTa	73.2	58.3	77.3	65.6	cascaded (RoBERTa)	39.1	39.6
ensemble	**75.9**	**63.5**	**78.8**	**68.4**	cascaded (ensemble)	**40.4**	**41.5**

Table 1: Results of our best system on test and validation set.

6 Experiments

We base our implementation[1] on the provided baseline code of the shared task [2]. Furthermore, we use the workflow manager Sisyphus (Peter et al., 2018) to organize our experiments.

For the first subtask, we use the base and large variants of RoBERTa (Liu et al., 2019) and ELECTRA (Clark et al., 2020) instead of BERT large uncased. In the second subtask, we use BART base instead of the large variant, which was used in the baseline code, since even after reducing the batch size to one, we were not able to run the baseline with a maximum sequence length of 1024 on our Nvidia GTX 1080 Ti and RTX 2080 Ti GPUs due to memory constraints. All models are fine-tuned with an initial learning rate of 3e-5. Base variants are trained for 10 epochs and large variants for 5 epochs.

We include agent follow-up turns in our training data, i.e. such turns u_t made by agents, where the preceding turn u_{t-1} was already taken by the agent. Similar to other agent turns, i.e. where the preceding turn was taken by the user, these turns are annotated with their grounding span and can be used as additional samples in both tasks. In the baseline implementation, these are excluded from training and evaluation. To maintain comparability, we do not include them in the validation or test data.

For evaluation, we use the same evaluation metrics as proposed in the baseline. In the first subtask, exact match (EM), i.e. the percentage of exact matches between the predicted and reference span (after lowercasing and removing punctuation, articles, and whitespace) and the token-level F1 score is used. The second subtask is evaluated using SacreBLEU (Post, 2018).

[1]Our code is made available at https://github.com/ndaheim/dialdoc-sharedtask-21

[2]Baseline code is available at https://github.com/doc2dial/sharedtask-dialdoc2021

6.1 Results

Table 1 summarizes our main results and submission to the shared task. The first line shows the results obtained by reproducing the baseline provided by the organizers (using BART base for Subtask 2). We note that these results differ from the ones reported in Feng et al. (2020) due to slightly different data conditions in the shared task and their paper. The second line shows the results of our best single model. In Subtask 1, we obtained our best results by using RoBERTa large, trained additionally on agent follow-up turns, and by restricting the model to phrases occurring in the document. Using an ensemble of this model, an ELECTRA large model trained with the same approach, and a RoBERTa base model trained with the span-based objective, we achieve our best result. In the second subtask, our cascaded approach using this model and BART base significantly outperforms the baseline by over 10% absolute in BLEU. Using the results of the ensemble in Subtask 2 also translates to a significant improvement in BLEU, which indicates a strong influence of the agent response grounding prediction task.

model	F1	EM	EM@5
baseline (BERT large)	70.8	56.3	68.2
ELECTRA large	75.1	63.1	79.5
RoBERTa large	<u>77.3</u>	<u>65.6</u>	82.1
– phrase restriction	77.0	65.1	79.7
– follow-up turns	76.5	64.5	80.9
– follow-up turns	75.7	63.2	80.3
RoBERTa base	74.8	63.1	79.5
+ span-based	73.6	62.5	<u>83.0</u>
ensemble	**78.8**	**68.4**	**85.0**

Table 2: Ablation analysis of our systems for subtask 1 on the validation set. The best single model results are underlined.

model	BLEU
baseline (ours)	32.9
span marginalization	38.4
cascaded (RoBERTa large)	<u>39.6</u>
+ section title	39.6
+ extended context	39.5
cascaded (ensemble)	41.2
+ follow-up turns	41.2
+ beam-size 6	41.3
+ repetition-penalty	**41.5**
cascaded (ground truth)	46.2

Table 3: Ablation analysis of our systems for subtask 2 on the validation set.

6.2 Ablation Analysis

Agent Response Grounding Prediction Table 2 gives an overview of our ablation analysis for the first subtask. In addition to F1 and EM, we report the EM@5 which we define as the percentage of turns where an exact match is part of the 5-best list predicted by the model. This metric gives an indication of the quality of the n-best list produced by the model. Both RoBERTa and ELECTRA large outperform BERT large concerning F1 and EM with RoBERTa large performing best. Removing agent follow-up turns in training consistently degrades the results for both models. Restricting the predictions of the model to valid phrases during training and evaluation gives consistent improvements in the EM and EM@5 scores.

Training RoBERTa base using the span-based objective, we observe degradations in F1 and EM but observe an improvement in EM@5 which indicates that it better models the distribution across phrases. Due to instabilities during training, we were not able to train a large model with the span-based objective. Additionally, we only did experiments with the biaffine classifier discussed in Section 3. It would be interesting to compare the results with other span-based objectives as the ones proposed by Fajcik et al. (2020).

Agent Response Generation Table 3 shows an ablation study of our results in response generation. The results show that our cascaded approach outperforms the baseline by a large margin. Further experiments with additional context, such as the title of a section or a window of 10 tokens to each side of the span, do not give improvements. This indicates that the selected spans seem to be sufficient to generate suitable responses. Furthermore, marginalizing over multiple spans leads to degradations, which might be because training is based on an n-best list from an uncertain model. We observe our best results when using only the predicted span and a beam size of 6. Furthermore, we add a repetition penalty of 1.2 (Keskar et al., 2019) to discourage repetitions in generated responses.

Finally, the last line of the table reports the results of the cascaded method when using ground truth spans instead of the spans predicted by a model. That is, a perfect model for the first subtask would additionally improve the results by 4.7 points absolute in BLEU.

7 Conclusion

In this paper, we have described our submissions to both subtasks of the first DialDoc shared task. In the first subtask, we have experimented with restricting the set of spans that can be predicted to valid phrases, which yields constant improvements in terms of EM. Furthermore, we have employed a model to directly hypothesize entire spans and shown the benefits of combining multiple models using Bayesian Model Averaging. In the second subtask, we have shown how cascading span selection and response generation improves results when compared to providing an entire document in generation. We have compared marginalizing over spans to just using a single span for generation, with which we obtain our best results in the shared task.

Acknowledgements

This work has received funding from the European Research Council (ERC) under the European Union's Horizon 2020 research and innovation programme (grant agreement No 694537, project "SEQCLAS"). The work reflects only the authors' views and the European Research Council Executive Agency (ERCEA) is not responsible for any use that may be made of the information it contains.

References

Paweł Budzianowski and Ivan Vulić. 2019. Hello, It's GPT-2 – How Can I Help You? Towards the Use of Pretrained Language Models for Task-Oriented Dialogue Systems. In *Proceedings of the 3rd Workshop on Neural Generation and Translation*, Hong Kong, China. Association for Computational Linguistics.

Kevin Clark, Minh-Thang Luong, Quoc V. Le, and Christopher D. Manning. 2020. ELECTRA: Pre-Training Text Encoders as Discriminators Rather Than Generators. In *ICLR*.

Jacob Devlin, Ming-Wei Chang, Kenton Lee, and Kristina Toutanova. 2019. BERT: Pre-training of deep bidirectional transformers for language understanding. In *Proceedings of the 2019 Conference of the North American Chapter of the Association for Computational Linguistics: Human Language Technologies, Volume 1 (Long and Short Papers)*, pages 4171–4186, Minneapolis, Minnesota. Association for Computational Linguistics.

Timothy Dozat and Christopher D Manning. 2017. Deep Biaffine Attention for Neural Dependency Parsing. In *ICLR*.

Martin Fajcik, Josef Jon, Santosh Kesiraju, and Pavel Smrz. 2020. Rethinking the Objectives of Extractive Question Answering.

Song Feng, Hui Wan, Chulaka Gunasekara, Siva Patel, Sachindra Joshi, and Luis Lastras. 2020. doc2dial: A goal-oriented document-grounded dialogue dataset. In *Proceedings of the 2020 Conference on Empirical Methods in Natural Language Processing (EMNLP)*, pages 8118–8128, Online. Association for Computational Linguistics.

Donghoon Ham, Jeong-Gwan Lee, Youngsoo Jang, and Kee-Eung Kim. 2020. End-to-End Neural Pipeline for Goal-Oriented Dialogue Systems using GPT-2. In *Proceedings of the 58th Annual Meeting of the Association for Computational Linguistics*, pages 583–592, Online. Association for Computational Linguistics.

Huang He, Hua Lu, Siqi Bao, Fan Wang, Hua Wu, Zhengyu Niu, and Haifeng Wang. 2021. Learning to select external knowledge with multi-scale negative sampling.

Jennifer A. Hoeting, David Madigan, Adrian E. Raftery, and Chris T. Volinsky. 1999. Bayesian model averaging: A tutorial. *Statistical Science*, 14(4):382–401.

Nitish Shirish Keskar, Bryan McCann, Lav R. Varshney, Caiming Xiong, and Richard Socher. 2019. CTRL: A conditional transformer language model for controllable generation.

Seokhwan Kim, Mihail Eric, Karthik Gopalakrishnan, Behnam Hedayatnia, Yang Liu, and Dilek Hakkani-Tur. 2020. Beyond domain APIs: Task-oriented conversational modeling with unstructured knowledge access. In *Proceedings of the 21th Annual Meeting of the Special Interest Group on Discourse and Dialogue*, pages 278–289, 1st virtual meeting. Association for Computational Linguistics.

Mike Lewis, Yinhan Liu, Naman Goyal, Marjan Ghazvininejad, Abdelrahman Mohamed, Omer Levy, Veselin Stoyanov, and Luke Zettlemoyer. 2020a. BART: Denoising sequence-to-sequence pre-training for natural language generation, translation, and comprehension. In *Proceedings of the 58th Annual Meeting of the Association for Computational Linguistics*, pages 7871–7880, Online. Association for Computational Linguistics.

Patrick Lewis, Ethan Perez, Aleksandara Piktus, Fabio Petroni, Vladimir Karpukhin, Naman Goyal, Heinrich Küttler, Mike Lewis, Wen-tau Yih, Tim Rocktäschel, Sebastian Riedel, and Douwe Kiela. 2020b. Retrieval-Augmented Generation for Knowledge-Intensive NLP Tasks. In *NeurIPS*.

Yinhan Liu, Myle Ott, Naman Goyal, Jingfei Du, Mandar Joshi, Danqi Chen, Omer Levy, Mike Lewis, Luke Zettlemoyer, and Veselin Stoyanov. 2019. Roberta: A robustly optimized bert pretraining approach.

Jan-Thorsten Peter, Eugen Beck, and Hermann Ney. 2018. Sisyphus, a Workflow Manager Designed for Machine Translation and Automatic Speech Recognition. In *Proceedings of the 2018 Conference on Empirical Methods in Natural Language Processing: System Demonstrations*, pages 84–89, Brussels, Belgium. Association for Computational Linguistics.

Matt Post. 2018. A call for clarity in reporting BLEU scores. In *Proceedings of the Third Conference on Machine Translation: Research Papers*, pages 186–191, Belgium, Brussels. Association for Computational Linguistics.

Siva Reddy, Danqi Chen, and Christopher D. Manning. 2019. CoQA: A conversational question answering challenge. *Transactions of the Association for Computational Linguistics*, 7:249–266.

Marzieh Saeidi, Max Bartolo, Patrick S. H. Lewis, Sameer Singh, Tim Rocktäschel, Mike Sheldon, Guillaume Bouchard, and Sebastian Riedel. 2018. Interpretation of natural language rules in conversational machine reading. In *Proceedings of the 2018 Conference on Empirical Methods in Natural Language Processing, Brussels, Belgium, October 31 - November 4, 2018*, pages 2087–2097. Association for Computational Linguistics.

David Thulke, Nico Daheim, Christian Dugast, and Hermann Ney. 2021. Efficient Retrieval Augmented Generation from Unstructured Knowledge for Task-Oriented Dialog. In *AAAI-21 : 9th Dialog System Technology Challenge (DSTC-9) Workshop*. 9th Dialog System Technology Challenge Workshop, online, 8 Feb 2021 - 9 Feb 2021.

Ensemble ALBERT and RoBERTa for Span Prediction in Question Answering

Sony Bachina, Spandana Balumuri and Sowmya Kamath S
Healthcare Analytics and Language Engineering (HALE) Lab,
Department of Information Technology,
National Institute of Technology Karnataka, Surathkal, Mangalore 575025, India
{bachina.sony, spandanabalumuri99}@gmail.com
sowmyakamath@nitk.edu.in

Abstract

Retrieving relevant answers from heterogeneous data formats, for given for questions, is a challenging problem. The process of pinpointing relevant information suitable to answer a question is further compounded in large document collections containing documents of substantial length. This paper presents the models designed as part of our submission to the DialDoc21 Shared Task (Document-grounded Dialogue and Conversational Question Answering) for span prediction in question answering. The proposed models leverage the superior predictive power of pretrained transformer models like RoBERTa, ALBERT and ELECTRA, to identify the most relevant information in an associated passage for the next agent turn. To further enhance the performance, the models were fine-tuned on different span selection based question answering datasets like SQuAD2.0 and Natural Questions (NQ) corpus. We also explored ensemble techniques for combining multiple models to achieve enhanced performance for the task. Our team SB_NITK ranked 6th on the leaderboard for the Knowledge Identification task, and our best ensemble model achieved an Exact score of 58.58 and an F1 score of 73.39.

1 Introduction

In recent years, deep learning based transformer models like BERT have accelerated research in the Natural Language Processing (NLP) domain, due to their outstanding performance in various NLP tasks like summarization, machine translation etc, against state-of-the-art models. Question-answering is one such text based Information Retrieval framework, focusing on generating relevant answers to natural language questions presented by humans. Extractive Question Answering models leverage document context to make decisions while identifying the most relevant answer and its location in a given passage or document. The applications of question answering systems include chat bots in medical science, search engines, personal assistants etc.

Several researchers have addressed the problem of answer generation for a given question, especially focusing on the challenge of dealing with descriptive answers. Some works deal with this challenge in a two-phased approach - first, classifying the question into opinion-based or yes/no questions and secondly, dealing with the issue of lengthy questions and generating relevant answers for them using deep neural models like LSTMs for the question answering task Upadhya et al. (2019). Agrawal et al. (2019) proposed a Question Answering model built on BiLSTMs pre-trained on the SquAD dataset, to obtain appropriate ranks for answers corresponding to a given question at hand. Additionally, ensemble techniques have proven well-suited due to better prediction performance, while reducing the variance and bias. Adopting ensemble techniques to combine multiple models can provide better predictions and boost the performance of Question Answering systems. As shown in Fig. 1, pretrained encoders such as BERT (Devlin et al., 2019) with an additional linear layer on top to predict spans have been shown to provide the advantage of transfer learning as they are pretrained on large, open datasets.

The DialDoc21 shared task aims to encourage the development of models that can detect the most relevant details in the grounding document and predict agent responses close to common human responses. DialDoc21 is composed of two different shared tasks –

- *Subtask1 - Knowledge Identification* : The aim of the task is to find where the answer is present (a text span) in the document context for the next agent turn. F1 metrics and Exact Match are the evaluation metrics for Subtask1.

Proceedings of the 1st Workshop on Document-grounded Dialogue and Conversational Question Answering, pages 63–68
August 5–6, 2021. ©2021 Association for Computational Linguistics

- *Subtask2 - Text Generation* : The task aims to generate responses close to human spoken language. The assessment metrics for Subtask2 are sacrebleu and individual evaluations.

Most recent Extractive Question Answering systems are predominantly BERT based models. Transformers like BERT, RoBERTa (Liu et al., 2019) and XLNet (Yang et al., 2020) are experimented for Extractive Question Answering task on datasets from multiple domains and languages like Stanford SQuAD v1.1 (Rajpurkar et al., 2016) and v2.0 (Rajpurkar et al., 2018), Natural Questions (Kwiatkowski et al., 2019), NewsQA (Trischler et al., 2017) and HotpotQA (Yang et al., 2018). Dua et al. (2019) experimented on the scenario of multiple answer spans.

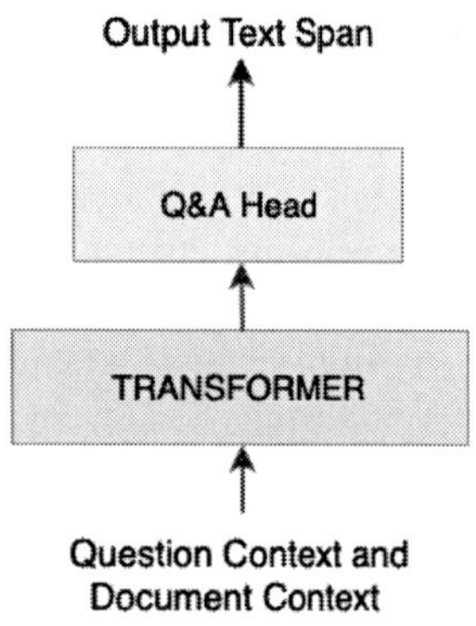

Figure 1: Base architecture for span prediction task using Transformers

In this paper, we describe various models and experiments that were developed and tested for the Knowledge Identification subtask. The models are built on fine-tuned, pretrained transformers like RoBERTa, ALBERT (Lan et al., 2020) and ELECTRA (Clark et al., 2020). We adopt ensembling techniques on multiple models to boost the prediction performance further. As part of our approach, we pretrained the transformer models considered on various question-answering datasets like SQuAD2.0, Natural Questions corpus, and CORD-19 dataset (Wang et al., 2020) prior to fine-tuning them for our dataset, and observe their performance.

The rest of this article is organized as follows. In Section 2, we provide information about the data used such as description of dataset and dataset pre-processing. Section 3 gives an overview of models used and their different versions. In Section 4, we describe the ensemble technique used and the various ensemble models submitted. Section 5 describes the system flow and experimental setup. In Section 6, we list the results and compare the performance of our proposed models in detail, followed by conclusion and directions for future work.

2 Data

2.1 Dataset Description

The organizers of the shared task provided the necessary training and testing data. The training data is taken from Doc2Dial dataset (Feng et al., 2020) which includes dialogues between an agent and an enduser, along with their base information in the associated documents provided. These documents were collected from different social websites such as `ssa.gov`, `va.gov`, `studentaid.gov` and DMV portal. The test dataset includes an unseen COVID-19 related domain's data (cdccov19), in addition to other domains that are available in the training dataset. Therefore, the unseen domain helps in testing the model performance on an unknown domain data.

2.2 Dataset Preprocessing

The average sequence length of the grounding document is 880 which is higher than the maximum sequence length of transformers. As a result the document text has been truncated into sliding windows with a stride value of 128. Each input sample to the encoder includes dialogue context, which is a combination of all previous utterances in reverse order and the corresponding document trunk. An example (a combination of a question and a document) can have multiple features (a pair of a question and a document trunk) in case of a lengthy context. Therefore, we have a map that links each feature to its associated example. Additionally, an offset map is maintained from each token to the position of the character in the actual context.

3 Models

For the DialDoc21 knowledge identification shared task, we experimented with various versions of three different transformer models by fine-tuning them on the Doc2Dial dataset. The details of these implementations are discussed in detail in subsequent sections.

3.1 RoBERTa

Facebook's RoBERTa (Robustly optimized BERT-pretraining approach) transformer model considers previously unexplored architecture options in BERT pre-training. To boost the training process, RoBERTa adopts dynamic masking approach. We experimented with the three different RoBERTa variants as listed below.

1. *roberta-large-squadv2* : RoBERTa large fine-tuned on SQuADv2.0 dataset.
2. *roberta-base-squadv2-nq* : RoBERTa base fine-tuned on NQ and SQuADv2.0 datasets.
3. *roberta-base-squadv2-covid* : RoBERTa base fine-tuned on SQuADv2.0 and CORD-19 datasets.

3.2 ALBERT

The key goal of Google's ALBERT(A Lite BERT) is to minimise the number of parameters in BERT (340M parameters) as training large models like BERT is computationally expensive and time-consuming. ALBERT implements 2 different techniques like factorization of the embedding parameterization and distributing all of its parameters across layers in order to decrease the number of parameters used in training. In our work, three ALBERT models were considered for the analysis.

1. *albert-base-squadv2* : ALBERT base fine-tuned on SQuADv2.0
2. *albert-xlarge-squadv2* : ALBERT xlarge fine-tuned on SQuADv2.0 dataset
3. *albert-xxlarge-squadv2* : ALBERT xxlarge fine-tuned on SQuADv2.0

3.3 ELECTRA

ELECTRA (Efficiently Learning an Encoder that Classifies Token Replacements Accurately) uses replaced token detection (RTD), which trains a bidirectional model such as an MLM while also learning from the input positions similar to an LM (Language Model). We considered two variants of ELECTRA for the benchmarking experiments.

1. *electra-base-squadv2* : electra-base fine-tuned on SQuAD 2.0 dataset.
2. *electra-large-squadv2* : electra-large language model fine-tuned on SQuAD2.0 dataset.

4 Ensemble Models

To further enhance the performance of the proposed models for the Knowledge Identification task, we employed ensembling techniques for leverage the predictive power of all the transformer models considered for the experiments. Various combinations of the models were designed and experimented with, in order to improve the predictions. The confidence score from different models is used as a measure to combine models. The predictions of the model with maximum confidence score is treated as best prediction and the same is considered for evaluation. Initially, various models from same groups of RoBERTa, ALBERT and ELECTRA are ensembled together, and based on the predictions on the validation set, few other models are added. The following are the different combinations of models submitted for testset evaluation.

1. *roberta-ensemble* : roberta-large-squadv2 + roberta-base-squadv2-nq + roberta-base-squadv2-covid
2. *albert-ensemble* : albert-base-squadv2 + albert-xlarge-squadv2 + albert-xxlarge-squadv2
3. *electra-ensemble* : electra-base-squadv2 + electra-large-squadv2
4. *Ensemble1* : alberta-ensemble + roberta-base-squadv2-covid
5. *Ensemble2* : alberta-ensemble + roberta-base-squadv2-nq + roberta-base-squadv2-covid

The performance of all the proposed models was measured using standard metrics, for both the validation and test set, the details of which are presented in Section 6. We also employed metrics like Exact Match and F1 score for individual pretrained models, and also *alberta-ensemble* with *roberta-base* pretrained on the *nq* and *covid* datasets.

5 Model Fine-tuning

In order to improve Exact Match and F1 scores, fine-tuning and ensemble techniques were considered. The dataset provided for the test-dev phase of the shared task is considered as validation set, which shares the same grounding document as training dataset. The test dataset is provided during the test phase of the task and contains 787 end-user questions.

During the training phase, the document trunk along with the corresponding dialogue context was input to the encoder model. The output obtained from the linear layer is a tuple representing the probabilities of the position being the start and end of the corresponding span. In case the ground truth span is not inside the considered trunk, the *begin* and *end* positions are taken as the start of the sequence. In the decoding phase, the probability tuples of all the trunks are considered by the model to obtain the optimum span.

We also conducted experiments by varying hyperparameters such as maximum sequence length (384, 512), batch size (4, 8, 16) and learning rate(3e-5, 1e-4) to select best performance. Each model has been trained for 5 epochs and during training, checkpoints were generated for every 2000 steps. Loss reduction was examined at every checkpoint to pick the best optimal checkpoint that could potentially generate optimal predictions for each model. All experiments were performed on NVIDIA V100 GPUs with 32GB RAM. In Section 6, the details of experiments conducted and the observed performance are described.

6 Experimental Results and Discussion

In this section, we discuss various versions of models submitted for consideration in the final phase on the leaderboard. Table 1 presents the observed results for the proposed transformer models for the metrics Exact Match and F1-score. It can be observed that, among the various RoBERTa models, fine-tuning *roberta-base-squadv2-nq* on Doc2Dial achieved the best performance, which proves that increasing the scope of data gives better results. From Table 1, it can seen that amongst the ALBERT models, fine-tuning *albert-xlarge-squadv2* resulted in improvements in performance when compared to those of *albert-base-squadv2*.

Table 2 tabulated the results of benchmarking of proposed ensemble models on test dataset. It is evindent that, combining different models through maximum confidence score ensembling technique helped in achieving increased performance when compared to the performance of individual models (Refer Table 1). The *albert-ensemble* model was the best-performing model among ensemble models belonging to same group such as *roberta-ensemble*, *albert-ensemble* and *electra-ensemble*. Therefore, we decided to combine cross-group models with *albert-ensemble* to improve predictions.

In case of *Ensemble1* and *Ensemble2*, applying ensembling techniques on best performing RoBERTa models like *roberta-base-squadv2-nq* and *roberta-base-squadv2-covid* with *albert-ensemble* resulted in further improvements as is

Table 1: Exact Match and F1 Scores of different pretrained models on validation set

Model	Exact Match	F1 Score
roberta-large-squadv2	52.02	67.57
roberta-base-squadv2-nq	**55.56**	**69.36**
roberta-base-squadv2-covid	54.54	68.09
albert-base-squadv2	44.44	59.01
albert-xlarge-squadv2	50.00	63.69
electra-base-squadv2	46.46	62.37

Table 2: Exact Match and F1 Scores of proposed ensemble models

Ensemble Model	Validation Set		Test Set	
	Exact Match	F1 Score	Exact Match	F1 Score
roberta-ensemble	56.56	69.91	54.76	70.17
electra-ensemble	53.53	69.47	47.65	65.14
Ensemble1	59.60	73.27	57.94	73.11
Ensemble2	**61.62**	**74.48**	**58.58**	**73.39**

Table 3: Sample question context generated by series of user and agent turns: "*user: what should I do if i go out in public? agent: Call 911 right away user: What if symptoms worsen? agent: you are at higher risk for more serious COVID-19 illness It is very important for you to take steps to stay healthy .s user: what if you are If you are an older adult or someone who has severe chronic medical conditions such as heart or lung disease , or diabetes agent: If you don t have soap and water , use an alcohol - based hand sanitizer with at least 60 % alcohol user: What if i do not have access to soap and water?*"

Model	Predicted Text Span
roberta-base-squadv2-nq	keep away from others who are sick, limit close contact, and wash your hands often. Consider steps you can take to stay away from other people. This is especially important for people who are at higher risk of getting very sick.
roberta-ensemble	keep away from others who are sick, limit close contact, and wash your hands often.
electra-ensemble	Avoid crowds as much as possible When you go out in public, keep away from others who are sick, limit close contact, and wash your hands often.
Ensemble1	keep away from others who are sick, limit close contact, and wash your hands often.
Ensemble2	keep away from others who are sick, limit close contact, and wash your hands often.

evident from the tabulated values shown in Table 2. The ensemble models performed well on both validation and test datasets, thus, underscoring the consistent performance of proposed models on different datasets.

Prediction metrics on the test set also emphasize the effectiveness of the proposed models on even completely new and unknown domain data. Table 3 shows predicted text span for a sample question context for different ensemble models. Amongst them, *Ensemble2* gave the optimal span followed by *Ensemble1*. The *Ensemble2* model gives the best scores on both validation and test datasets with an Exact Match score of 58.58 and F1 Score of 73.39 on test dataset which show significant increase over the baseline (Feng et al., 2020) 55.4 Exact Match score and an F1 score of 65.0 respectively.

7 Conclusion and Future Work

In this paper, the application of transfer learning by utilizing transformer models like RoBERTa, ALBERT and ELECTRA for Question Answering Span Prediction task was explored. We also experimented with pretrained models on several other datasets prior to fine-tuning it on the DialDoc21 dataset, provided as part of the DialDoc21 Shared task. Maximum confidence score based ensemble techniques were employed to combine various base transformer models to further boost the performance. We plan to extend our approach and experiment with other ensembling techniques for further enhancing the performance and also explore avenues for improved scalability when applied to larger datasets.

References

Anumeha Agrawal, Rosa Anil George, Selvan Suntiha Ravi, Sowmya Kamath, and Anand Kumar. 2019. Ars_nitk at mediqa 2019: Analysing various methods for natural language inference, recognising question entailment and medical question answering system. In *Proceedings of the 18th BioNLP Workshop and Shared Task*, pages 533–540.

Kevin Clark, Minh-Thang Luong, Quoc V. Le, and Christopher D. Manning. 2020. Electra: Pre-training text encoders as discriminators rather than generators.

Jacob Devlin, Ming-Wei Chang, Kenton Lee, and Kristina Toutanova. 2019. Bert: Pre-training of deep bidirectional transformers for language understanding.

Dheeru Dua, Yizhong Wang, Pradeep Dasigi, Gabriel Stanovsky, Sameer Singh, and Matt Gardner. 2019. DROP: A reading comprehension benchmark requiring discrete reasoning over paragraphs. In *Proceedings of the 2019 Conference of the North American Chapter of the Association for Computational Linguistics: Human Language Technologies, Volume 1 (Long and Short Papers)*, pages 2368–2378, Minneapolis, Minnesota. Association for Computational Linguistics.

Song Feng, Hui Wan, Chulaka Gunasekara, Siva Sankalp Patel, Sachindra Joshi, and Luis A. Lastras. 2020. doc2dial: A goal-oriented document-grounded dialogue dataset.

Tom Kwiatkowski, Jennimaria Palomaki, Olivia Redfield, Michael Collins, Ankur Parikh, Chris Alberti, Danielle Epstein, Illia Polosukhin, Matthew Kelcey, Jacob Devlin, Kenton Lee, Kristina N. Toutanova, Llion Jones, Ming-Wei Chang, Andrew Dai, Jakob Uszkoreit, Quoc Le, and Slav Petrov. 2019. Natural questions: a benchmark for question answering research. *Transactions of the Association of Computational Linguistics*.

Zhenzhong Lan, Mingda Chen, Sebastian Goodman, Kevin Gimpel, Piyush Sharma, and Radu Soricut. 2020. Albert: A lite bert for self-supervised learning of language representations.

Yinhan Liu, Myle Ott, Naman Goyal, Jingfei Du, Mandar Joshi, Danqi Chen, Omer Levy, Mike Lewis, Luke Zettlemoyer, and Veselin Stoyanov. 2019. Roberta: A robustly optimized bert pretraining approach.

Pranav Rajpurkar, Robin Jia, and Percy Liang. 2018. Know what you don't know: Unanswerable questions for squad.

Pranav Rajpurkar, Jian Zhang, Konstantin Lopyrev, and Percy Liang. 2016. Squad: 100,000+ questions for machine comprehension of text.

Adam Trischler, Tong Wang, Xingdi Yuan, Justin Harris, Alessandro Sordoni, Philip Bachman, and Kaheer Suleman. 2017. NewsQA: A machine comprehension dataset. In *Proceedings of the 2nd Workshop on Representation Learning for NLP*, pages 191–200, Vancouver, Canada. Association for Computational Linguistics.

Akshay Upadhya, Swastik Udupa, and S Sowmya Kamath. 2019. Deep neural network models for question classification in community question-answering forums. In *2019 10th International Conference on Computing, Communication and Networking Technologies (ICCCNT)*, pages 1–6. IEEE.

Lucy Lu Wang, Kyle Lo, Yoganand Chandrasekhar, Russell Reas, Jiangjiang Yang, Darrin Eide, Kathryn Funk, Rodney Michael Kinney, Ziyang Liu, William Merrill, P. Mooney, D. Murdick, Devvret Rishi, J. Sheehan, Zhihong Shen, Brandon Brandon Stilson Stilson, Alex D Wade, Kuansan Wang, Christopher Wilhelm, Boya Xie, Douglas A. Raymond, Daniel S. Weld, Oren Etzioni, and Sebastian Kohlmeier. 2020. Cord-19: The covid-19 open research dataset. *ArXiv*.

Zhilin Yang, Zihang Dai, Yiming Yang, Jaime Carbonell, Ruslan Salakhutdinov, and Quoc V. Le. 2020. Xlnet: Generalized autoregressive pretraining for language understanding.

Zhilin Yang, Peng Qi, Saizheng Zhang, Yoshua Bengio, William Cohen, Ruslan Salakhutdinov, and Christopher D. Manning. 2018. HotpotQA: A dataset for diverse, explainable multi-hop question answering. In *Proceedings of the 2018 Conference on Empirical Methods in Natural Language Processing*, pages 2369–2380, Brussels, Belgium. Association for Computational Linguistics.

WeaSuL$^{\pi}$: Weakly Supervised Dialogue Policy Learning: Reward Estimation for Multi-turn Dialogue

Anant Khandelwal
India Machine Learning
Amazon
anantkha@amazon.com

Abstract

An intelligent dialogue system in a multi-turn setting should not only generate the responses which are of good quality, but it should also generate the responses which can lead to long-term success of the dialogue. Although, the current approaches improved the response quality, but they over-look the training signals present in the dialogue data. We can leverage these signals to generate the weakly supervised training data for learning dialog policy and reward estimator, and make the policy take actions (generates responses) which can foresee the future direction for a successful (rewarding) conversation. We simulate the dialogue between an agent and a user (modelled similar to an agent with supervised learning objective) to interact with each other. The agent uses dynamic blocking to generate ranked diverse responses and exploration-exploitation to select among the Top-K responses. Each simulated state-action pair is evaluated (works as a weak annotation) with three quality modules: Semantic Relevant, Semantic Coherence and Consistent Flow. Empirical studies with two benchmarks indicate that our model can significantly out-perform the response quality and lead to a successful conversation on both automatic evaluation and human judgment.[1]

1 Introduction

Dialog policy for multi-turn dialogue decides the next best action to take on the environment so as to complete the conversation based on various success criteria. Reinforcement learning can help to learn such a policy where the environment can be users (human or model) and the policy takes action on the environment from which it gets a reward signal (Fatemi et al., 2016; Peng et al., 2017; Chen et al., 2017; Yarats and Lewis, 2018; Lei et al., 2018; He et al., 2018; Su et al., 2018).

Learning a dialogue policy using reinforcement learning can be challenging with humans users, since it requires a large set of samples with a reward to train. Since there are a lot of previous works on neural response generation (Gu et al., 2020; Zhao et al., 2020; Zhang et al., 2019; Xing et al., 2018; Serban et al., 2016) we can model the users also, using any of these encoder-decoder architectures. This helps to simulate the conversations between the simulated user and the agent (policy model) replying to each other (Zhao and Eskenazi, 2016; Dhingra et al., 2016; Shah et al., 2018). Reward signal for policy learning can be as simple as the small constant negative reward at each turn and a large reward at the end (if the goal completes) to encourage shorter conversations (Takanobu et al., 2019).

However, reward estimation for dialogue is challenging, the small constant negative reward at each turn may lead to ending the conversation prematurely. Instead of handcrafting the reward at the end based on success or failure, it is more useful if we can evaluate reward at every turn to guide the policy to dynamically change actions as per the need for the user and end the conversation naturally. With the growing complexity of the system across different topics, it is required to build a more sophisticated reward function to avoid manual intervention for accounting different factors towards conversation success.

In this work, we proposed a novel model for contextual response generation in multi-turn dialogue. The model includes the turn-level reward estimator, which combines the weak supervision signals obtained from three basic modules 1) Semantic Coherence, 2) Consistent Flow, 3) Semantic Relevance. These modules are learned jointly with the response generation model with the counterfactual examples obtained from negative sampling. Leveraging the weak supervision signals obtained from these models, we further update the reward

[1]Work done prior to joining Amazon

Proceedings of the 1st Workshop on Document-grounded Dialogue and Conversational Question Answering, pages 69–80
August 5–6, 2021.

estimator and dialog policy jointly in an alternative way, thus improving each other.

Our proposed approach integrates semantic understanding of utterances using encoder-decoder systems with the power of Reinforcement Learning (RL) to optimize long-term success. We test the proposed approach with two benchmarks: DailyDialog (Li et al., 2017b) and PersonaChat (Zhang et al., 2018). Experimental results demonstrate on both datasets indicate that our model can significantly outperform state-of-the-art generation models in terms of both automatic evaluation and human judgment.

2 Related Work

Open-domain dialogue in a multi-turn setting has been widely explored with different encoder-decoder architectures (Gu et al., 2020; Feng et al., 2021; Kottur et al., 2017; Li et al., 2016; Shah et al., 2018; Shang et al., 2015; Vinyals and Le, 2015; Wu et al., 2019; Zhao et al., 2020; Zhong et al., 2019). The basic encoder-decoder architectures like Seq-to-Seq models have been widely extended and modified to generate the generic responses, context modelling and grounding by persona/emotion/knowledge (Li et al., 2015; Xing et al., 2017; Serban et al., 2016; Xing et al., 2018; Zhang et al., 2019, 2018; Zhou et al., 2018; Dinan et al., 2018).

The dialogue literature widely applies reinforcement learning, including the recent ones based on deep architectures (Takanobu et al., 2019, 2020; Li et al., 2020; Takanobu et al., 2020; Li et al., 2020; Gordon-Hall et al., 2020a,b). But these task-oriented RL dialogue systems often model the dialogue with limited parameters and assumptions specific to the dataset, targeted for that task. The dataset includes hand-built templates with state, action and reward signals designed by humans for each new domain making this setting difficult for extending these to open domain dialogue systems.

Our goal in this work is to integrate the state-of-the-art encoder-decoder architectures like in Gu et al. (2020); Zhao et al. (2020); Csaky and Recski (2020) and reinforcement learning paradigms to efficiently learn the dialogue policy optimized for long-term success in the multi-turn dialogue scenarios. We are recently inspired by the works in Takanobu et al. (2019); Li et al. (2020, 2016) to jointly learn the reward function and dialogue policy, and reduce the effort and cost for manual labelling the conversations for building the reward model. Specifically, we leverage the weak supervision inspired from Chang et al. (2021a,b) to generate the labelled dataset to facilitate this joint learning and building reward estimation model.

3 Approach

We represent dialog sessions $\mathcal{D} = \{\tau_1, \tau_2, \tau_3, ...\tau_n\}$ where each dialog session τ represents the trajectory of state-action pairs as $\{s_0^u, a_0^u, s_0, a_0, s_1^u, a_1^u, s_1, a_1, ...\}$. The user in our case is a simulator which utters a response a^u given the state s^u denoted as $\mu(a^u, e^u|s^u)$ where e^u denotes the binary signal indicating the end of a dialog session, in that case the response a^u is empty. The dialog policy $\pi_\theta(a|s)$ decides the action a according to the current state s after the agent interacts with the user simulator μ. At each time, the state given to the either dialog party is updated after recording the action uttered by the other party. The reward estimator f evaluates the quality of response/action uttered by the dialog policy π. The dialog policy π is based on the BERT (Devlin et al., 2019) encoder-decoder model and the reward function f is the MLP model parameterized by θ and ω respectively. We have modeled the user simulator exactly in the same way as the agent but trained only using supervised learning objective.

In the subsequent section, we will introduce the components action, state, policy, quality modules and reward estimator. Further, sections explain the setup we have used for weakly supervised learning and, finally, the experimental results.

3.1 Action

An action a is the dialogue utterance generated by the encoder-decoder model as shown in Figure 1. The model takes as input the context history (state), and outputs the probability distribution over a set of possible actions denoted as $\pi_\theta(a|s)$ parameterized by θ. The user simulator generates the action a^u, policy generates the action a, and the input state for the agent and the user is s and s^u respectively.

3.2 State

The state is the past conversation history between an agent and a user denoted as, $s_t = \{q_1, a_1, q_2, a_2, q_3, a_3, ..., q_t\}$. The state for an agent and a user are differently denoted as s and s^u respectively. Let's say the agent utter-

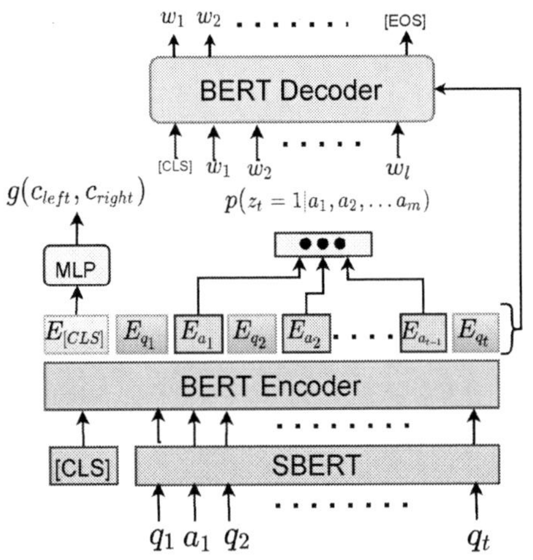

Figure 1: BERT based Encoder-Decoder with Semantic Coherence and Relevance. Similarly, Consistent Flow loss is also calculated using encoder.

ances are denoted by a's, then state, $s = s_t$ and the agent utters a_t. Similarly, the user state $s_t^u = \{q_1, a_1, q_2, a_2, q_3, a_3, ..., q_t, a_t\}$ and the user utters q_{t+1}. Each of the utterances is mapped to a fixed-length sentence vector using SBERT (Reimers and Gurevych, 2019).

3.3 Dialogue Policy

The dialogue policy takes the form of a BERT based encoder-decoder (i.e. $\pi_\theta(a|s)$) (Gu et al., 2020) as shown in Figure 1. Similar to Xu et al. (2020), we have used the BERT based encoder and transformer decoder, but instead of feeding the utterance at word level, we instead fed the utterance representation (obtained from SBERT) into the encoder. The encoder takes as input the previous context history as s_t and output the response a_t at the output of the decoder.

3.4 User Simulator

We have modelled the user simulator in exactly the same way as the BERT based encoder-decoder shown in Figure 1. However, the user simulator is trained only (with supervised learning objective) for utterances in dialog corpus and predicting user response (Gu et al., 2020).

3.5 Conversation Quality Modules

We calculate the reward for each state-action pair (see Section. 3.8) and use this signal to train the dialogue policy so that it can avoid reaching bad states so as to reach the successful end of the conversation between a user and an agent. We have leveraged the signals from three basic modules, namely, Semantic Coherence, Consistent Flow and Semantic Relevance (which are jointly learned with the dialogue policy). For each of the three modules, the data for the positive class is obtained from the source corpus while for the negative class it has been generated dynamically during training. We describe each of the three modules in the following sections.

3.5.1 Semantic Relevance

We need to filter out the utterances generated with high confidence by the dialog policy but are semantically irrelevant to the previous context. To quantify such a characteristic, we modeled the general response relevance prediction task which utilizes the sequential relationship of the dialog data fed to the encoder side of BERT encoder-decoder framework. Since, the task of semantic relevance is to match the two sequences of conversation, so instead of matching the context and response, we have measured the relevance of two fragments of dialogue session.

Specifically, given a context $c = \{q_1, a_1, q_2, a_2, ...q_m\}$, we randomly split c into two consecutive pieces $c_{left} = \{q_1, a_1, q_2, a_2, ...q_t, a_t\}$ and $c_{right} = \{q_{t+1}, a_{t+1}, ...q_m\}$. Similar to Xu et al. (2020), we replaced the left or right part with the sampled piece from the corpus. Also, we additionally generate the negative samples by internal shuffling in the left or right part. The whole model is trained like a classifier with corresponding labels $y_{sr} \in \{0, 1\}$. Since the individual utterances are fed after obtaining their vector representation, the aggregated representation of two pieces is represented by E_{CLS}^{sr} over which the non-linear transformation is applied, the score for semantic relevance is given by $g(c_{\text{left}}, c_{\text{right}})$, and similar to Xu et al. (2020), it has been trained using the binary cross-entropy loss as:

$$L_{sr} = -y_{sr} \log(g(c_{\text{left}}, c_{\text{right}})) - (1 - y_{sr}) \log(1 - g(c_{\text{left}}, c_{\text{right}})) \quad (1)$$

3.5.2 Semantic Coherence

The response generated should be rewarded only if it is coherent despite having adequate content. This makes the model to generate the coherent responses while avoiding the incoherent ones. Specifically, given a context $c = \{q_1, a_1, q_2, a_2, ...q_m\}$, we randomly select any of the agent response at time t, denoted as a_t, and replace it with any random utterance from the corpus. We also generate the incoherent samples by internal shuffling of bi-grams. The incoherent utterance is labelled as $y_t^{coh} = 0$ and coherent samples as $y_t^{coh} = 1$. The semantic coherence model is also trained like a classifier for each of the utterance representations obtained at the output of BERT encoder as shown in Figure 1. The probability of the t-th utterance being incoherent is given as:

$$\begin{aligned} p(z_t = 1|a_1, .., a_t) &= softmax(W_{coh}E_{a_t} + b_{coh}) \\ &= \frac{exp(W_{coh}E_{a_t} + b_{coh})}{\sum_{l=1}^{m} exp(W_{coh}E_{a_l} + b_{coh})} \end{aligned} \quad (2)$$

and the loss function is given as:

$$L_{coh} = -\sum_{t=1}^{m} z_t \log p(z_t = 1|a_1, a_2.....a_m) \quad (3)$$

3.5.3 Consistent Flow

We want the agent to continuously add the information to keep the conversation going in the forward direction. To determine the flowing conversation, we take the cosine similarity between the last two agent utterances denoted as $E_{a_{i-1}}$ and E_{a_i} denoted as $g(a_{i-1}, a_i)$, and we measure the similarity with randomly sampled utterance v in place of a_{i-1} given as $g(a_{i-1}, v)$. We would like $g(a_{i-1}, a_i)$ to be larger than $g(a_{i-1}, v)$ by at least a margin Δ and define the learning objective as a hing loss function:

$$L_{cf} = max\{0, \Delta - g(a_{i-1}, a_i) + g(a_{i-1}, v)\} \quad (4)$$

3.6 Joint Training of Agent and Reward Modules

To initialize the parameters of agent and reward modules $\mathcal{M}$ ={Semantic Relevance, Semantic Coherence, Consistent Flow}, we used the supervised learning objective since all the state-action pairs obtained from the pre-training corpus are the ground-truth and can be used as close approximation for further fine-tuning on other dialog corpus. We used the pre-training corpus $\mathcal{P}$ as Gutenberg dialog corpus (Csaky and Recski, 2020). Since the agent model in our case is based on BERT encoder-decoder parameterized by θ similar to Gu et al. (2020), the probability of generating agent's response $\mathbf{a}$ is given as:

$$p_\theta(\mathbf{a}|\mathbf{s}) = \prod_{j=1}^{N} p_\theta(a_j|a_{<j}, \mathbf{s}), \quad (5)$$

where a_j is the j-th word generated at the output of decoder and $\mathbf{s}$ is the whole context history utterances fed to the encoder and N is the maximum sequence length of decoder. The loss function for generating agent response $\mathbf{a}$ is given as:

$$L_a = J(\theta) = -\sum_{i=1}^{N} \log p_\theta(a_j|a_{<j}, \mathbf{s}) \quad (6)$$

The joint loss function is defined as:

$$L_{full} = L_a + \alpha * (L_{sr} + L_{coh} + L_{cf}) \quad (7)$$

The policy π_θ is also parameterized by θ, and the probability of action a is given by $\pi_\theta(a|s)$ similar to $p_\theta(a|s)$, since the probability distribution is learned only from (s, a) pairs obtained from the corpus with human demonstrations. It is a good approximation to initialize the parameters of policy $\pi_\theta(a|s)$ with parameters of $p_\theta(a|s)$. Furthermore, we update the policy π_θ (Step 13 in the Algorithm. 1) to avoid actions a which do not lead to rewarding conversations.

3.7 Dialogue Simulation between Agent and User

We setup simulation between virtual agent and user, and let them take turns talking to each other. The simulation is started with a starter utterance obtained from the dialog samples D_H (Step 5 of Algorithm 1) and fed to the agent, it then encodes the utterance and generates the response a, the state s^u is then updated with previous history and fed to the user model to obtain the next response a^u. The response a^u is appended to s^u to obtain the updated state s. Similarly, the process is repeated until one of the following conditions occurs after a few number of turns[2]: a) When agent starts to produce dull responses like "I don't know" [3]. b) When agent starts to generate repetitive response consecutively [4] c) Or, the conversation achieved

[2]The number of turns after these rules applied is average number of turns in the corpus

[3]Used simple rule matching method with 9 phrases collected from the corpus, instead of having false positives and negatives this works well in practice.

[4]If by rule two consecutive utterances matched more than 80% it is said to be repetitive.

the maximum number of turns handled by agent and user models.[5]

3.8 Weakly Supervised Learning Algorithm

Learning with weak supervision is widely used with the rise of data-driven neural approaches (Ratner et al., 2020; Mrkšić et al., 2017; Chang et al., 2020; Bach et al., 2017; Wu et al., 2018; Chang et al., 2021a). Our approach incorporates a similar line of work by providing noisy text to a pre-trained model which incorporates prior knowledge from general-domain text and small in-domain text (Peng et al., 2020; Chen et al., 2019; Harkous et al., 2020) and use it as a weak annotator similar to Ratner et al. (2020). The primary challenge with the synthetic data is the noise introduced during the generation process, and the noisy labels tend to bring little to no improvement (Frénay and Verleysen, 2013). To train on such noisy data, we employ three step training process: a) pre-training b) generate data with weighted categories c) fine-tuning similar to Chang et al. (2021a); Dehghani et al. (2017).

Step 1: Pre-train Generation and Quality Modules Jointly. This step involves pre-training the agent with quality modules jointly as explained in Section 3.6. Quality modules trained on clean data as well as automatically generated negative samples by random sampling. These modules are further fine-tuned on the sampled dialogues from target dialogue corpus at each training iteration. Similarly, we initialized the user also by supervised training on the pre-training dialogue corpus with fine-tuning on target dialogue corpus. (see steps 2-7 of Algorithm 1). The fine-tuning steps make use of continual learning to avoid catastrophic forgetting (Madotto et al., 2020; Lee, 2017).

Step 2: Generates the Weakly Labelled data with Reward categories. After the models are initialized with trained parameters, the dialogue simulation has been started between the agent and the user (see Section. 3.7) to interact with each other and generates the synthetic data with annotated scores with each quality module for every state-action pair in sampled dialogues. During dialogue simulation, we employ Dynamic Blocking mechanism(Niu et al., 2020) to generate novel words and paraphrased responses. Specifically, we generate Top-7 response at each turn and set the agent to exploration for 60 percent of the times and for the rest of the times it exploits by selecting the response from top two ranked responses. We specifically filter the state-action pairs into three reward categories namely, *VeryHigh*, *High* and *Low*. For the state-action pairs whose scores by each module are greater than or equal to 0.8 are put into the *VeryHigh* category. Other, state-action pairs whose scores by each module are between 0.6 and 0.8 are put into the *High* reward category. The rest of all state-action pairs are put into the *Low* reward category. Additionally, we include state-action pairs sampled from target dialog corpus in Step 1. into the *VeryHigh* category.

Step 3: Update the reward estimator and policy. The reward estimator maximizes the log likelihood state-action pairs of higher rewards than the lower ones. The reward estimator f_ω, parameterized by ω, and let's say H, V and L represents the collection of all state action pairs of *High*, *VeryHigh* and *Low* reward category respectively.

$$\begin{aligned} \omega^* &= \arg\max \mathbb{E}_{(s_k,a_k)\sim\{H,V\}}[f_\omega(s_k,a_k)] \\ f_\omega(s_k,a_k) &= \log p_\omega(s_k,a_k) = \log \frac{e^{R_\omega(s_k,a_k)}}{Z_\omega} \\ R_\omega(s_k,a_k) &= \sum_{t=k}^{T} \gamma^{t-k} r_\omega(s_t,a_t) \\ Z_\omega &= \sum_{\forall(s_k,a_k)} e^{R_\omega(s_k,a_k)} \end{aligned} \tag{8}$$

where f models state-action pairs of H, V and L category as a Boltzmann distribution (Takanobu et al., 2019). The cost function for reward estimator in terms of trajectories obtained from respective reward categories is given as:

$$\begin{aligned} J_f(\omega) = -0.5 * KL(p_H(s,a) \parallel p_\omega(s,a)) \\ - KL(p_V(s,a) \parallel p_\omega(s,a)) \\ + KL(p_L(s,a) \parallel p_\omega(s,a)) \end{aligned} \tag{9}$$

It minimize the KL-divergence between reward distribution and the state-action pairs of high and very high reward but maximize the distribution from the ones with low category. The gradient yields:

$$\begin{aligned} \nabla_\omega J_f = 0.5 * \mathbb{E}_{(s,a)\sim H}[\nabla_\omega f_\omega(s,a)] \\ + \mathbb{E}_{(s,a)\sim V}[\nabla_\omega f_\omega(s,a)] - \mathbb{E}_{(s,a)\sim L}[\nabla_\omega f_\omega(s,a)] \end{aligned} \tag{10}$$

[5]The maximum number of turn is set as 20.

Since, the dialog policy is required to put the actions atleast to that of high category, i.e. maximize the entropy regularized expected reward $(\mathbb{E}_{\pi}[R] + H(\pi))$ which is effectively minimizes the KL divergence between the policy distribution and Boltzmann distribution.

$$\begin{aligned} J_{\pi}(\theta) &= -KL(\pi_{\theta}(a|s) \parallel p_{\omega}(s,a)) \\ &= \mathbb{E}_{(s,a)\sim\pi}[f_{\omega}(s,a) - \log \pi_{\theta}(a|s)] \\ &= \mathbb{E}_{(s,a)\sim\pi}[R_{\omega}(s,a)] - \log Z_{\omega} + H(\pi_{\theta}) \end{aligned} \quad (11)$$

where the term $\log Z_{\omega}$ is independent to θ, and $H(\cdot)$ denotes the entropy of a model. Using likelihood ratio trick the gradient for policy is given as:

$$\begin{aligned} \nabla_{\theta} J_{\pi} = \mathbb{E}_{(s,a)\sim\pi}[(f_{\omega}(s,a) \\ - \log \pi_{\theta}(a|s))\nabla_{\theta} \log \pi_{\theta}(a|s)]. \end{aligned} \quad (12)$$

Hence, the reward is $r_{\omega}(s,a) = f_{\omega}(s,a) - \log \pi_{\theta}(a|s)$ for each state-action pair and the loss function re-written as:

$$\begin{aligned} J_{\pi}(\theta) = \mathbb{E}_{(s,a)\sim\pi}[\sum_{k=t}^{T} \gamma^{k-t}(f_{\omega}(s_k,a_k) \\ - \log \pi_{\theta}(a_k|s_k))] \end{aligned} \quad (13)$$

Like in Takanobu et al. (2019) the reward estimator f_{ω} includes the shaping term. Formally, we include next state s_{t+1} also instead of just (s_t, a_t)

$$f_{\omega}(s_t, a_t, s_{t+1}) = g_{\omega}(s_t, a_t) + \gamma h(s_{t+1}) - h(s_t) \quad (14)$$

where h is the MLP network with input as pre-sigmoid scores from each quality modules, and g_{ω} is also the MLP network with input as the concatenation of E_{CLS} as state vector and SBERT sentence embedding of action a.

Algorithm 1 Dialogue Policy Learning

Require: Pre-Training corpus P, Dialogue Corpus $\mathcal{D}$.

Modules $\mathcal{M}$ = {Semantic Relevance, Semantic Coherence, Consistent Flow}

Do Agent training on $\mathcal{P}$ as in Section 3.6 jointly with modules $\mathcal{M}$

User μ supervised training on $\mathcal{P}$.

for each *training iteration* **do**

    Sample dialogues $\mathcal{D}_H$ from $\mathcal{D}$ randomly.

    Fine-tune user simulator μ on $\mathcal{D}_H$.

    Fine-tune Agent and $\mathcal{M}$ on $\mathcal{D}_H$ jointly.

    Collect dialog samples $\mathcal{D}_{\pi}$ by executing the dialog policy π and interacting with μ, $a^u \sim \mu(\cdot|s^u)$, $a \sim \pi(\cdot|s)$ where s and s^u is updated each time after getting response from user and agent respectively.

    Get weak annotation scores for all $(s,a) \in \mathcal{D}_{\pi}$ from each of the modules $\mathcal{M}$.

    Filtering the (s,a) pairs into {*VeryHigh*, *High* and *Low*} reward categories.

    Update the reward estimator f by minimizing J_f w.r.t ω (Eq.10)

    Compute reward for each $(s,a) \in \mathcal{D}_{\pi}$ as,

$$\hat{r} = f_{\omega}(s_t, a_t, s_{t+1}) - \log \pi(a_t|s_t)$$

    Update the policy π_{θ} by minimizing J_{π} w.r.t θ (Eq. 13).

end for

4 Experiments

We conduct experiments on DailyDialog (Li et al., 2017b), PersonaChat (Zhang et al., 2018) and used Gutenberg Dialogue Dataset (Csaky and Recski, 2020) as a pre-training corpus. We compare our model performance with baselines on various aspects of response quality.

4.1 Datasets

We considered DailyDialog (Li et al., 2017b) and PersonaChat (Zhang et al., 2018) which are open domain dialog corpus to evaluate our system. DailyDialog contains conversation revolving around various topics pertaining to daily life, and PersonaChat contains conversations between people with their respective persona profiles. These dialogues can be of varying length, we limit the maximum length to 20, that can be fed to the BERT Encoder-Decoder model. Since average length of DailyDialog is 7.9 and that of PersonaChat is 9.4, so most of the dialogues fit easily without truncation from the history. For rest of the dialogues, it can be slided across to include the more recent utterances and remove it from the starting. Since we are mapping the utterances to their corresponding vectors using SBERT, the length of individual utterances truncated automatically and retain only first 512 word pieces in case of longer utterances. For pre-training corpus the vocabulary is limited to 100,000 while the vocabularies for DailyDialog and PersonaChat are 25,000 and 32,768 respectively.

4.2 Baselines

We select various multi-turn response generation baselines. The baselines which are not included pre-training are (1) **HRED**[6]: Hierarchical encoder-decoder framework (Serban et al., 2016) (2) **VHRED**[7]: an extension of HRED that generates response with latent variables (Serban et al., 2017) (3) **HRAN**[8]: Hierarchical attention mechanism based encoder-decoder framework (Xing et al., 2018) (4) **ReCoSa**[9]: Hierarchical transformer based model (Zhang et al., 2019) (5) **SSN**: dialogue generation learning with self-supervision signals extracted from utterance order (Wu et al., 2019) (6) **Transformer-Auxiliary Tasks**: A recent state-of-the are model leaning language generation with joint learning of transformer with auxiliary tasks (Zhao et al., 2020). The another two baselines from Csaky and Recski (2020) which involve pre-training on the Gutenberg corpus are: (1)**Transformer**[10]: 50M parameters version and (2) **GPT-2**[11]: Pre-trained model with version of 117M parameters. The repository[12] contains these two trained models.

4.3 Evaluation Metrics

We evaluate the performance of our model on various aspects of response quality using both automatic and human evaluation. Although, most of the automatic metrics poorly correlate with human evaluation (Liu et al., 2016), and the recently proposed metrics (Li et al., 2017a; Lowe et al., 2017; Tao et al., 2018) are harder to evaluate than perplexity and BLEU (Papineni et al., 2002). Additionally, human evaluation has its inherent limitation of bias, cost and replication difficulty (Tao et al., 2018). Due to this consensus, some used only automatic metrics (Xing and Fernández, 2018; Xu et al., 2018b) and some used only human evaluation (Krause et al., 2017; Fang et al., 2018) while some used both (Shen et al., 2018; Xu et al., 2018a; Baheti et al., 2018; Ram et al., 2018).

We mainly used the automatic metrics using the DIALOG-EVAL repository[13], it contains 17 different metrics, but we measure only a few metrics to facilitate the comparison with the published baselines results. We specifically follow (Zhao et al., 2020) to measure automatic evaluation and human evaluation. For response content quality we measured BLEU-4 (Papineni et al., 2002) and Perplexity(PPL) (Sutskever et al., 2014). Like in Zhao et al. (2020) used embedding metrics average (AVG), extrema (EXT), and greedy (GRE) measuring similarity between response and target embedding. Similar to Zhao et al. (2020) we also measured the informativeness of responses with distinct-1 and distinct-2 that are calculated as the ratios of distinct unigrams and bigrams.

Since our main objective is not to judge the response quality but to predict the response for long-term success of dialogue. We follow the guidelines as in Li et al. (2016) to explore both single-turn and multi-turn settings. We picked 500 dialogues from the test set and asked 3 native speakers for their judgement. In the first setting, we asked judges to pick the better response among the one generated by our model and a baseline model (**Pre-Trained GPT2**) based on various criteria like answerability and semantics. In the second setting, in case of multi-turn we used 200 simulated conversations between RL agent and a user model to judge the whole conversation for responses uttered by agent. In a complete end-to-end conversation we asked the judges to decide which of the simulated conversations are of higher quality. To compare against the RL model we employ baseline model to simulate the 200 conversations with the same starter utterance used by RL model. Automatic and Human evaluation are shown in Table. 1 and 2 respectively.

4.4 Results and Discussions

Table. 1 reports automatic evaluation metrics on the baseline and the proposed model. Our model outperforms for most of the metrics on both datasets. Since our main idea is to generate the responses for successful conversation in the long run than just evaluating the response quality at each of the turn. This is the main reason of why our model outperforms on both distinct-1 and distinct-2 metrics, in comparison to Transformer-auxiliary task model which also trained jointly with the similar tasks but lacks fine-tuning with the weak supervision signals indicate that an additional training with weakly labelled data improves the generalization performance. Although, we see the perplexity also improves since our model is generating the responses

[6]https://github.com/hsgodhia/hred

[7]https://github.com/julianser/hed-dlg-truncated

[8]https://github.com/LynetteXing1991/HRAN

[9]https://github.com/zhanghainan/ReCoSa

[10]https://github.com/tensorflow/tensor2tensor

[11]https://github.com/huggingface/transfer-learning-conv-ai

[12]https://github.com/ricsinaruto/gutenberg-dialog

[13]https://github.com/ricsinaruto/ dialog-eval

Dataset	Model	PPL	BLEU	Distinct-1	Distinct-2	Average	Greedy	Extrema
DailyDialog	HRED	56.22	0.535	1.553	3.569	81.393	65.546	48.109
	HRAN	47.23	0.447	1.953	7.400	83.460	67.239	49.599
	VHRED	44.79	0.997	1.299	6.113	83.866	67.186	48.570
	SSN	44.28	1.250	2.309	7.266	72.796	73.069	44.260
	ReCoSa	42.34	1.121	1.987	10.180	84.763	67.557	48.957
	Transformer-Auxiliary Tasks	38.60	1.658	3.457	14.954	85.224	69.518	49.069
	Pre-Trained Transformer	-	11.5	2.92	14.7	55.1	53.5	59.8
	Pre-Trained GPT2	-	12.8	4.07	25.9	56.8	54.0	59.6
	Our Model	**20.13**	**15.171**	**6.316**	**28.422**	85.417	**73.118**	**61.539**
	Our Model w/o weak supervision	20.51	14.718	4.611	26.752	**86.481**	73.003	59.911
PersonaChat	HRED	46.04	1.279	0.164	0.450	83.329	65.546	48.109
	HRAN	41.94	1.997	0.235	0.771	82.850	67.239	49.599
	VHRED	42.07	2.181	0.312	1.915	82.995	67.186	48.570
	SSN	47.90	2.288	0.637	2.623	85.002	73.069	44.260
	ReCoSa	34.19	2.258	0.915	4.217	83.963	67.557	48.957
	Transformer-Auxiliary Tasks	33.23	2.434	1.279	5.816	83.632	69.518	49.069
	Pre-Trained Transformer	-	15.5	1.04	4.8	51.3	57.5	57.1
	Pre-Trained GPT2	-	15.3	1.82	12.9	53.6	55.9	55.8
	Our Model	**19.78**	**16.651**	**2.434**	**13.912**	84.941	**73.081**	**59.241**
	Our Model w/o weak supervision	21.49	16.017	2.318	13.274	**85.018**	72.438	58.816

Table 1: Automatic metrics comparison with baselines. Results in bold indicate the best performing model on the corresponding metrics.

DailyDialog			
Setting	**RL-Win**	**RL-Lose**	**Tie**
Single-Turn general quality	0.41	0.28	0.31
Single-Turn ease to answer	0.55	0.12	0.33
Multi-turn general quality	0.76	0.13	0.11
PersonaChat			
Setting	**RL-Win**	**RL-Lose**	**Tie**
Single turn general quality	0.36	0.22	0.42
Single-Turn ease to answer	0.51	0.14	0.35
Multi-turn general quality	0.71	0.17	0.12

Table 2: Human Evaluation Results. Ratios are calculated after taking majority vote among the decisions made by three judges.

more like humans to optimize the conversation in long run. Similarly, embedding metrics also shown the improvement but little on average since it capturing the sense but due to length mismatch which occurs owing to the fact that our model is generating more novel words with futuristic sense. However, Distinct-{1,2} scores shows improvement because of the large pre-trained vocabulary, it gives the model more flexibility to generate novel words without disturbing the sense of the sentence.

We also note the results for our model without weak supervision training, namely, **Our Model w/o Weak Supervision**, this model just fine-tunes on the DailyDialog (Li et al., 2017b) and PersonaChat (Zhang et al., 2018) without generating the weak labelled data. Clearly, the distinct-1 and distinct-2 metrics are lower than the proposed model, because the model tends to generate the repetitive words more frequently. Similarly, the embedding metrics and PPL does not show any improvement over the proposed model except on embedding metric based on Average. However, it performs well on BLEU scores since it learns well to reproduce the responses as in the ground truth but not optimized for a successful conversation in the long run.

Table 1 also reports the results of another two baselines which are pre-trained models on Gutenberg Dialogue Corpus (Csaky and Recski, 2020). These models are fine-tuned on DailyDialog and PersonaChat dataset respectively. These models although improved much on BLEU scores and distinct-1 and distinct-2 scores since it gets the larger vocab and more enhanced training for learning the language structure. But lags in the embedding metrics indicating the response quality is low.

Table 2 reports the human evaluation results, the objective for which our model training is to generate the response for a successful conversation in the long run for the multi-turn scenario. Clearly, the evaluation results are up to our expectation, since the RL system does not bring a significant boost in single-turn response quality than the case of multi-turn setting.

5 Conclusions

We proposed a weak supervision framework for policy and reward estimation for long-term success of the dialogue by simulating the conversation between a virtual agent and user. Empirical studies on two benchmarks proves the effectiveness of our approach.

Acknowledgments

We thank the three anonymous reviewers for their helpful comments and invaluable suggestions. We also thank the members of [24]7.ai Innovation Labs - Pataparla Raga Ashritha and Rishav Sahay for their work in building Dialogue agents, and especially Satyajit Banerjee for the detailed concepts in Reinforcement Learning. We also thank Satyajit Banerjee and [24]7.ai, India for providing access to necessary resources.

References

Stephen H Bach, Bryan He, Alexander Ratner, and Christopher Ré. 2017. Learning the structure of generative models without labeled data. In *International Conference on Machine Learning*, pages 273–282. PMLR.

Ashutosh Baheti, Alan Ritter, Jiwei Li, and Bill Dolan. 2018. Generating more interesting responses in neural conversation models with distributional constraints. *arXiv preprint arXiv:1809.01215*.

Ernie Chang, David Ifeoluwa Adelani, Xiaoyu Shen, and Vera Demberg. 2020. Unsupervised pidgin text generation by pivoting english data and self-training. *arXiv preprint arXiv:2003.08272*.

Ernie Chang, Vera Demberg, and Alex Marin. 2021a. Jointly improving language understanding and generation with quality-weighted weak supervision of automatic labeling. *arXiv preprint arXiv:2102.03551*.

Ernie Chang, Xiaoyu Shen, Dawei Zhu, Vera Demberg, and Hui Su. 2021b. Neural data-to-text generation with lm-based text augmentation. *arXiv preprint arXiv:2102.03556*.

Lu Chen, Xiang Zhou, Cheng Chang, Runzhe Yang, and Kai Yu. 2017. Agent-aware dropout dqn for safe and efficient on-line dialogue policy learning. In *Proceedings of the 2017 Conference on Empirical Methods in Natural Language Processing*, pages 2454–2464.

Zhiyu Chen, Harini Eavani, Wenhu Chen, Yinyin Liu, and William Yang Wang. 2019. Few-shot nlg with pre-trained language model. *arXiv preprint arXiv:1904.09521*.

Richard Csaky and Gabor Recski. 2020. The gutenberg dialogue dataset. *arXiv preprint arXiv:2004.12752*.

Mostafa Dehghani, Arash Mehrjou, Stephan Gouws, Jaap Kamps, and Bernhard Schölkopf. 2017. Fidelity-weighted learning. *arXiv preprint arXiv:1711.02799*.

Jacob Devlin, Ming-Wei Chang, Kenton Lee, and Kristina Toutanova. 2019. BERT: Pre-training of deep bidirectional transformers for language understanding. In *Proceedings of the 2019 Conference of the North American Chapter of the Association for Computational Linguistics: Human Language Technologies, Volume 1 (Long and Short Papers)*, pages 4171–4186, Minneapolis, Minnesota. Association for Computational Linguistics.

Bhuwan Dhingra, Lihong Li, Xiujun Li, Jianfeng Gao, Yun-Nung Chen, Faisal Ahmed, and Li Deng. 2016. Towards end-to-end reinforcement learning of dialogue agents for information access. *arXiv preprint arXiv:1609.00777*.

Emily Dinan, Stephen Roller, Kurt Shuster, Angela Fan, Michael Auli, and Jason Weston. 2018. Wizard of wikipedia: Knowledge-powered conversational agents. *arXiv preprint arXiv:1811.01241*.

Hao Fang, Hao Cheng, Maarten Sap, Elizabeth Clark, Ari Holtzman, Yejin Choi, Noah A. Smith, and Mari Ostendorf. 2018. Sounding board: A user-centric and content-driven social chatbot. In *Proceedings of the 2018 Conference of the North American Chapter of the Association for Computational Linguistics: Demonstrations*, pages 96–100, New Orleans, Louisiana. Association for Computational Linguistics.

Mehdi Fatemi, Layla El Asri, Hannes Schulz, Jing He, and Kaheer Suleman. 2016. Policy networks with two-stage training for dialogue systems. *arXiv preprint arXiv:1606.03152*.

Shaoxiong Feng, Xuancheng Ren, Kan Li, and Xu Sun. 2021. Multi-view feature representation for dialogue generation with bidirectional distillation. *arXiv preprint arXiv:2102.10780*.

Benoît Frénay and Michel Verleysen. 2013. Classification in the presence of label noise: a survey. *IEEE transactions on neural networks and learning systems*, 25(5):845–869.

Gabriel Gordon-Hall, Philip John Gorinski, and Shay B Cohen. 2020a. Learning dialog policies from weak demonstrations. *arXiv preprint arXiv:2004.11054*.

Gabriel Gordon-Hall, Philip John Gorinski, Gerasimos Lampouras, and Ignacio Iacobacci. 2020b. Show us the way: Learning to manage dialog from demonstrations. *arXiv preprint arXiv:2004.08114*.

Xiaodong Gu, Kang Min Yoo, and Jung-Woo Ha. 2020. Dialogbert: Discourse-aware response generation via learning to recover and rank utterances. *arXiv preprint arXiv:2012.01775*.

Hamza Harkous, Isabel Groves, and Amir Saffari. 2020. Have your text and use it too! end-to-end neural data-to-text generation with semantic fidelity. *arXiv preprint arXiv:2004.06577*.

He He, Derek Chen, Anusha Balakrishnan, and Percy Liang. 2018. Decoupling strategy and generation in negotiation dialogues. *arXiv preprint arXiv:1808.09637*.

Satwik Kottur, Xiaoyu Wang, and Vítor Carvalho. 2017. Exploring personalized neural conversational models. In *IJCAI*, pages 3728–3734.

Ben Krause, Marco Damonte, Mihai Dobre, Daniel Duma, Joachim Fainberg, Federico Fancellu, Emmanuel Kahembwe, Jianpeng Cheng, and Bonnie Webber. 2017. Edina: Building an open domain socialbot with self-dialogues. *arXiv preprint arXiv:1709.09816*.

Sungjin Lee. 2017. Toward continual learning for conversational agents. *arXiv preprint arXiv:1712.09943*.

Wenqiang Lei, Xisen Jin, Min-Yen Kan, Zhaochun Ren, Xiangnan He, and Dawei Yin. 2018. Sequicity: Simplifying task-oriented dialogue systems with single sequence-to-sequence architectures. In *Proceedings of the 56th Annual Meeting of the Association for Computational Linguistics (Volume 1: Long Papers)*, pages 1437–1447.

Jiwei Li, Michel Galley, Chris Brockett, Jianfeng Gao, and Bill Dolan. 2015. A diversity-promoting objective function for neural conversation models. *arXiv preprint arXiv:1510.03055*.

Jiwei Li, Will Monroe, Alan Ritter, Michel Galley, Jianfeng Gao, and Dan Jurafsky. 2016. Deep reinforcement learning for dialogue generation. *arXiv preprint arXiv:1606.01541*.

Jiwei Li, Will Monroe, Tianlin Shi, Sébastien Jean, Alan Ritter, and Dan Jurafsky. 2017a. Adversarial learning for neural dialogue generation. *arXiv preprint arXiv:1701.06547*.

Yanran Li, Hui Su, Xiaoyu Shen, Wenjie Li, Ziqiang Cao, and Shuzi Niu. 2017b. Dailydialog: A manually labelled multi-turn dialogue dataset. In *Proceedings of The 8th International Joint Conference on Natural Language Processing (IJCNLP 2017)*.

Ziming Li, Sungjin Lee, Baolin Peng, Jinchao Li, Shahin Shayandeh, and Jianfeng Gao. 2020. Guided dialog policy learning without adversarial learning in the loop. *arXiv preprint arXiv:2004.03267*.

Chia-Wei Liu, Ryan Lowe, Iulian V Serban, Michael Noseworthy, Laurent Charlin, and Joelle Pineau. 2016. How not to evaluate your dialogue system: An empirical study of unsupervised evaluation metrics for dialogue response generation. *arXiv preprint arXiv:1603.08023*.

Ryan Lowe, Michael Noseworthy, Iulian V Serban, Nicolas Angelard-Gontier, Yoshua Bengio, and Joelle Pineau. 2017. Towards an automatic turing test: Learning to evaluate dialogue responses. *arXiv preprint arXiv:1708.07149*.

Andrea Madotto, Zhaojiang Lin, Zhenpeng Zhou, Seungwhan Moon, Paul Crook, Bing Liu, Zhou Yu, Eunjoon Cho, and Zhiguang Wang. 2020. Continual learning in task-oriented dialogue systems. *arXiv preprint arXiv:2012.15504*.

Nikola Mrkšić, Diarmuid Ó Séaghdha, Tsung-Hsien Wen, Blaise Thomson, and Steve Young. 2017. Neural belief tracker: Data-driven dialogue state tracking. In *Proceedings of the 55th Annual Meeting of the Association for Computational Linguistics (Volume 1: Long Papers)*, pages 1777–1788, Vancouver, Canada. Association for Computational Linguistics.

Tong Niu, Semih Yavuz, Yingbo Zhou, Huan Wang, Nitish Shirish Keskar, and Caiming Xiong. 2020. Unsupervised paraphrase generation via dynamic blocking. *arXiv preprint arXiv:2010.12885*.

Kishore Papineni, Salim Roukos, Todd Ward, and Wei-Jing Zhu. 2002. Bleu: a method for automatic evaluation of machine translation. In *Proceedings of the 40th annual meeting of the Association for Computational Linguistics*, pages 311–318.

Baolin Peng, Xiujun Li, Lihong Li, Jianfeng Gao, Asli Celikyilmaz, Sungjin Lee, and Kam-Fai Wong. 2017. Composite task-completion dialogue policy learning via hierarchical deep reinforcement learning. *arXiv preprint arXiv:1704.03084*.

Baolin Peng, Chenguang Zhu, Chunyuan Li, Xiujun Li, Jinchao Li, Michael Zeng, and Jianfeng Gao. 2020. Few-shot natural language generation for task-oriented dialog. *arXiv preprint arXiv:2002.12328*.

Ashwin Ram, Rohit Prasad, Chandra Khatri, Anu Venkatesh, Raefer Gabriel, Qing Liu, Jeff Nunn, Behnam Hedayatnia, Ming Cheng, Ashish Nagar, et al. 2018. Conversational ai: The science behind the alexa prize. *arXiv preprint arXiv:1801.03604*.

Alexander Ratner, Stephen H Bach, Henry Ehrenberg, Jason Fries, Sen Wu, and Christopher Ré. 2020. Snorkel: Rapid training data creation with weak supervision. *The VLDB Journal*, 29(2):709–730.

Nils Reimers and Iryna Gurevych. 2019. Sentence-bert: Sentence embeddings using siamese bert-networks. *arXiv preprint arXiv:1908.10084*.

Iulian Serban, Alessandro Sordoni, Yoshua Bengio, Aaron Courville, and Joelle Pineau. 2016. Building end-to-end dialogue systems using generative hierarchical neural network models. In *Proceedings of the AAAI Conference on Artificial Intelligence*, volume 30.

Iulian Vlad Serban, Alessandro Sordoni, Ryan Lowe, Laurent Charlin, Joelle Pineau, Aaron Courville, and Yoshua Bengio. 2017. A hierarchical latent variable encoder-decoder model for generating dialogues. In *Proceedings of the Thirty-First AAAI Conference on Artificial Intelligence*, AAAI'17, page 3295–3301. AAAI Press.

Pararth Shah, Dilek Hakkani-Tur, Bing Liu, and Gokhan Tur. 2018. Bootstrapping a neural conversational agent with dialogue self-play, crowdsourcing and on-line reinforcement learning. In *Proceedings of the 2018 Conference of the North American Chapter of the Association for Computational Linguistics: Human Language Technologies, Volume 3 (Industry Papers)*, pages 41–51.

Lifeng Shang, Zhengdong Lu, and Hang Li. 2015. Neural responding machine for short-text conversation. *arXiv preprint arXiv:1503.02364*.

Xiaoyu Shen, Hui Su, Wenjie Li, and Dietrich Klakow. 2018. Nexus network: Connecting the preceding and the following in dialogue generation. In *Proceedings of the 2018 Conference on Empirical Methods in Natural Language Processing*, pages 4316–4327.

Shang-Yu Su, Xiujun Li, Jianfeng Gao, Jingjing Liu, and Yun-Nung Chen. 2018. Discriminative deep dyna-q: Robust planning for dialogue policy learning. *arXiv preprint arXiv:1808.09442*.

Ilya Sutskever, Oriol Vinyals, and Quoc V Le. 2014. Sequence to sequence learning with neural networks. *arXiv preprint arXiv:1409.3215*.

Ryuichi Takanobu, Runze Liang, and Minlie Huang. 2020. Multi-agent task-oriented dialog policy learning with role-aware reward decomposition. *arXiv preprint arXiv:2004.03809*.

Ryuichi Takanobu, Hanlin Zhu, and Minlie Huang. 2019. Guided dialog policy learning: Reward estimation for multi-domain task-oriented dialog. *arXiv preprint arXiv:1908.10719*.

Chongyang Tao, Lili Mou, Dongyan Zhao, and Rui Yan. 2018. Ruber: An unsupervised method for automatic evaluation of open-domain dialog systems. In *Proceedings of the AAAI Conference on Artificial Intelligence*, volume 32.

Oriol Vinyals and Quoc Le. 2015. A neural conversational model. *arXiv preprint arXiv:1506.05869*.

Thomas Wolf, Lysandre Debut, Victor Sanh, Julien Chaumond, Clement Delangue, Anthony Moi, Pierric Cistac, Tim Rault, Rémi Louf, Morgan Funtowicz, Joe Davison, Sam Shleifer, Patrick von Platen, Clara Ma, Yacine Jernite, Julien Plu, Canwen Xu, Teven Le Scao, Sylvain Gugger, Mariama Drame, Quentin Lhoest, and Alexander M. Rush. 2020. Huggingface's transformers: State-of-the-art natural language processing.

Jiawei Wu, Xin Wang, and William Yang Wang. 2019. Self-supervised dialogue learning. *arXiv preprint arXiv:1907.00448*.

Yu Wu, Wei Wu, Zhoujun Li, and Ming Zhou. 2018. Learning matching models with weak supervision for response selection in retrieval-based chatbots. *arXiv preprint arXiv:1805.02333*.

Chen Xing, Wei Wu, Yu Wu, Jie Liu, Yalou Huang, Ming Zhou, and Wei-Ying Ma. 2017. Topic aware neural response generation. In *Proceedings of the AAAI Conference on Artificial Intelligence*, volume 31.

Chen Xing, Yu Wu, Wei Wu, Yalou Huang, and Ming Zhou. 2018. Hierarchical recurrent attention network for response generation. In *Proceedings of the AAAI Conference on Artificial Intelligence*, volume 32.

Yujie Xing and Raquel Fernández. 2018. Automatic evaluation of neural personality-based chatbots. *arXiv preprint arXiv:1810.00472*.

Can Xu, Wei Wu, and Yu Wu. 2018a. Towards explainable and controllable open domain dialogue generation with dialogue acts. *arXiv preprint arXiv:1807.07255*.

Ruijian Xu, Chongyang Tao, Daxin Jiang, Xueliang Zhao, Dongyan Zhao, and Rui Yan. 2020. Learning an effective context-response matching model with self-supervised tasks for retrieval-based dialogues.

Xinnuo Xu, Ondřej Dušek, Ioannis Konstas, and Verena Rieser. 2018b. Better conversations by modeling, filtering, and optimizing for coherence and diversity. *arXiv preprint arXiv:1809.06873*.

Denis Yarats and Mike Lewis. 2018. Hierarchical text generation and planning for strategic dialogue. In *International Conference on Machine Learning*, pages 5591–5599. PMLR.

Hainan Zhang, Yanyan Lan, Liang Pang, Jiafeng Guo, and Xueqi Cheng. 2019. Recosa: Detecting the relevant contexts with self-attention for multi-turn dialogue generation. *arXiv preprint arXiv:1907.05339*.

Saizheng Zhang, Emily Dinan, Jack Urbanek, Arthur Szlam, Douwe Kiela, and Jason Weston. 2018. Personalizing dialogue agents: I have a dog, do you have pets too? *arXiv preprint arXiv:1801.07243*.

Tiancheng Zhao and Maxine Eskenazi. 2016. Towards end-to-end learning for dialog state tracking and management using deep reinforcement learning. *arXiv preprint arXiv:1606.02560*.

Yufan Zhao, Can Xu, and Wei Wu. 2020. Learning a simple and effective model for multi-turn response generation with auxiliary tasks. *arXiv preprint arXiv:2004.01972*.

Peixiang Zhong, Di Wang, and Chunyan Miao. 2019. An affect-rich neural conversational model with biased attention and weighted cross-entropy loss. In *Proceedings of the AAAI Conference on Artificial Intelligence*, volume 33, pages 7492–7500.

Hao Zhou, Minlie Huang, Tianyang Zhang, Xiaoyan Zhu, and Bing Liu. 2018. Emotional chatting machine: Emotional conversation generation with internal and external memory. In *Proceedings of the AAAI Conference on Artificial Intelligence*, volume 32.

A Implementation Details

Our implementation uses the open source Huggingface Transformer repository (Wolf et al., 2020). Specifically, we have used the base version from sentence transformers pre-trained on millions of paraphrase examples, named as *'paraphrase-distilroberta-base-v1'*. The encoder-decoder framework is initialized with the base version *'bert-base-uncased'* but with configuration of smaller size. The smaller sized model reduces the *'bert-base-uncased'* configuration to 6 transformer layers, has a hidden size of 768, and contains 2 attention heads, {L=6, H=768, A=2}. Similar to Gu et al. (2020) we sum the position embeddings to the output sentence embeddings of size 768 to indicate the user or agent utterances. Odd ones indicate the user utterances and even ones are that of an agent. The MLP network for semantic relevance and semantic coherence used a hidden dimension of 128. The Δ has been set to best value of 0.54 after performing a grid search in the range of $\{0.4, 0.7\}$ with step size of 0.02. The reward estimator models g_ω using two hidden layers of size 512 and 256 respectively. And, h is modelled using a single hidden layer of size one. In each training iteration the policy and reward estimator are updated with continual learning to avoid catastrophic forgetting mechanism using EWC modified loss, the λ value used as a parameter is set to 0.4. Also, at each training iteration the policy and reward parameters are saved if it reduces the perplexity on the validation set (calculated after running for all the batches of the training dataset) and patience is set to 3 as a stopping criterion before we terminate the training.

Summary-Oriented Question Generation for Informational Queries

Xusen Yin[*]
USC/ISI
xusenyin@isi.edu

Li Zhou
Amazon
lizhouml@amazon.com

Kevin Small
Amazon
smakevin@amazon.com

Jonathan May
USC/ISI
jonmay@isi.edu

Abstract

Users frequently ask simple factoid questions for question answering (QA) systems, attenuating the impact of myriad recent works that support more complex questions. Prompting users with automatically generated *suggested questions* (SQs) can improve user understanding of QA system capabilities and thus facilitate more effective use. We aim to produce self-explanatory questions that focus on main document topics and are answerable with variable length passages as appropriate. We satisfy these requirements by using a BERT-based Pointer-Generator Network trained on the Natural Questions (NQ) dataset. Our model shows SOTA performance of SQ generation on the NQ dataset (20.1 BLEU-4). We further apply our model on out-of-domain news articles, evaluating with a QA system due to the lack of gold questions and demonstrate that our model produces better SQs for news articles – with further confirmation via a human evaluation.

1 Introduction

Question answering (QA) systems have experienced dramatic recent empirical improvements due to several factors including novel neural architectures (Chen and Yih, 2020), access to pre-trained contextualized embeddings (Devlin et al., 2019), and the development of large QA training corpora (Rajpurkar et al., 2016; Trischler et al., 2017; Yu et al., 2020). However, despite technological advancements that support more sophisticated questions (Yang et al., 2018; Joshi et al., 2017; Choi et al., 2018; Reddy et al., 2019), many consumers of QA technology in practice tend to ask simple factoid questions when engaging with these systems. Potential explanations for this phenomenon include low expectations set by previous QA systems, limited coverage for more complex questions not changing these expectations, and users simply not possessing sufficient knowledge of the subject of interest to ask more challenging questions. Irrespective of the reason, one potential solution to this dilemma is to provide users with automatically generated *suggested questions* (SQs) to help users better understand QA system capabilities.

Generating SQs is a specific form of question generation (QG), a long-studied task with many applied use cases – the most frequent purpose being data augmentation for mitigating the high sample complexity of neural QA models (Alberti et al., 2019a). However, the objective of such existing QG systems is to produce large quantities of question/answer pairs for training, which is contrary to that of SQs. The latter seeks to guide users in their research of a particular subject by producing engaging and understandable questions. To this end, we aim to generate questions that are *self-explanatory* and *introductory*.

Self-explanatory questions require neither significant background knowledge nor access to documents used for QG to understand the SQ context. For example, existing QG systems may use the text *"On December 13, 2013, Beyoncé unexpectedly released her eponymous fifth studio album on the iTunes store without any prior announcement or promotion."* to produce the question *"Where was the album released?"* This kind of question is not uncommon in crowd-sourced datasets (e.g., SQuAD (Rajpurkar et al., 2016)) but do not satisfy the self-explanatory requirement. Clark and Gardner (2018) estimate that 33 % of SQuAD questions are context-dependent. This context-dependency is not surprising, given that annotators observe the underlying documents when generating questions.

Introductory questions are best answered by a larger passage than short spans such that users can learn more about the subject, possibly inspiring follow-up questions (e.g., "Can convalescent

[*]Work was done as an intern at Amazon.

Proceedings of the 1st Workshop on Document-grounded Dialogue and Conversational Question Answering, pages 81–97
August 5–6, 2021. ©2021 Association for Computational Linguistics

plasma help COVID patients?"). However, existing QG methods mostly generate questions while reading the text corpus and tend to produce narrowly focused questions with close syntactic relations to associated answer spans. TriviaQA (Joshi et al., 2017) and HotpotQA (Yang et al., 2018) also provide fine-grained questions, even though reasoning from a larger document context via multi-hop inference. This narrower focus often produces factoid questions peripheral to the main topic of the underlying document and is less useful to a human user seeking information about a target concept.

Conversely, the Natural Question (NQ) dataset (Kwiatkowski et al., 2019) (and similar ones such as MS Marco (Bajaj et al., 2016), GooAQ (Khashabi et al., 2021)) is significantly closer to simulating the desired information-seeking behavior. Questions are generated independently of the corpus by processing search query logs, and the resulting answers can be entities, spans in texts (aka short answers), or entire paragraphs (aka long answers). Thus, the NQ dataset is more suitable as QG training data for generating SQs as long-answer questions that tend to satisfy our self-explanatory and introductory requirements.

To this end, we propose a novel BERT-based Pointer-Generator Network (BERTPGN) trained with the NQ dataset to generate introductory and self-explanatory questions as SQs. Using NQ, we start by creating a QG dataset that contains questions with both short and long answers. We train our BERTPGN model with these two types of context-question pairs together. During inference, the model can generate either short- or long-answer questions as determined by the context. With automatic evaluation metrics such as BLEU (Papineni et al., 2002), we show that for long-answer question generation, our model can produce state-of-the-art performance with 20.1 BLEU-4, 6.2 higher than (Mishra et al., 2020), the current state-of-the-art on this dataset. The short answer question generation performance can reach 28.1 BLEU-4.

We further validate the generalization ability of our BERTPGN model by creating an out-of-domain test set with the CNN/Daily Mail (Hermann et al., 2015). Without human-generated reference questions, automatic evaluation metrics such as BLEU are not usable. We propose to evaluate these questions with a pretrained QA system that produces two novel metrics. The first is *answerability*, measuring the possibility to find answers from given contexts. The second is *granularity*, indicating whether the answer would be passages or short spans. Finally, we conduct a human evaluation with generated questions of the test set and demonstrate that our BERTPGN model can produce introductory and self-explanatory questions for information-seeking scenarios, even for a new domain that differs from the training data.

The novel contributions of our paper include:

- We generate questions, aiming to be both introductory and self-explanatory, to support human information seeking QA sessions.
- We propose to use the BERT-based Pointer-Generator Network to generate questions by encoding larger contexts capable of resulting in answer forms including entities, short text spans, and even whole paragraphs.
- We evaluate our method, both automatically and with human evaluation, on in-domain Natural Questions and out-of-domain news datasets, providing insights into question generation for information seeking.
- We propose a novel evaluation metric with a pretrained QA system for generated SQs when there is no reference question.

2 Related Work

QG has been studied in multiple application contexts (e.g., generating questions for reading comprehension tests (Heilman and Smith, 2010), generating questions about an image (Mostafazadeh et al., 2016), recommending questions with respect to a news article (Laban et al., 2020)), evaluating summaries (Deutsch et al., 2020; Wang et al., 2020), and using multiple methods (see (Pan et al., 2019) for a recent survey). Early neural models focused on sequence-to-sequence generation based solutions (Serban et al., 2016; Du et al., 2017). The primary directions for improving these early works generally fall into the categories of providing mechanisms to inject answer-aware information into the neural encoder-decoder architectures (Du and Cardie, 2018; Li et al., 2019; Liu et al., 2019; Wang et al., 2020; Sun et al., 2018), encoding larger portions of the answer document as context (Zhao et al., 2018; Tuan et al., 2020), and incorporating richer knowledge sources (Elsahar et al., 2018).

These QG methods and the work described in this paper focus on using single-hop QA datasets such as SQuAD (Rajpurkar et al., 2016, 2018),

NewsQA (Trischler et al., 2017; Hermann et al., 2015), and MS Marco (Bajaj et al., 2016). However, there has also been recent interest in multi-hop QG settings (Yu et al., 2020; Gupta et al., 2020; Malon and Bai, 2020) by using multi-hop QA datasets including HotPotQA (Yang et al., 2018), TriviaQA (Joshi et al., 2017), and FreebaseQA (Jiang et al., 2019). Finally, there has been some recent interesting work regarding *unsupervised* QG, where the goal is to generate QA training data without an existing QG corpus to train better QA models (Lewis et al., 2019; Li et al., 2020).

Most directly related to our work from a motivation perspective is recent research regarding providing SQs in the context of supporting a news chatbot (Laban et al., 2020). However, the focus of this work is not QG, where they essentially use a GPT-2 language model (Radford et al., 2019) trained on SQuAD data for QG and do not evaluate this component independently. Qi et al. (2020) generates questions for information-seeking but not focuses on introductory questions. Most directly related to our work from a conceptual perspective is regarding producing questions for long answer targets (Mishra et al., 2020), which we contrast directly in Section 3. As QG is a generation task, automated evaluation frequently uses metrics such as BLEU (Papineni et al., 2002), METEOR (Lavie and Agarwal, 2007), and ROUGE (Lin, 2004). As these do not explicitly evaluate the requirements of our information-seeking use case, we also evaluate using the output of a trained QA system and conduct human annotator evaluations.

3 Problem Definition

Given a context X and an answer A, we want to generate a question $\tilde{Q}$ that satisfies

$$\tilde{Q} = \arg\max_{Q} P(Q|X, A),$$

where the context X could be a paragraph or a document that contains answers, rather than sentences as used in (Du and Cardie, 2018; Tuan et al., 2020), while A could be either short spans in X such as entities or noun phrases (referred to as a *short answer*), or the entire context X (referred to as a *long answer*).

The *long answer* QG task targets generating questions that are best answered by the entire context (i.e., paragraph or document) or a summary of the context, which is notably different from most QG settings where the answer is a short text span and the context is frequently a single sentence. Mishra et al. (2020) also work on the *long answer* QG setting using the NQ dataset, but their task definition is $\arg\max_Q P(Q|X)$ where they refer to the context X as the *long answer*. We use their models as baselines.

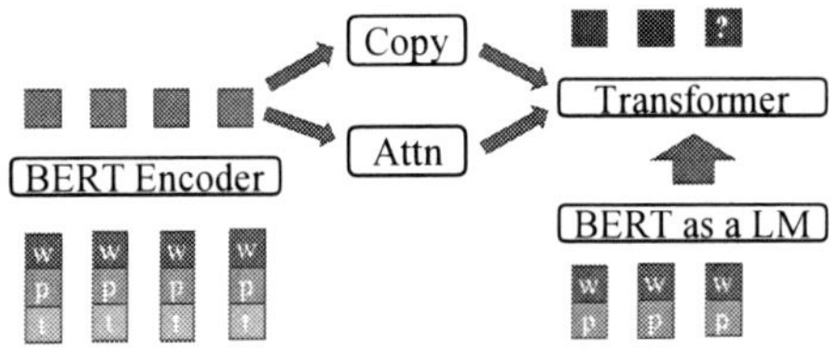

Figure 1: The BERTPGN architecture. The input for the BERT encoder is the context (w/p: word and position embeddinngs) with answer spans (or the whole context in the long answer setting) marked with the answer tagging (t: answer tagging embeddings). The decoder is a combination of BERT as a language model (i.e. has only self-attentions) and a Transformer-based pointer-generator network.

4 Methods

We use the BERT-based Pointer-Generator Network (BERTPGN) to generate questions. Tuan et al. (2020) use two-layer cross attentions between contexts and answers to encode contexts such as paragraphs when generating questions and show improved results. However, they show that three-layer cross attentions produce worse results. We will show later in the experiment that this is due to a lack of better initialization and that a higher layer is better for long answer question generation. Zhao et al. (2018) use answer tagging from the context instead of combining context and answer. Our model is motivated by these two works (Figure 1).

4.1 Context and Answer Encoding

Given context $X = \{x_i\}_{i=1}^{L}$, we add positional embeddings $P = \{p_i\}_{i=1}^{L}$ and type embeddings $T = \{t_i\}_{i=1}^{L}$ as the input for BERT. We use type embeddings to discriminate between a context and an answer, following Zhao et al. (2018); Tuan et al. (2020). We use $t_i = 0$ to represent *'context-only'* and $t_i = 1$ to represent *'both context and answer'* for token x_i. We do not apply the `[CLS]` in the beginning since we do not need the pooled output from BERT. We do not use the `[SEP]` to combine contexts and answers as inputs for BERT since we mark answers in the context with type embeddings.

The sequence output from BERT which forms our context-answer encoding is given by

$$H = f_{\text{BERT}}(X + P + T).$$

4.2 Question Decoding

The transformer-based Pointer-Generator Network is derived from (See et al., 2017) with adaptations to support transformers (Vaswani et al., 2017). Denoting $\text{LN}(\cdot)$ as layer normalization, $\text{MHA}(Q, K, V)$ as the multi-head attention with three parameters—query, key, and value, $\text{FFN}(\cdot)$ as a linear function, and the decoder input at time t: $Y^{(t)} = \{y_j\}_{j=1}^{t}$, the decoder self-attention at time t is given by (illustrated with a single-layer transformer simplification)

$$A_S^{(t)} = \text{LN}\left(\text{MHA}\left(Y^{(t)}, Y^{(t)}, Y^{(t)}\right) + Y^{(t)}\right),$$

the cross-attention between encoder and decoder is

$$A_C^{(t)} = \text{LN}\left(\text{MHA}\left(A_S^{(t)}, H, H\right) + A_S^{(t)}\right),$$

and the final decoder output is

$$O^{(t)} = \text{LN}\left(\text{FFN}\left(A_C^{(t)}\right) + A_C^{(t)}\right).$$

Using the LSTM (Hochreiter and Schmidhuber, 1997) encoder-decoder model, See et al. (2017) compute a generation probability using the encoder context, decoder state, and decoder input. While the transformer decoder cross-attention $A_C^{(t)}$ already contains a linear combination between self-attention of decoder input and encoder-decoder cross attention. Thus, we use the combination of the decoder input and cross-attention to compute the generation probability

$$P_G^{(t)} = \text{FFN}\left(\left[Y^{(t)}, A_C^{(t)}\right]\right).$$

To improve generalization, we also use a separate BERT model as a language model (LM) for the decoder. Even though BERT is not trained to predict the next token (Devlin et al., 2019) as with typical language models (e.g., GPT-2), we still choose BERT as our LM to ensure the COPY mechanism shares the same vocabulary between the encoder and the decoder.[1] We also do not need to process out-of-vocabulary words because we use the BPE (Sennrich et al., 2016; Devlin et al., 2019) tokenization in both the encoder and decoder.

[1]Note that we change the masking for the original BERT when using BERT as a LM, since the decoder at step t should not read inputs at steps $t + i$ where $i \geq 0$.

5 Dataset

5.1 Natural Questions dataset

We use Natural Questions dataset (Kwiatkowski et al., 2019) for training as NQ questions are independent of their supporting documents. NQ has 307,000 training examples, answered and annotated from Wikipedia pages, in a format of a question, a Wikipedia link, long answer candidates, and short answer annotations. 51 % of these questions have no answer for either being invalid or non-evidence in their supporting documents. Another 36 % have long answers that are paragraphs and have corresponding short answers that either spans long answers or being masked as yes-or-no. The remaining 13 % questions only have long answers. We are most interested in the last portion of questions as they are best answered by summaries of their long answers, reflecting the coarse-grained information-seeking behavior.[2]

We use paragraphs that contain long answers or short answers in NQ as the context. We do not consider using the whole Wikipedia page, i.e., the document, as the context as most Wikipedia pages are too long to encode: In the NQ training set, there are 8407 tokens at document level on average, while for news articles in the CNN/Daily Mail that we will discuss in Section 5.2, the average document size is 583 (Tuan et al., 2020), which is not much larger than the average size of long answers in NQ (384 tokens).

We also consider the ratio between questions and the context-answer pairs to avoid generating multiple questions based on the same context-answer. After removing questions that have no answers, there are 152,148 questions and 136,450 unique long answers. The average ratio between questions and long answers is around 1.1 questions per *paragraph* (ratios are in a range of 1 to 47). The average ratio is more reasonable for question generation, comparing to the SQuAD where there are 1.4 questions per *sentence* on average (Du et al., 2017).

5.1.1 NQ Preprocessing

We extract questions, long answers, and short answer spans from the NQ dataset. We also extract the Wikipedia titles since long answers alone do not

[2]Data annotation is a *subjective* task where different annotators could have different opinions for whether there is a short answer or not. NQ uses multi-fold annotations (e.g., a 5-fold annotation for the dev set). However, the training data only has the 1-fold annotation, so whether there is a short answer is not 100 % accurate.

data	type	count
train	mix	99,725
dev	mix	11,140
NQ-SA	long and short	3364
NQ-LA	long only	1495
News-LA	long only	3048

Table 1: QG Data summary. *-LA contains questions that only have long answers, while NQ-SA contains questions having both long and short answers.

always contain the words from their corresponding titles. We add brackets (' [' and '] ') for all possible short answer spans such that we can later extract these spans accordingly to avoid potential position changes due to context preprocessing (e.g., different tokenization).[3] When there is no short answer, we add brackets to the whole long answer. We then concatenate the titles with long answers as contexts. For details, see examples from Figure 5 and Figure 6 in Appendix A.

As in (Mishra et al., 2020), we only keep questions with long answers starting from the HTML paragraph tag. After preprocessing (Table 1), we get 110,865 question-context pairs, while Mishra et al. (2020) gets 77,501 pairs since they only keep long answer questions. We split the dataset with a 90/10 ratio for training/validation.

We use the original NQ dev set, which contains 7830 questions, as our test set. We follow the same extraction procedure as with the training and validation data modulo two new steps. First, noting that 79 % of Wikipedia pages appearing in the NQ dev set are also present in the NQ training set, we filter all overlapped contexts from the NQ dev set when creating our test set. Second, the original NQ dev set is 5-way annotated; thus, each question may have up to five different long/short answers. We treat each annotation as an independent context, even though they are associated with the same target question. To separately evaluate the QG performance for long answers and short answers, we split test data into *long-answer* questions (NQ-LA) and *short-answer* questions (NQ-SA). Finally, we get 4859 test data in total, with 1495 of them only have long answers while the remaining 3364 have both long and short answers while Mishra et al. (2020) gets 2136 test data from the original dev set.

[3]Using brackets here is an arbitrary but functional choice.

5.2 News dataset

We use the 12,744 CNN news articles from the CNN/Daily Mail dataset (Hermann et al., 2015)) for the out-of-domain evaluation. We apply the same preprocessing method as in the NQ dataset to create a long-answer test set — News-LA. We use whole news articles, instead of paragraphs, as contexts, considering to generate questions that lead to entire news articles as answers. For each news article, we first remove *highlights*, which is a human-generated summary, and datelines (e.g., NEW DELHI, India (CNN)). We filter out those news articles that are longer than 490 tokens with the BEP tokenization and those overlapped context-question pairs. Finally, we get 3048 data in the News-LA test set.

6 In-Domain Evaluation with Generation Metrics

6.1 Experiment Setup and Training

We use a BERT-base uncased model (Devlin et al., 2019) that contains 12 hidden layers. The vocabulary contains 30,522 tokens. We create the PGN decoder with another BERT model from the same setting, followed by a 2-layer transformer with 12 heads and 3072 intermediate sizes. The maximum allowed context length is 500, while the maximum question length is 50. We train our model on an Amazon EC2 P3 machine with one Tesla V100 GPU, with the batch size 10, and the learning rate 5×10^{-5} with the Adam optimizer (Kingma and Ba, 2015) on all parameters of the BERTPGN model (both BERT models are trainable). We train 20 epochs of our model and evaluate with the dev set to select the model according to perplexity. Each epoch takes around 20 minutes to finish. Throughout the paper, we use the implementation of BLEU, METEOR, and ROUGE_L by Sharma et al. (2017).

6.2 In-Domain Evaluation

We first evaluate our model using BLEU, METEOR, and ROUGE_L to compare with Mishra et al. (2020) on long answers (first two rows in Table 2). The transformer-based iwslt_de_en is a German to English translation model with 6 encoder and decoder layers, 16 encoder and decoder attention heads, 1024 embedding dimension, and 4096 embedding dimension of feed forward network. The other transformer-based multi-source method, which is based on (Libovický et al., 2018), combines each context with a retrieval-based summary

	B1	B4	ME	RL
TX iwslt_de_en	36.8	13.9	17.5	35.6
TX Multi-Source	36.0	13.3	16.8	34.6
BERTPGN LA	**43.9**	**20.1**	**22.6**	**42.2**
BERTPGN SA	**54.7**	**28.1**	**27.9**	**53.2**

Table 2: Comparing our model (BERTPGN) on NQ-LA and NQ-SA with two models in (Mishra et al., 2020)—their best performing Transformer_iwslt_de_en and multi-source transformer combining contexts and automatically generated summaries, with automatic evaluation BLEU-1, BLEU-4, METEOR, and Rouge_L.

B4	NQ-LA	NQ-SA
no-pointer	17.1	23.6
no-BERT-LM (*)	18.9	26.5
* - no-type-id	19.0	20.8
* - no-init	15.3	19.3
* - 2-layer	14.9	19.1

Table 3: Ablation study of the BERTPGN. Removing the pointer network drops BLEU-4 by around 3 points for both test sets. Removing BERT initialization affects both the NQ-LA and NQ-SA substantially but more mildly than removing the pointer. Removing type IDs affects the NQ-SA by 5.7 drop in BLEU-4.

as input. We decode questions from our model using beam search (beam=3).[4] Evaluating on NQ-LA, our BERTPGN model outperforms both existing models substantially with near seven points for all metrics. The performance for short answer questions NQ-SA is even better, with near eight more BLEU-4 points than NQ-LA.

6.3 Ablation Study

We first examine the effect of the pointer network from the BERTPGN. We then run ablation study by first removing BERT-LM in the decoder, and independently

- removing type IDs from BERT encoder
- removing BERT initialization for BERT encoder
- substituting BERT encoder with a 2-layer transformer

We train our BERTPGN models from scratch for each setting and conduct these ablation studies for NQ-LA and NQ-SA separately (Table 3).

Removing the pointer from the BERTPGN makes the BLEU-4 scores drop for both NQ-LA and NQ-SA more than removing the BERT as the LM in the decoder. Type IDs are more helpful for NQ-SA (approximately a 5-point drop in BLEU-4) than NQ-LA since NQ-SA needs to use type IDs to mark answers. Removing BERT initialization causes notable drops for both NQ-LA (3.6 drops in BLEU-4) and NQ-SA (7.2 in BLEU-4), which implies that BERT achieves better generalization when encoding these considerably long contexts. Another interesting finding is that the NQ-LA is more sensitive to the number of layers of the encoder than NQ-SA. When decreasing the layers to two from twelve, NQ-LA drops by 0.4 in BLEU-4 while NQ-SA drops by 0.2.

[4]Mishra et al. (2020) have not described the decoding method and possible beam size, but they use models from (Ott et al., 2018) that uses beam=4.

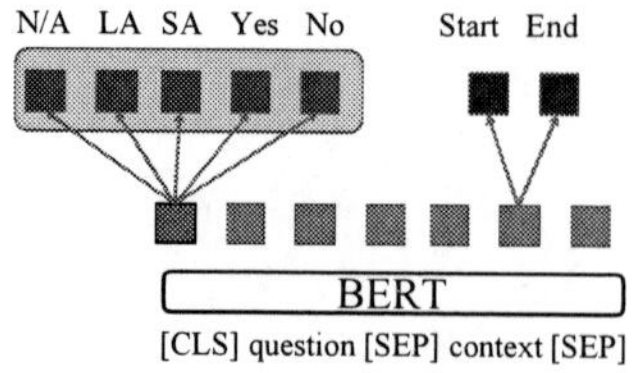

Figure 2: The BERT-joint architecture (Alberti et al., 2019b). Input is the combined question and context, and the outputs are an answer-type classification from the `[CLS]` token and start/end of answer spans for each token from the context.

7 Out-of-Domain Evaluation with QA Systems

We use a well-trained question answering system as the evaluation method, given that the automated scoring metrics have two notable drawbacks when evaluating long-answer questions: (1) There are usually multiple valid questions for long-answer question generation as contexts are much longer than previous work. However, most datasets only have one gold question for each context; (2) They cannot measure generated questions when there is no gold question, which is the right problem that we encountered for our News-LA dataset.

7.1 The QA Metrics

We use the BERT-joint model (Alberti et al., 2019b) (Figure 2) for NQ question answering to evaluate our long answer question generation. The BERT-joint model takes the combination a question and the corresponding context as an input, outputs the probability of answer spans and the probability of answer types. For a context of size n, it produces p_{start} and p_{end} for each token, indicating whether this token is a start or end token of an answer span. It then chooses the answer span (i, j) where $i < j$

	B1	B4	ME	RL
Du-17 best	43.1	12.3	16.6	39.8
M_{SD}	**46.0**	**14.8**	**19.2**	**42.0**

Table 4: The performance of our answer-free baseline, compared with the best model from (Du et al., 2017).

that maximizes $p_{start}(i) \cdot p_{end}(j)$ as the probability of the answer. It also defines the probability of no answer to be $p_{start}([CLS]) \cdot p_{end}([CLS])$, i.e., an answer span that starts then stops at the [CLS] token. Furthermore, the BERT-joint model computes the probability of *types* of the question—*undetermined, long answer, short answer*, and *YES-or-NO*. This model achieves 66.2 % F1 on NQ long answer test set, which is 10 % better compared to models used in (Kwiatkowski et al., 2019; Parikh et al., 2016). We define the *answerability* score (s_{ans}) as $\log(p_{ans}/p_{no\_ans})$, and the *granularity* score (s_{gra}) as $\log(p_{la}/p_{sa})$ when evaluating our long answer question generation with the BERT-joint model.

7.2 QG Models to Compare

We construct a baseline model to compare as follows. Using the same BERTPGN architecture, we train a model on the SQuAD sentence-question pairs prepared by Du et al. (2017). When generating questions for news articles, we use the first line of each news article as the context, with the assumption that the first line is a genuine summary produced by humans. Notice that the resulting baseline is the state-of-the-art for answer-free (the model does not know the whereabouts of answer spans) question generation with SQuAD (Table 4). We refer to the model as M_{SD} hereafter. Similarly, we call our BERTPGN model trained on the NQ dataset as M_{NQ}. We use beam search (beam=3) for both models.

7.3 Evaluation Results

We show the QA evaluation results in Figure 3. In the context column, M_{NQ} shows a lower answerability score than the baseline model M_{SD}. While granularity scores show a reverse trend, i.e., higher scores for M_{NQ} than those of M_{SD}. This result implies that M_{NQ} generates more coarse-style questions that have long answers, but these questions are considerably more difficult to answer by the QA model, comparing to short-answer questions.

It is also reasonable to assume that news articles' summaries are proper answer-candidates for

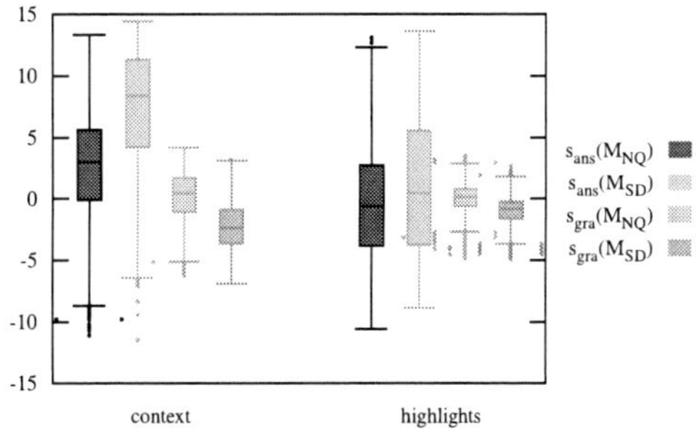

Figure 3: Answerability and granularity scores of generated questions for News-LA with the BERT-joint model (Alberti et al., 2019b) as the evaluation QA model by answering generated questions from either news article *context* or news article *highlights*. We compare two models: (1) NQ: BERTPGN trained with NQ dataset and generate on whole news articles; (2) SD: BERTPGN trained with SQuAD dataset and generate on the first line of each news article.

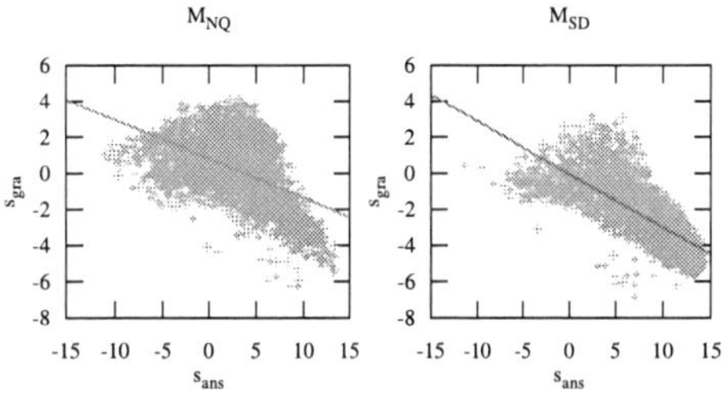

Figure 4: Scatter plots of generated questions of the News-LA from M_{NQ} (left) and M_{SD} (right). s_{ans} and s_{gra} are negatively correlated, but the M_{NQ} model tends to generate more questions with positive anserability and granularity. Straight lines show fitted linear regressions.

long-answer questions. Highlights in news articles are human-generated summaries, so we also combine the same set of questions with their corresponding highlights as input for the BERT-joint QA system with results shown as the highlights column in Figure 3. The answerability scores drop for both models comparing the column highlights to the column of context, which is reasonable as the models never see highlights when generating questions. However, the baseline method M_{SD} drops more significantly than M_{NQ}, suggesting that the baseline model is more context-dependent while our model M_{NQ} generates more self-explanatory questions. From the granularity scores of highlights, we find that confidence to determine answer types is lower for both models than that of the context column. However, the M_{NQ} still shows higher granularity scores than the M_{SD}.

We map generated questions for the News-LA on a 2D plot with x-axis the answerability score and y-axis the granularity score for both models in Figure 4. They also confirm the negative correlation between answerability and granularity of generated questions. However, the M_{NQ} generates more questions with both positive s_{ans} and s_{gra} than those from M_{SD}, indicating the effectiveness of our model to generate introductory and self-explanatory questions.

8 Out-of-Domain Human Evaluation

(%)	Context		Span		Entire	
	T	F	T	F	T	F
M_{NQ}	38	62	77	23	49	51
M_{SD}	70	30	89	11	40	60

Table 5: Ratios (shown as a percentage) between *True* and *False* for human evaluation with three statements (*Context*, *Span*, and *Entire*) on generated questions. We count true/false marked by annotators with unanimity amongst all three annotators for each statement.

We further conduct a human evaluation using MTurk for the News-LA test set to verify that we can generate self-explanatory and introductory questions and that the automatic evaluation in Section 7 agrees with human evaluation. We ask annotators to read news articles and mark true or false for seven statements regarding generated questions. For each context-question pair, these statements include (see examples in Appendix B)

- Question is *context* dependent
- Question is *irrelevant* to the article
- Question implies a *contradiction* to facts present in the article
- Question focuses on a *peripheral* topic
- There is a short *span* to answer the question
- The *entire* article can be an answer
- *None* answer in the article

We randomly select 1000 news articles in News-LA to perform our human evaluation with three different annotators per news article. We received three valid annotations for 943 news articles from a set of 224 annotators. We first consider true/false results regarding three metrics – *Context*, *Span*, and *Entire* – considering only when unanimity is reached among annotators (Table 5). M_{NQ} questions are more context-free than M_{SD} ones, with 38 % true and 62 % false towards the *Context* statement. Second, the M_{NQ} questions are more likely to be answered by entire news articles (49 % true of *Entire* vs. 40 %) while less likely to be answered by spans from news articles (77 % true of *Span* vs. 89 %) comparing with M_{SD} questions. These human evaluation results confirm that M_{NQ} questions are more self-explanatory and introductory than M_{SD}.

	s_{ans}		s_{gra}	
	M_{NQ}	M_{SD}	M_{NQ}	M_{SD}
Context	0.1	−0.1	0.1	0.5
Irrelevant	−1.0	−0.6	**0.7**	0.4
Contradiction	−0.5	−0.3	0.4	0.2
Peripheral	−0.3	−0.3	0.2	0.2
Span	**1.5**	**1.1**	**−0.8**	**−0.6**
Entire	0.4	0.3	0.4	0.3
None	**−1.5**	**−1.2**	0.6	**0.6**

Table 6: Pearson correlation (1×10^{-1}) between human (Section 8) and automatic (Section 7) evaluation. For each column, we mark the most positive and negative correlated scores in bold text.

We compute the s_{ans} and s_{gra} for the 943 generated questions (Section 7). We then normalize these two scores and conduct a Pearson correlation analysis (Benesty et al., 2009) with human evaluation results. We use all human evaluation results, regardless of agreements among annotators. From Table 6, we find that *Span* has the strongest positive correlation with the s_{ans}, while *None* shows the strongest negative correlation – aligning with the findings for answerability. *Span* also shows the strongest negative correlation with the s_{gra} for both M_{NQ} and M_{SD}, but the highest positive correlation with granularity varies, with *Irrelevant* for M_{NQ} questions and *None* for M_{SD} questions.

9 Conclusion

We tackle the problem of question generation targeted for human information seeking using automatic question answering technology. We focus on generating questions for news articles that can be answered by longer passages rather than short text spans as suggested questions. We build a BERT-based Pointer-Generator Network as the QG model, trained with the Natural Questions dataset. Our method shows state-of-the-art performance in terms of BLEU, METEOR, and ROUGE_L scores on our NQ question generation dataset. We then apply our model to the out-of-domain news articles without further training. We use a QA system to evaluate our QG models as there are no gold questions for comparison. We also conduct a human evaluation to confirm the QA evaluation results.

Broader Impact

We describe a method for an autonomous agent to suggest questions based on machine-reading and question generation technology. Operationally, this work focuses on newswire-sourced data where the generated questions are answered by the text – and is applicable to multi-turn search settings. Thus, there are several potentially positive social impacts. By presenting questions with known answers in the text, users can more efficiently learn about topics in the source documents. Our focus on *self-explanatory* and *introductory* questions increases the utility of questions for this purpose.

Conversely, there is potential to bias people toward a subset of the news chosen by a purported fair search engine, which may be more difficult to detect as the provided questions remove some of the article contexts. In principle, this is mitigated by selecting content that maintains high journalistic standards – but such a risk remains if the technology is deployed by bad-faith actors.

The data for our experiments was derived from the widely used Natural Questions (Kwiatkowski et al., 2019) and CNN/Daily Mail (Hermann et al., 2015) datasets, which in turn were derived from public news sourced data. Our evaluation annotations were performed on Amazon Mechanical Turk, where three authors completed a sample task and set a wage corresponding to an expected rate of 15 $/h.

References

Chris Alberti, Daniel Andor, Emily Pitler, Jacob Devlin, and Michael Collins. 2019a. Synthetic QA corpora generation with roundtrip consistency. In *Proceedings of the 57th Annual Meeting of the Association for Computational Linguistics*, pages 6168–6173, Florence, Italy. Association for Computational Linguistics.

Chris Alberti, Kenton Lee, and Michael Collins. 2019b. A bert baseline for the natural questions.

Payal Bajaj, Daniel Campos, Nick Craswell, Li Deng, Jianfeng Gao, Xiaodong Liu, Rangan Majumder, Andrew McNamara, Bhaskar Mitra, Tri Nguyen, Mir Rosenberg, Xia Song, Alina Stoica, Saurabh Tiwary, and Tong Wang. 2016. Ms marco: A human generated machine reading comprehension dataset.

Jacob Benesty, Jingdong Chen, Yiteng Huang, and Israel Cohen. 2009. Pearson correlation coefficient. In *Noise reduction in speech processing*, pages 37–40. Springer.

Danqi Chen and Wen-tau Yih. 2020. Open-domain question answering. In *Proceedings of the 58th Annual Meeting of the Association for Computational Linguistics: Tutorial Abstracts*, pages 34–37.

Eunsol Choi, He He, Mohit Iyyer, Mark Yatskar, Wen-tau Yih, Yejin Choi, Percy Liang, and Luke Zettlemoyer. 2018. QuAC: Question answering in context. In *Proceedings of the 2018 Conference on Empirical Methods in Natural Language Processing*, pages 2174–2184, Brussels, Belgium. Association for Computational Linguistics.

Christopher Clark and Matt Gardner. 2018. Simple and effective multi-paragraph reading comprehension. In *Proceedings of the 56th Annual Meeting of the Association for Computational Linguistics (Volume 1: Long Papers)*, pages 845–855, Melbourne, Australia. Association for Computational Linguistics.

Daniel Deutsch, Tania Bedrax-Weiss, and Dan Roth. 2020. Towards question-answering as an automatic metric for evaluating the content quality of a summary.

Jacob Devlin, Ming-Wei Chang, Kenton Lee, and Kristina Toutanova. 2019. BERT: Pre-training of deep bidirectional transformers for language understanding. In *Proceedings of the 2019 Conference of the North American Chapter of the Association for Computational Linguistics: Human Language Technologies, Volume 1 (Long and Short Papers)*, pages 4171–4186, Minneapolis, Minnesota. Association for Computational Linguistics.

Xinya Du and Claire Cardie. 2018. Harvesting paragraph-level question-answer pairs from Wikipedia. In *Proceedings of the 56th Annual Meeting of the Association for Computational Linguistics (Volume 1: Long Papers)*, pages 1907–1917, Melbourne, Australia. Association for Computational Linguistics.

Xinya Du, Junru Shao, and Claire Cardie. 2017. Learning to ask: Neural question generation for reading comprehension. In *Proceedings of the 55th Annual Meeting of the Association for Computational Linguistics (Volume 1: Long Papers)*, pages 1342–1352, Vancouver, Canada. Association for Computational Linguistics.

Hady Elsahar, Christophe Gravier, and Frederique Laforest. 2018. Zero-shot question generation from knowledge graphs for unseen predicates and entity types. In *Proceedings of the 2018 Conference of the North American Chapter of the Association for Computational Linguistics: Human Language Technologies, Volume 1 (Long Papers)*, pages 218–228, New Orleans, Louisiana. Association for Computational Linguistics.

Deepak Gupta, Hardik Chauhan, Asif Ekbal, and Pushpak Bhattacharyya. 2020. Reinforced multi-task approach for multi-hop question generation.

Michael Heilman and Noah A Smith. 2010. Good question! statistical ranking for question generation. In *Human Language Technologies: The 2010 Annual Conference of the North American Chapter of the Association for Computational Linguistics*, pages 609–617.

Karl Moritz Hermann, Tomáš Kočiský, Edward Grefenstette, Lasse Espeholt, Will Kay, Mustafa Suleyman, and Phil Blunsom. 2015. Teaching machines to read and comprehend. In *Proceedings of the 28th International Conference on Neural Information Processing Systems - Volume 1*, NIPS'15, page 1693–1701. MIT Press.

Sepp Hochreiter and Jürgen Schmidhuber. 1997. Long short-term memory. *Neural computation*, 9:1735–80.

Ari Holtzman, Jan Buys, Li Du, Maxwell Forbes, and Yejin Choi. 2019. The curious case of neural text degeneration.

Kelvin Jiang, Dekun Wu, and Hui Jiang. 2019. FreebaseQA: A new factoid QA data set matching trivia-style question-answer pairs with Freebase. In *Proceedings of the 2019 Conference of the North American Chapter of the Association for Computational Linguistics: Human Language Technologies, Volume 1 (Long and Short Papers)*, pages 318–323, Minneapolis, Minnesota. Association for Computational Linguistics.

Mandar Joshi, Eunsol Choi, Daniel Weld, and Luke Zettlemoyer. 2017. TriviaQA: A large scale distantly supervised challenge dataset for reading comprehension. In *Proceedings of the 55th Annual Meeting of the Association for Computational Linguistics (Volume 1: Long Papers)*, pages 1601–1611, Vancouver, Canada. Association for Computational Linguistics.

Daniel Khashabi, Amos Ng, Tushar Khot, Ashish Sabharwal, Hannaneh Hajishirzi, and Chris Callison-Burch. 2021. Gooaq: Open question answering with diverse answer types.

Diederik P. Kingma and Jimmy Ba. 2015. Adam: A method for stochastic optimization. In *3rd International Conference on Learning Representations, ICLR 2015, San Diego, CA, USA, May 7-9, 2015, Conference Track Proceedings*.

Tom Kwiatkowski, Jennimaria Palomaki, Olivia Redfield, Michael Collins, Ankur Parikh, Chris Alberti, Danielle Epstein, Illia Polosukhin, Jacob Devlin, Kenton Lee, Kristina Toutanova, Llion Jones, Matthew Kelcey, Ming-Wei Chang, Andrew M. Dai, Jakob Uszkoreit, Quoc Le, and Slav Petrov. 2019. Natural questions: A benchmark for question answering research. *Transactions of the Association for Computational Linguistics*, 7:453–466.

Philippe Laban, John Canny, and Marti A. Hearst. 2020. What's the latest? a question-driven news chatbot. In *Proceedings of the 58th Annual Meeting of the Association for Computational Linguistics: System Demonstrations*, pages 380–387, Online. Association for Computational Linguistics.

Alon Lavie and Abhaya Agarwal. 2007. Meteor: An automatic metric for mt evaluation with high levels of correlation with human judgments. In *Proceedings of the Second Workshop on Statistical Machine Translation*, StatMT '07, page 228–231, USA. Association for Computational Linguistics.

Patrick Lewis, Ludovic Denoyer, and Sebastian Riedel. 2019. Unsupervised question answering by cloze translation. In *Proceedings of the 57th Annual Meeting of the Association for Computational Linguistics*, pages 4896–4910, Florence, Italy. Association for Computational Linguistics.

Jingjing Li, Yifan Gao, Lidong Bing, Irwin King, and Michael R. Lyu. 2019. Improving question generation with to the point context. In *Proceedings of the 2019 Conference on Empirical Methods in Natural Language Processing and the 9th International Joint Conference on Natural Language Processing (EMNLP-IJCNLP)*, pages 3216–3226, Hong Kong, China. Association for Computational Linguistics.

Zhongli Li, Wenhui Wang, Li Dong, Furu Wei, and Ke Xu. 2020. Harvesting and refining question-answer pairs for unsupervised qa. *Proceedings of the 58th Annual Meeting of the Association for Computational Linguistics*.

Jindřich Libovický, Jindřich Helcl, and David Mareček. 2018. Input combination strategies for multi-source transformer decoder. In *Proceedings of the Third Conference on Machine Translation: Research Papers*, pages 253–260, Brussels, Belgium. Association for Computational Linguistics.

Chin-Yew Lin. 2004. ROUGE: A package for automatic evaluation of summaries. In *Text Summarization Branches Out*, pages 74–81, Barcelona, Spain. Association for Computational Linguistics.

Bang Liu, Mingjun Zhao, Di Niu, Kunfeng Lai, Yancheng He, Haojie Wei, and Yu Xu. 2019. Learning to generate questions by learningwhat not to generate. In *The World Wide Web Conference*, WWW '19, page 1106–1118, New York, NY, USA. Association for Computing Machinery.

Christopher Malon and Bing Bai. 2020. Generating followup questions for interpretable multi-hop question answering.

Shlok Kumar Mishra, Pranav Goel, Abhishek Sharma, Abhyuday Jagannatha, David Jacobs, and Hal Daumé III. 2020. Towards automatic generation of questions from long answers.

Nasrin Mostafazadeh, Ishan Misra, Jacob Devlin, Margaret Mitchell, Xiaodong He, and Lucy Vanderwende. 2016. Generating natural questions about an image. In *Proceedings of the 54th Annual Meeting of the Association for Computational Linguistics (Volume 1: Long Papers)*, pages 1802–1813, Berlin, Germany. Association for Computational Linguistics.

Myle Ott, Sergey Edunov, David Grangier, and Michael Auli. 2018. Scaling neural machine translation. In *Proceedings of the Third Conference on Machine Translation: Research Papers*, pages 1–9, Brussels, Belgium. Association for Computational Linguistics.

Liangming Pan, Wenqiang Lei, Tat-Seng Chua, and Min-Yen Kan. 2019. Recent advances in neural question generation. *CoRR*, abs/1905.08949.

Kishore Papineni, Salim Roukos, Todd Ward, and Wei-Jing Zhu. 2002. Bleu: A method for automatic evaluation of machine translation. In *Proceedings of the 40th Annual Meeting on Association for Computational Linguistics*, ACL '02, page 311–318, USA. Association for Computational Linguistics.

Ankur Parikh, Oscar Täckström, Dipanjan Das, and Jakob Uszkoreit. 2016. A decomposable attention model for natural language inference. In *Proceedings of the 2016 Conference on Empirical Methods in Natural Language Processing*, pages 2249–2255, Austin, Texas. Association for Computational Linguistics.

Peng Qi, Yuhao Zhang, and Christopher D. Manning. 2020. Stay hungry, stay focused: Generating informative and specific questions in information-seeking conversations.

Alec Radford, Jeff Wu, Rewon Child, David Luan, Dario Amodei, and Ilya Sutskever. 2019. Language models are unsupervised multitask learners.

Pranav Rajpurkar, Robin Jia, and Percy Liang. 2018. Know what you don't know: Unanswerable questions for SQuAD. In *Proceedings of the 56th Annual Meeting of the Association for Computational Linguistics (Volume 2: Short Papers)*, pages 784–789, Melbourne, Australia. Association for Computational Linguistics.

Pranav Rajpurkar, Jian Zhang, Konstantin Lopyrev, and Percy Liang. 2016. SQuAD: 100,000+ questions for machine comprehension of text. In *Proceedings of the 2016 Conference on Empirical Methods in Natural Language Processing*, pages 2383–2392, Austin, Texas. Association for Computational Linguistics.

Siva Reddy, Danqi Chen, and Christopher D. Manning. 2019. CoQA: A conversational question answering challenge. *Transactions of the Association for Computational Linguistics*, 7:249–266.

Abigail See, Peter J. Liu, and Christopher D. Manning. 2017. Get to the point: Summarization with pointer-generator networks. In *Proceedings of the 55th Annual Meeting of the Association for Computational Linguistics (Volume 1: Long Papers)*, pages 1073–1083, Vancouver, Canada. Association for Computational Linguistics.

Rico Sennrich, Barry Haddow, and Alexandra Birch. 2016. Neural machine translation of rare words with subword units. In *Proceedings of the 54th Annual Meeting of the Association for Computational Linguistics (Volume 1: Long Papers)*, pages 1715–1725, Berlin, Germany. Association for Computational Linguistics.

Iulian Vlad Serban, Alberto García-Durán, Caglar Gulcehre, Sungjin Ahn, Sarath Chandar, Aaron Courville, and Yoshua Bengio. 2016. Generating factoid questions with recurrent neural networks: The 30M factoid question-answer corpus. In *Proceedings of the 54th Annual Meeting of the Association for Computational Linguistics (Volume 1: Long Papers)*, pages 588–598, Berlin, Germany. Association for Computational Linguistics.

Shikhar Sharma, Layla El Asri, Hannes Schulz, and Jeremie Zumer. 2017. Relevance of unsupervised metrics in task-oriented dialogue for evaluating natural language generation. *CoRR*, abs/1706.09799.

Xingwu Sun, Jing Liu, Yajuan Lyu, Wei He, Yanjun Ma, and Shi Wang. 2018. Answer-focused and position-aware neural question generation. In *Proceedings of the 2018 Conference on Empirical Methods in Natural Language Processing*, pages 3930–3939, Brussels, Belgium. Association for Computational Linguistics.

Adam Trischler, Tong Wang, Xingdi Yuan, Justin Harris, Alessandro Sordoni, Philip Bachman, and Kaheer Suleman. 2017. NewsQA: A machine comprehension dataset. In *Proceedings of the 2nd Workshop on Representation Learning for NLP*, pages 191–200, Vancouver, Canada. Association for Computational Linguistics.

Luu Anh Tuan, Darsh Shah, and Regina Barzilay. 2020. Capturing greater context for question generation. *Proceedings of the AAAI Conference on Artificial Intelligence*, 34(05):9065–9072.

Ashish Vaswani, Noam Shazeer, Niki Parmar, Jakob Uszkoreit, Llion Jones, Aidan N Gomez, Ł ukasz Kaiser, and Illia Polosukhin. 2017. Attention is all you need. In *Advances in Neural Information Processing Systems*, volume 30. Curran Associates, Inc.

Alex Wang, Kyunghyun Cho, and Mike Lewis. 2020. Asking and answering questions to evaluate the factual consistency of summaries. In *Proceedings of the 58th Annual Meeting of the Association for Computational Linguistics*, pages 5008–5020, Online. Association for Computational Linguistics.

Zhilin Yang, Peng Qi, Saizheng Zhang, Yoshua Bengio, William Cohen, Ruslan Salakhutdinov, and Christopher D. Manning. 2018. HotpotQA: A dataset for diverse, explainable multi-hop question answering. In *Proceedings of the 2018 Conference on Empirical Methods in Natural Language Processing*, pages 2369–2380, Brussels, Belgium. Association for Computational Linguistics.

Jianxing Yu, Xiaojun Quan, Qinliang Su, and Jian Yin. 2020. Generating multi-hop reasoning questions to improve machine reading comprehension. In *Proceedings of The Web Conference 2020*, WWW '20, page 281–291, New York, NY, USA. Association for Computing Machinery.

Yao Zhao, Xiaochuan Ni, Yuanyuan Ding, and Qifa Ke. 2018. Paragraph-level neural question generation with maxout pointer and gated self-attention networks. In *Proceedings of the 2018 Conference on Empirical Methods in Natural Language Processing*, pages 3901–3910, Brussels, Belgium. Association for Computational Linguistics.

A Appendix

We show several generated questions here. Each frame box contains a news article, with two questions generated by M_{NQ} (showing in bold texts) and M_{SD} respectively. News articles are selected from the CNN/Daily Mail dataset with preprocessing described in Section 5.2. We also compare these generated questions in Table 7.

> Two Italians, a Dane, a German, a Frenchman and a Brit walk into a space station... or will, in 2013, if all goes according to European Space Agency plans. Europe's six new astronauts hope to join their American counterparts on the Internation Space Station. The six new astronauts named Wednesday were chosen from more than 8,400 candidates, and are the first new ESA astronauts since 1992, the space agency said in a statement. They include two military test pilots, one fighter pilot and one commercial pilot, plus an engineer and a physicist. "This is a very important day for human spaceflight in Europe," said Simonetta Di Pippo, Director of Human Spaceflight at ESA. "These young men and women are the next generation of European space explorers. They have a fantastic career ahead, which will put them right on top of one of the ultimate challenges of our time: going back to the Moon and beyond as part of the global exploration effort." Humans have not walked on the moon since 1972, just over three years after the first manned mission to Earth's nearest neighbor. The six will begin space training in Germany, with an eye to being ready for future missions to the International Space Station and beyond in four years. They are: Samantha Cristoforetti of Italy, a fighter pilot with degrees in engineering and aeronautical sciences; Alexander Gerst, a German researcher with degrees in physics and earth science; Andreas Mogensen, a Danish engineer with the private space firm HE Space Operations; Luca Parmitano of Italy, an Air Force pilot with a degree in aeronautical sciences; Timothy Peake, an English test pilot with the British military; and Frenchman Thomas Pesquet, an Air France pilot who previously worked as an engineer at the French space agency.

- **who are the new astronauts on the moon**
- how many italians walk into a space station in 2013

> After several delays, NASA said Friday that space shuttle Discovery is scheduled for launch in five days. The space shuttle Discovery, seen here in January, is now scheduled to launch Wednesday. Commander Lee Archambault and his six crewmates are now scheduled to lift off to the International Space Station at 9:20 p.m. ET Wednesday. NASA said its managers had completed a readiness review for Discovery, which will be making the 28th shuttle mission to the ISS. The launch date had been delayed to allow "additional analysis and particle impact testing associated with a flow-control valve in the shuttle's main engines," the agency said. According to NASA, the readiness review was initiated after damage was found in a valve on the shuttle Endeavour during its November 2008 flight. Three valves have been cleared and installed on Discovery, it said. Discovery is to deliver the fourth and final set of "solar array wings" to the ISS. With the completed array the station will be able to provide enough electricity when the crew size is doubled to six in May, NASA said. The Discovery also will carry a replacement for a failed unit in a system that converts urine to drinkable water, it said. Discovery's 14-day mission will include four spacewalks, NASA said.

- **when is the space shuttle discovery coming out**
- how many days is the space shuttle discovery scheduled to launch

> Unemployment in Spain has reached 20 percent, meaning 4.6 million people are out of work, the Spanish government announced Friday. The figure, from the first quarter, is up from 19 percent and 4.3 million people in the previous quarter. It represents the second-highest unemployment rate in the European Union, after Latvia, according to figures Friday from Eurostat, the EU's statistics service. Spanish Prime Minister Jose Luis Rodriguez Zapatero told Parliament on Wednesday he believes the jobless rate has peaked and will now start to decline. The first quarter of the year is traditionally poor for Spain because of a drop in labor-intensive activity like construction, agriculture and tourism. This week, Standard & Poor's downgraded Spain's long-term credit rating and said the outlook is negative. "We now believe that the Spanish economy's shift away from credit-fuelled economic growth is likely to result in a more protracted period of sluggish activity than we previously assumed," Standard & Poor's credit analyst Marko Mrsnik said. Gross domestic product growth in Spain is expected to average 0.7 percent annually through 2016, compared with previous expectations of 1 percent annually, he said. Spain's economic problems are closely tied to the housing bust there, according to The Economist magazine. Many of the newly unemployed worked in construction, it said. The recession revealed how dependent public finances were on housing-related tax revenues, it said. Another problem in Spain is that wages are set centrally and most jobs are protected, making it hard to shift skilled workers from one industry to another, the magazine said. Average unemployment for the 27-member European Union stayed stable in March at 9.6 percent, Eurostat said Friday. That percentage represents 23 million people, it said. The lowest national unemployment rates were in the Netherlands and Austria, which had 4.1 and 4.9 percent respectively, Eurostat said.

- **what is the average unemployment rate in spain**
- what percentage of spain's population is out of work

> Atlanta rapper DeAndre Cortez Way, better known by his stage name Soulja Boy Tell 'Em or just Soulja Boy, was charged with obstruction after running from police despite an order to stop, a police spokesman said Friday. Rapper Soulja Boy was arrested in Georgia after allegedly running from police. The 19-year-old singer was among a large group that had gathered at a home in Stockbridge, 20 miles south of Atlanta, said Henry County, Georgia, police Capt. Jason Bolton. Way was arrested Wednesday night along with another man, Bolton said. Police said Way left jail Thursday after posting a $550 bond. Bolton said officers responded to a complaint about a group of youths milling around the house, which appeared to be abandoned. When police arrived, they saw about 40 people. Half of them

President of the United Nations General Assembly [Miroslav Lajčák of Slovakia] has been elected as the United Nations General Assembly President of its 72nd session beginning in September 2017.
who is the current president of un general assembly

Learner 's permit Typically , a driver operating with a learner 's permit must be accompanied by [an adult licensed driver who is at least 21 years of age or older and in the passenger seat of the vehicle at all times] .
who needs to be in the car with a permit driver

Java development Kit [The Java Development Kit (JDK) is an implementation of either one of the Java Platform , Standard Edition , Java Platform , Enterprise Edition , or Java Platform , Micro Edition platforms released by Oracle Corporation in the form of a binary product aimed at Java developers on Solaris , Linux , macOS or Windows . The JDK includes a private JVM and a few other resources to finish the development of a Java Application . Since the introduction of the Java platform , it has been by far the most widely used Software Development Kit (SDK) . On 17 November 2006 , Sun announced that they would release it under the GNU General Public License (GPL) , thus making it free software . This happened in large part on 8 May 2007 , when Sun contributed the source code to the OpenJDK .]
what is the use of jdk in java

Figure 5: Examples of the NQ data preprocessing from the training set. Orange texts are Wikipedia titles that added in the front the each long answers. In first two examples, annotators mark there are short answers represented in cyan; while for the last example, there is no short answer marked by annotators so we mark the whole paragraph as the answer. Cyan texts are tagged with type ID '1' during preprocessing.

Context	Therefore sign [**(1)** In logical argument and mathematical proof, [**(2)** [**(3)** the [**(4)** therefore sign **(/4)**] **(/3)**] (∴) is generally used before [**(5)** a logical consequence, such as the conclusion of a syllogism. **(/5)**] **(/2)**] The symbol consists of three dots placed in an upright triangle and is read therefore. It is encoded at U+2234 ∴ therefore (HTML ∴ ∴). For common use in Microsoft Office hold the ALT key and type "8756". While it is not generally used in formal writing, it is used in mathematics and shorthand. It is complementary to U+2235 ∵ because (HTML ∵). **(/1)**]
Question	*what do the 3 dots mean in math*
SA 1	whole paragraph
Predicted	*what is the therefore sign in a syllogism*
SA 2	[the therefore sign (∴) is generally used before a logical consequence, such as the conclusion of a syllogism.]
Predicted	*what is the meaning of therefore in triangle*
SA 3	[the therefore sign]
Predicted	*what is the name of the three dots in a triangle called*
SA 4	[therefore sign]
Predicted	*what is the name of the three dots in a triangle called*
SA 5	[a logical consequence , such as the conclusion of a syllogism]
Predicted	*when is the therefore sign used in a syllogism*

Figure 6: Example of the question generation from Natural Questions dataset with BERTPGN. We use '[(i)' and '(/i)]' to represent the start and end position of the *i*-th answer span. The context is the long answer for the question *what do the 3 dots mean in math.* Five short answers (SA) marked by five different annotators. Our BERTPGN model with nucleus sampling (Holtzman et al., 2019) with temperature of 0.1 produces different but related questions for each short answers as well as the whole context with brackets over each of them.

ran away, including Way, Bolton said. The ones who remained told officers they were at the home to film a video. Way was arrested when he returned to the house to get his car, Bolton said. He said the house was dark inside and looked abandoned. "He just ran from the police, and then he decided to come back," according to Bolton. The second man who returned for his vehicle was arrested after police found eight $100 counterfeit bills inside, according to the officer. Way broke into the music scene two years ago with his hit "Crank That (Soulja Boy)." The rapper also describes himself as a producer and entrepreneur.

- **what is the meaning of soulja boy tell em**
- what was deandre cortez way known as

The U.S. military is gearing up for a possible influx of Haitians fleeing their earthquake-stricken country at an Army facility not widely known for its humanitarian missions: Guantanamo Bay. Soldiers at the base have set up tents, beds and toilets, awaiting possible orders from the secretary of defense to proceed, according to Maj. Diana Haynie, a spokeswoman for Joint Task Force Guantanamo Bay. "There's no indication of any mass migration from Haiti," Haynie stressed. "We have not been told to conduct migrant operations." But the base is getting ready "as a prudent measure," Haynie said, since "it takes some time to set things up." Guantanamo Bay is about 200 miles from Haiti. Currently, military personnel at the base are helping the earthquake relief effort by shipping bottled water and food from its warehouse. In addition, Gen. Douglas Fraser, commander of U.S. Southern Command, said the Navy has set up a "logistics field," an area to support bigger ships in the region. The military can now use that as a "lily pad" to fly supplies from ships docked at Guantanamo over to Haiti, he said. "Guantanamo Bay proves its value as a strategic hub for the movement of supplies and personnel to the affected areas in Haiti," Haynie said. As part of the precautionary measures to prepare for possible refugees, the Army has

BERTPGN-NQ-whole-article	BERTPGN-SQuAD-first-line
who are the new astronauts on the moon	how many italians walk into a space station in 2013
when is the space shuttle discovery coming out	how many days is the space shuttle discovery scheduled to launch
what is the average unemployment rate in spain	what percentage of spain's population is out of work
what is the meaning of soulja boy tell em	what was deandre cortez way known as
where does the us refugees at guantanamo bay come from	what is the name of the us military facility in the us
what happened to the girl in the texas polygamist ranch	what was the name of the texas polygamist ranch
who scored the first goal in the premier league	which team did everton fc beat to win the premier league's home draw with tottenham on sunday

Table 7: Comparing generated questions side-by-side. Our model uses uncased vocabulary and omits the final question mark.

erected 100 tents, each holding 10 beds, according to Haynie. Toilet facilities are nearby. If needed, hundreds more tents are stored in Guantanamo Bay and can be erected, she said. The refugees would be put on the leeward side of the island, more than 2 miles from some 200 detainees being held on the other side, Haynie said. The refugees would not mix with the detainees. Joint Task Force Guantanamo Bay is responsible for planning for any kind of Caribbean mass immigration, according to Haynie. In the early 1990s, thousands of Haitian refugees took shelter on the island, she said.

- **where does the us refugees at guantanamo bay come from**
- what is the name of the us military facility in the us

A Colorado woman is being pursued as a "person of interest" in connection with phone calls that triggered the raid of a Texas polygamist ranch, authorities said Friday. Rozita Swinton, 33, has been arrested in a case that is not directly related to the Texas raid. Texas Rangers are seeking Rozita Swinton of Colorado Springs, Colorado, "regarding telephone calls placed to a crisis center hot line in San Angelo, Texas, in late March 2008," the Rangers said in a written statement. The raid of the YFZ (Yearning for Zion) Ranch in Eldorado, Texas, came after a caller – who identified herself as a 16-year-old girl – said she had been physically and sexually abused by an adult man with whom she was forced into a "spiritual marriage." The release said a search of Swinton's home in Colorado uncovered evidence that possibly links her to phone calls made about the ranch, run by the Fundamentalist Church of Jesus Christ of Latter-day Saints. "The possibility exists that Rozita Swinton, who has nothing to do with the FLDS church, may have been a woman who made calls and pretended she was the 16-year-old girl named Sarah," CNN's Gary Tuchman reported. Swinton, 33, has been charged in Colorado with false reporting to authorities and is in police custody. Police said that arrest was not directly related to the Texas case. Authorities raided the Texas ranch April 4 and removed 416 children. Officials have been trying to identify the 16-year-old girl, referred to as Sarah, who claimed she had been abused in the phone calls. FLDS members have denied the girl, supposedly named Sarah Jessop Barlow, exists. Some of the FLDS women who spoke with CNN on Monday said they believed the calls were a hoax. While the phone calls initially prompted the raid, officers received a second search warrant based on what they said was evidence of sexual abuse found at the compound. In court documents, investigators described seeing teen girls who appeared pregnant, records that showed men marrying multiple women and accounts of girls being married to adult men when they were as young as 13. A court hearing began Thursday to determine custody of children who were removed from the ranch.

- **what happened to the girl in the texas polygamist ranch**
- what was the name of the texas polygamist ranch

Everton scored twice late on and goalkeeper Tim Howard saved an injury-time penalty as they fought back to secure a 2-2 Premier League home draw with Tottenham on Sunday. Jermain Defoe gave the visitors the lead soon after the interval when nipping in front of Tony Hibbert to convert Aaron Lennon's cross at the near post for his 13th goal of the season. And they doubled their advantage soon after when defender Michael Dawson headed home a Niko Kranjcar corner. But Everton got a foothold back in the game when Seamus Coleman's run and cross was converted by fellow-substitute Louis Saha in the 78th minute. And Tim Cahill rescued a point for the home side with four minutes remaining when he stooped low to head home Leighton Baines' bouncing cross. However, there was still further drama to come when Hibbert was penalized for crashing into Wilson Palacios in the area. However, England striker Defoe smashed his penalty too close to Howard and the keeper pulled off a fine save to give out-of-form Everton a morale-boosting point. The result means Tottenham remain in fourth place, behind north London rivals Arsenal, while Everton have now won just one of their last nine league games. In the day's other match, Bobby Zamora scored the only goal of the game as Fulham beat Sunderland 1-0 to move up to eighth place in the table.

- **who scored the first goal in the premier league**
- which team did everton fc beat to win the premier league's home draw with tottenham on sunday

B Human Evaluation Criteria

Question is context dependent

Some questions are context-dependent, e.g.,

- "who intends to boycott the election" - which election?

- “where did the hijackers go to” - what hijackers?
- “what type of hats did they use” - who are they?
- “how many people were killed in the quake” - which quake?

Compared to these context-independent, self-contained questions:

- “what was toyota’s first-ever net loss”
- “who is hillary’s secretary of state”
- “what is the name of the motto of the new york times ”

Question is irrelevant to the article

Given a news article:

> "Usually when I mention suspended animation people will flash me the Vulcan sign and laugh," says scientist Mark Roth. But he's not referring to the plot of a "Star Trek" episode. Roth is completely serious about using lessons he's learned from putting some organisms into suspended animation to help people survive medical trauma. He spoke at the TED2010 conference in Long Beach, California, in February. The winner of a MacArthur genius fellowship in 2007, Roth described the thought process that led him and fellow researchers to explore ways to lower animals' metabolism to the point where they showed no signs of life – and yet were not dead. More remarkably, they were able to restore the animals to normal life, with no apparent damage. Read more about Roth on TED.com The Web site of Roth's laboratory at the Fred Hutchinson Cancer Research Center in Seattle, Washington, describes the research this way: "We use the term suspended animation to refer to a state where all observable life processes (using high resolution light microscopy) are stopped: The animals do not move nor breathe and the heart does not beat. We have found that we are able to put a number of animals (yeast, nematodes, drosophila, frogs and zebrafish) into a state of suspended animation for up to 24 hours through one basic technique: reducing the concentration of oxygen." Visit Mark Roth's laboratory Roth is investigating the use of small amounts of hydrogen sulfide, a gas that is toxic in larger quantities, to lower metabolism. In his talk, he imagined that "in the not too distant future, an EMT might give an injection of hydrogen sulfide, or some related compound, to a person suffering severe injuries, and that person might de-animate a bit ... their metabolism will fall as though you were dimming a switch on a lamp at home. "That will buy them the time to be transported to the hospital to get the care they need. And then, after they get that care ... they'll wake up. A miracle? We hope not, or maybe we just hope to make miracles a little more common."

The question: “what is the meaning of suspended animation in star trek” is irrelevant to the news since the news is not talking about Star Trek.

However, the question “what is the meaning of suspended animation” is related.

Question implies a contradiction to facts present in the article

Given a news article:

> At least 6,000 Christians have fled the northern Iraqi city of Mosul in the past week because of killings and death threats, Iraq's Ministry of Immigration and Displaced Persons said Thursday. A Christian family that fled Mosul found refuge in the Al-Sayida monastery about 30 miles north of the city. The number represents 1,424 families, at least 70 more families than were reported to be displaced on Wednesday. The ministry said it had set up an operation room to follow up sending urgent aid to the displaced Christian families as a result of attacks by what it called "terrorist groups." Iraqi officials have said the families were frightened by a series of killings and threats by Muslim extremists ordering them to convert to Islam or face death. Fourteen Christians have been slain in the past two weeks in the city, which is about 260 miles (420 kilometers) north of Baghdad. Mosul is one of the last Iraqi cities where al Qaeda in Iraq has a significant presence and routinely carries out attacks. The U.S. military said it killed the Sunni militant group's No. 2 leader, Abu Qaswarah, in a raid in the northern city earlier this month. In response to the recent attacks on Christians, authorities have ordered more checkpoints in several of the city's Christian neighborhoods. The attacks may have been prompted by Christian demonstrations ahead of provincial elections, which are to be held by January 31, authorities said. Hundreds of Christians took to the streets in Mosul and surrounding villages and towns, demanding adequate representation on provincial councils, whose members will be chosen in the local elections. Thursday, Iraq's minister of immigration and displaced persons discussed building housing complexes for Christian families in northern Iraq and allocating land to build the complexes. Abdel Samad Rahman Sultan brought up the issue when he met with a representative of Iraq's Hammurabi Organization for Human Rights and with the head of the Kojina Organization for helping displaced persons. A curfew was declared Wednesday in several neighborhoods of eastern Mosul as authorities searched for militants behind the attacks.

The question “how many christians fled to mosul in the past” is contradicted to the fact — 6000 christians fled from Mosul — in the news.

Question focuses on a peripheral topic

Given a news article:

> One of the Marines shown in a famous World War II photograph raising the U.S. flag on Iwo Jima was posthumously awarded a certificate of U.S. citizenship on Tuesday. The Marine Corps War Memorial in Virginia depicts Strank and five others raising a flag on Iwo Jima. Sgt. Michael Strank, who was born in Czechoslovakia and came to the United States when he was 3, derived U.S. citizenship when his father was naturalized in 1935. However, U.S. Citizenship and Immigration Services recently discovered that Strank never was given citizenship papers. At a ceremony Tuesday at the Marine Corps Memorial – which depicts the flag-raising – in Arlington, Virginia, a certificate of citizenship was presented to Strank's younger sister, Mary Pero. Strank and five other men became national icons when an Associated Press photographer captured the image of them planting an American flag on top of Mount Suribachi on February 23, 1945. Strank was killed in action on the island on March 1, 1945, less than a month before the battle between Japanese and U.S. forces there ended.

> Jonathan Scharfen, the acting director of CIS, presented the citizenship certificate Tuesday. He hailed Strank as "a true American hero and a wonderful example of the remarkable contribution and sacrifices that immigrants have made to our great republic throughout its history."

The question "who presented the american flag raising on iwo jima" focuses on a peripheral topic — the name of the one raising the flag.

While the question "who was awarded a certificate of citizenship raising the u.s. flag" focuses on the main topic - getting a citizenship.

There is a short span to answer the question

Given a news:

> Los Angeles police have launched an internal investigation to determine who leaked a picture that appears to show a bruised and battered Rihanna. Rihanna was allegedly attacked by her boyfriend, singer Chris Brown, before the Grammys on February 8. The close-up photo – showing a woman with contusions on her forehead and below her eyes, and cuts on her lip – was published on the entertainment Web site TMZ Thursday. TMZ said it was a photo of Rihanna. Twenty-one-year-old Rihanna was allegedly attacked by her boyfriend, singer Chris Brown, on a Los Angeles street before the two were to perform at the Grammys on February 8. "The unauthorized release of a domestic violence photograph immediately generated an internal investigation," an L.A. police spokesman said in a statement. "The Los Angeles Police Department takes seriously its duty to maintain the confidentiality of victims of domestic violence. A violation of this type is considered serious misconduct, with penalties up to and including termination." A spokeswoman for Rihanna declined to comment. The chief investigator in the case had told CNN earlier that authorities had tried to guard against leaks. Detective Deshon Andrews said he had kept the case file closely guarded and that no copies had been made of the original photos and documents. Brown was arrested on February 8 in connection with the case and and booked on suspicion of making criminal threats. Authorities are trying to determine whether Brown should face domestic violence-related charges. Brown apologized for the incident this week. "Words cannot begin to express how sorry and saddened I am over what transpired," the 19-year-old said in a statement released by his spokesman. "I am seeking the counseling of my pastor, my mother and other loved ones and I am committed, with God's help, to emerging a better person."

The question "who have launched an internal investigation of the leaked rihanna's picture" can be answered by "Los Angeles police".

The entire article can be an answer

Given a news:

> A high court in northern India on Friday acquitted a wealthy businessman facing the death sentence for the killing of a teen in a case dubbed "the house of horrors." Moninder Singh Pandher was sentenced to death by a lower court in February. The teen was one of 19 victims – children and young women – in one of the most gruesome serial killings in India in recent years. The Allahabad high court has acquitted Moninder Singh Pandher, his lawyer Sikandar B. Kochar told CNN. Pandher and his domestic employee Surinder Koli were sentenced to death in February by a lower court for the rape and murder of the 14-year-old. The high court upheld Koli's death sentence, Kochar said. The two were arrested two years ago after body parts packed in plastic bags were found near their home in Noida, a New Delhi suburb. Their home was later dubbed a "house of horrors" by the Indian media. Pandher was not named a main suspect by investigators initially, but was summoned as co-accused during the trial, Kochar said. Kochar said his client was in Australia when the teen was raped and killed. Pandher faces trial in the remaining 18 killings and could remain in custody, the attorney said.

The question "what was the case of the house of horrors in northern india" can be answered by the whole news article. There is no short span can be extracted as an answer.

None answer in the article

Given a news:

> Buy a $175,000 package to attend the Oscars and you might buy yourself trouble, lawyers for the Academy Awards warn. The 81st annual Academy Awards will be held on February 22 from Hollywood's Kodak Theatre. The advertising of such packages – including four tickets to the upcoming 81st annual Academy Awards and a hotel stay in Los Angeles, California – has prompted the Academy of Motion Picture Arts and Sciences to sue an Arizona-based company. The Academy accused the company Experience 6 of selling "black-market" tickets, because tickets to the lavish movie awards show cannot be transferred or sold. Selling tickets could become a security issue that could bring celebrity stalkers or terrorists to the star-studded event, says the lawsuit, which was filed Monday in federal court in the Central District of California. "Security experts have advised the Academy that it must not offer tickets to members of the public and must know identities of the event attendees," the lawsuit says. "In offering such black-market tickets, defendants are misleading the public and the ticket buyers into thinking that purchasers will be welcomed guests, rather than as trespassers, when they arrive for the ceremony." Experience 6 did not return calls from CNN for comment. On Tuesday morning, tickets to the event were still being advertised on the company's Web site. The Oscars will be presented February 22 from Hollywood's Kodak Theatre. The Academy Awards broadcast will air on ABC. Hugh Jackman is scheduled to host.

The questions "where does the 81st annual academy awards come from" and "how much did the academy pay to attend the oscars" cannot be answered from the news.

Document-Grounded Goal-Oriented Dialogue Systems on Pre-Trained Language Model with Diverse Input Representation

Boeun Kim*, **Dohaeng Lee***, **Yejin Lee** and **Harksoo Kim**
Konkuk University / Seoul, South Korea
{boeun, dsdhlee, jinjin096, nlpdrkim}@konkuk.ac.kr

Sihyung Kim
Kangwon National University / Chuncheon, South Korea
sureear@kangwon.ac.kr

Jin-Xia Huang, Oh-Woog Kwon
Electronics and Telecommunications Research Institute / Daejeon, South Korea
{hgh, ohwoog}@etri.re.kr

Abstract

Document-grounded goal-oriented dialog system understands users' utterances, and generates proper responses by using information obtained from documents. The Dialdoc21 shared task consists of two subtasks; subtask1, finding text spans associated with users' utterances from documents, and subtask2, generating responses based on information obtained from subtask1. In this paper, we propose two models (i.e., a knowledge span prediction model and a response generation model) for the subtask1 and the subtask2. In the subtask1, dialogue act losses are used with RoBERTa, and title embeddings are added to input representation of RoBERTa. In the subtask2, various special tokens and embeddings are added to input representation of BART's encoder. Then, we propose a method to assign different difficulty scores to leverage curriculum learning. In the subtask1, our span prediction model achieved F1-scores of 74.81 (ranked at top 7) and 73.41 (ranked at top 5) in test-dev phase and test phase, respectively. In the subtask2, our response generation model achieved sacreBLEUs of 37.50 (ranked at top 3) and 41.06 (ranked at top 1) in in test-dev phase and test phase, respectively.

1 Introduction

The Dialdoc21 shared task is a task that generates a proper response by finding a knowledge span from a document associated with a dialogue history. It consists of two subtasks; subtask1 for finding useful knowledge spans from a document and subtask2 for generating proper responses based on the knowledge spans. The doc2dial dataset, the dataset for the Dialdoc21 shared task, contains conversations between users and agents in real-world situations. The user and the agent engage in a conversation associated with a document, and the agent should provide the user with document-grounded information in order to guide the user. In this paper, we propose two models to perform the Dialdoc21 shared task using a pre-trained language model. In particular, we show that in the process of fine-tuning the pre-trained model, the proposed input representations significantly contribute to improving performances.

*equal contribution

2 Related Work

The baseline models for the subtask1 and the subtask2 were proposed by Feng et al. (2020), the composers of doc2dial datasets. They formulated the subtask1 as a span selection, inspired by extractive question answering tasks such as SQuAD task (Rajpurkar et al., 2016, 2018). Zheng et al. (2020) proposed a method to reflect the differences between knowledge spans used for each turn and current knowledge span candidates. The differential information is fused with or disentangled from the contextual information to facilitate final knowledge selection. Wolf et al. (2019) constructed input presentation using word, dialog state and positional embedding.

3 Task Description

In the subtask1, our goal is to find a relevant knowledge span required for agent's response in a conversation composed of multi-turns from a given document. Inspired by Feng et al. (2020), we propose a joint model to perform both dialogue act prediction and knowledge span prediction. In the subtask2, our goal is to generate agent's response

Proceedings of the 1st Workshop on Document-grounded Dialogue and Conversational Question Answering, pages 98–102
August 5–6, 2021. ©2021 Association for Computational Linguistics

Title	Section ID	Span ID	Text
For Your Surviving Divorced Spouse	8	31	For Your Surviving Divorced Spouse
	9	32	If you have a surviving divorced spouse
		33	they could get the same benefits as your widow or widower provided that your marriage lasted 10 years or more.
	10	34	Benefits paid to a surviving divorced spouse won't affect the benefit amounts your other survivors will receive based on your earnings record.
	11	35	If your former spouse is caring for your child who is under age 16 or disabled and gets benefits on your record ,
		36	they will not have to meet the length - of - marriage rule.
		37	The child must be your natural or legally adopted child.

Table 1: Example of span extensions from a sentence to a title. The red cell denotes an answer span predicted by the subtask1 model. The green cell denotes a section span containing the answer span. The blue cell denotes a title span containing the predicted span.

in natural language based on a dialogue history and a document associated with the dialogue history. The dialogue history consists of speakers and utterances. Then, the document consists of sentences, tags, titles, and so on. Based on these structural information of the dialogue history and the document, we define special tokens and embeddings. Then, we propose a method to reflect these special tokens and embeddings to the well-known BART model (Lewis et al., 2020). The doc2dial dataset contains goal-oriented dialogues and knowledge documents. For developing models, three sub-datasets in four domains (DMV, VA, SSA, and studentaid) were deployed; a train dataset, a validation dataset, and a test-dev dataset. For evaluating the models, a test dataset in five domains (i.e., four seen domains (DMV, VA, SSA, studentaid) and an unseen domain (COVID-19)) was used. The test-dev dataset embodied 30% of the test dataset except for the unseen domain.

4 Key Components of Our Model

4.1 Subtask1

We adopt pre-trained RoBERTa-large model (Liu et al., 2019) as a backbone. Each dialogue turn in the train dataset and the validation dataset has a dialogue act label. We assume that agent's dialogue act aids to find a proper knowledge span. For dialogue act prediction, we use a fully connected layer added on the [CLS] output vector of the RoBERTa-large model. Then, we pointwise add special embeddings called title embeddings to conventional input representation of the RoBERTa-large model. As shown in Table 1, each span in a knowledge document has its own title. By adding the title embedding, we expect that spans sharing the same title will be tied together to help find a knowledge span. For knowledge span prediction, we use the well-known machine reading comprehension (MRC) architecture proposed by (Devlin et al., 2019). In the MRC model, each output vector of the RoBERTa-large model is fed into a bidirectional gated recurrent unit (Bi-GRU) (Cho et al., 2014) layer. Then, each output of the Bi-GRU layer is again fed into a fully connected layer for predicting a starting position and an ending position of a knowledge span. Finally, the knowledge span prediction model expands predicted spans (a sequence of words) into span segments predefined with span IDs. In this paper, these predefined span segments are called answer spans. The final loss function of the proposed span prediction model, L_{total}, is the weighted sum of the dialogue act prediction loss, $L_{dialogueact}$, and the span prediction loss, L_{span}, as follows:

$$L_{total} = \alpha * L_{dialogueact} + \beta * L_{span}$$

where α and β are weighting parameters that are set to 0.3 and 0.7, respectively. Then, the dialogue act prediction loss and the span prediction loss are calculated by minimizing cross-entropies between predicted values and gold values, respectively.

4.2 Subtask2

Token	Meaning
<user>	Beginning of user's utterance
<agent>	Beginning of agent's utterance
<doc>	Beginning of a knowledge document
<title>	Beginning of a knowledge document's title
<rank>	Bordering between answer spans
<u>	Ending of underline markup that is existed in a knowledge document
<h>	Ending of heading markup that is existed in a knowledge document

Table 2: Special tokens and their meanings.

We adopt pre-trained BART-base model (Lewis

et al., 2020) as a backbone. An input of BART's encoder consists of a dialogue history and a knowledge document. We use a current utterance and 7 previous utterances, $u_i, u_{i-1}, \ldots, u_{i-7}$, as a dialogue history. Then, we use answer spans that are constructed from 100 span candidates predicted by the knowledge span prediction model, $\hat{s}_0, \hat{s}_1, \ldots, \hat{s}_{100}$, as a knowledge document. For enriching input representation of BART's encoder, we use special tokens and additional embeddings. We first add some special tokens to BART's input, as shown in Table 2. Then, we pointwise add the following special embeddings to input representation of BART's encoder:

Type-of-Input embedding: Embedding to distinguish between a dialogue history and a knowledge document.

Rank Embedding: Embedding for representing rankings of title spans containing answer spans that are returned by the knowledge span prediction model.

Rank-in-Section Embedding: Embedding for representing rankings of answer spans in each title.

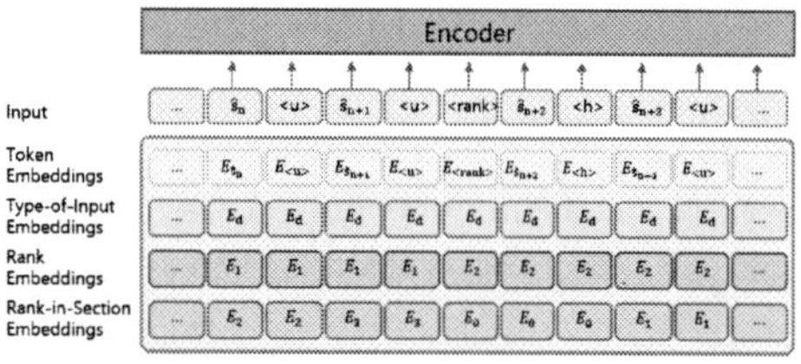

Figure 1: Special tokens and embeddings.

Figure 1 illustrates the proposed special tokens and embeddings.

5 Curriculum Learning

To improve performances, we train the proposed models through curriculum learning (Xu et al., 2020). Figure 2 illustrates the training process by curriculum learning. We first divide the training dataset into *N* buckets and train *N* teacher model (i.e., a teacher model per bucket). In this paper, *N* is set to four. Then, we measure performances of each teacher model by using *N-1* dataset except for those used for training each teacher model. Based on the performances of the teacher models, we assign each data to difficulty levels.

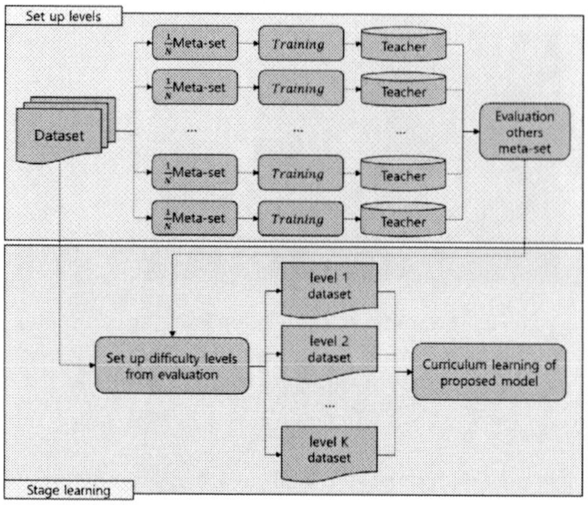

Figure 2: Curriculum learning process. *K* denotes the number of difficulty levels.

5.1 Difficulty level for subtask1

In the subtask1, we implement four teacher model based on the RoBERTa-base model (Liu et al., 2019). Each teacher model calculates an average of F1-score and EM-score (i.e., F1-score + EM score / 2) per input data. Then, the average scores of three teacher models are summed. According to the summed average scores, we divide the training dataset into an easiest level (the summed average score of 300), an easy level (the summed average score of (200,300)), a median level (the summed average score of (100,200]), and a difficult level (the summed average score of (0,100]). The numbers of data in each level are 5,390, 3,215, 6,538 and 9,260, respectively.

5.2 Difficulty level for subtask2

In the subtask2, we implement four teacher models based on the BART-base model (Lewis et al., 2020). We compute an average sum of sacreBLEUs evaluated by each teacher model. Then, we perform human evaluations on the computed average sums. Based on the human evaluations, we divide the training dataset into an easy level (sacreBLEU of [30,100]), a median level (sacreBLEU of [15,30)), and a difficult level (sacreBLEU of [0,15)). The numbers of data in each level are 8,165, 3,976, and 12,262, respectively.

5.3 Training detail

Based on the measured difficulty scoring, the total training stage consists of *K+1* phases. For instance, if *K* is set to two, the difficulty level comprises of two levels, i.e., "easy" and "difficult", and the training stage is composed of three phases. Concisely, we sort training datasets through difficulty levels. In the first stage, we train the model by using *1/K* dataset of "easy" level. In the second stage, we train the model by using *1/K* dataset of "easy" level and *1/K* dataset of "difficult" level excluding data used for the previous training stage. In the last stage, we train the model by using the entire training dataset until convergence. Since we use K as 4 in subtask1 and K as 3 in subtask2, each stage is composed of five phases and four phases.

6 Experiments

Models	F1	EM
BERT-large	67.96	52.02
+ DA	69.29	54.04
RoBERTa-large	-	-
+ DA	72.23	56.06
+ DA + T	72.91	57.07
+ DA + T + CL	74.81	59.59

Table 3: Subtask1 test-dev phase results. DA denotes the dialogue act prediction, T denotes the title embedding, and CL denotes the curriculum learning.

As shown in Table 3, the span prediction model based on RoBERTa-large showed better performances than that based on BERT-large (Devlin et al., 2019). The dialogue act contributed to improving performances: "BERT-large+DA" showed F1-score of 1.33%p higher and EM score of 2.02%p higher than "BERT-large". The title embedding contributed to improving performances: "RoBERTa-large+DA+T" showed F1-score of 0.68%p higher and EM score of 1.01%p higher than "RoBERTa-large+DA". Moreover, the curriculum learning significantly contributed to improving performances: "RoBERTa-large+DA+T+CL" showed F1-score of 1.9%p higher and EM score of 2.52%p higher than "RoBERTa-large+DA+T". Table 4 lists results of the subtask2 in the test-dev phase.
As shown in Table 4, the Type-of-Input embedding contributed to improving the sacreBLEU of 2.74%p compared to BART-base. Adding the Rank embedding improved the score by 5.39%p, and adding the Rank-in-Section embedding boosts the performance by another 4.47%p. Finally, the curriculum learning improved the sacreBLEU of 1.81%p.

Models	SacreBLEU
BART-base	23.09
+ TI	25.83
+ TI + R	31.22
+ TI + R + RS	35.69
+ TI + R + RS + CL	37.50

Table 4: Subtask2 test-dev phase results. TI denotes the Type-of-Input embedding, R denotes the Rank embedding, RS denotes the Rank-in-Section embedding, and CL denotes the curriculum learning.

7 Conclusion

We proposed a document-grounded goal-oriented dialogue system for the Dialdoc21 shared task. The proposed model used various special tags and embeddings for enriching input representation of pre-trained language models, RoBERTa-large for knowledge span prediction and BART for response generation. In addition, curriculum learning was adopted to achieve performance improvements. In the subtask1, our span prediction model achieved F1-scores of 74.81 (ranked at top 7) and 73.41 (ranked at top 5) in test-dev phase and test phase, respectively. In the subtask2, our response generation model achieved sacreBLEUs of 37.50 (ranked at top 3) and 41.06 (ranked at top 1) in test-dev phase and test phase, respectively.

Acknowledgments

This work was supported by Institute of Information & Communications Technology Planning & Evaluation(IITP) grant funded by the Korea government(MSIT) (2019-0-00004, Development of semi-supervised learning language intelligence technology and Korean tutoring service for foreigners). Also, this work was supported by Institute of Information & communications Technology Planning & Evaluation(IITP) grant funded by the Korea government(MSIT) (No.2020-0-00368, A Neural-Symbolic Model for Knowledge Acquisition and Inference Techniques)

References

Kyunghyun Cho, Bart van Merrienboer, Çaglar Gülçehre, Dzmitry Bahdanau, Fethi Bougares, Holger Schwenk, and Yoshua Bengio. 2014. Learning phrase representations using rnn encoder-decoder for statistical machine translation. In *EMNLP*.

Jacob Devlin, Ming-Wei Chang, Kenton Lee, and Kristina Toutanova. 2019. Bert: Pre-training of deep bidirectional transformers for language understanding. In *Proceedings of the 2019 Conference of the North American Chapter of the Association for Computational Linguistics: Human Language Technologies, Volume 1 (Long and Short Papers)*, pages 4171–4186.

Song Feng, Hui Wan, Chulaka Gunasekara, Siva Patel, Sachindra Joshi, and Luis Lastras. 2020. Doc2dial: A goal-oriented document-grounded dialogue dataset. In *Proceedings of the 2020 Conference on Empirical Methods in Natural Language Processing (EMNLP)*, pages 8118–8128.

Mike Lewis, Yinhan Liu, Naman Goyal, Marjan Ghazvininejad, Abdelrahman Mohamed, Omer Levy, Veselin Stoyanov, and Luke Zettlemoyer. 2020. Bart: Denoising sequence-to-sequence pretraining for natural language generation, translation, and comprehension. In *Proceedings of the 58th Annual Meeting of the Association for Computational Linguistics*, pages 7871–7880.

Yinhan Liu, Myle Ott, Naman Goyal, Jingfei Du, Mandar Joshi, Danqi Chen, Omer Levy, Mike Lewis, Luke Zettlemoyer, and Veselin Stoyanov. 2019. Roberta: A robustly optimized bert pretraining approach. *arXiv preprint arXiv:1907.11692*.

Pranav Rajpurkar, Robin Jia, and Percy Liang. 2018. Know what you don't know: Unanswerable questions for squad. In *Proceedings of the 56th Annual Meeting of the Association for Computational Linguistics (Volume 2: Short Papers)*, pages 784–789.

Pranav Rajpurkar, Jian Zhang, Konstantin Lopyrev, and Percy Liang. 2016. Squad: 100,000+ questions for machine comprehension of text. In *Proceedings of the 2016 Conference on Empirical Methods in Natural Language Processing*, pages 2383–2392.

Thomas Wolf, Victor Sanh, Julien Chaumond, and Clement Delangue. 2019. Transfertransfo: A transfer learning approach for neural network based conversational agents. *arXiv preprint arXiv:1901.08149*.

Benfeng Xu, Licheng Zhang, Zhendong Mao, Quan Wang, Hongtao Xie, and Yongdong Zhang. 2020. Curriculum learning for natural language understanding. In *Proceedings of the 58th Annual Meeting of the Association for Computational Linguistics*, pages 6095–6104.

Chujie Zheng, Yunbo Cao, Daxin Jiang, and Minlie Huang. 2020. Difference-aware knowledge selection for knowledge-grounded conversation generation. In *Proceedings of the 2020 Conference on Empirical Methods in Natural Language Processing: Findings*, pages 115–125.

Team JARS: DialDoc Subtask 1 - Improved Knowledge Identification with Supervised Out-of-Domain Pretraining

Sopan Khosla, Justin Lovelace, Ritam Dutt, Adithya Pratapa
Language Technologies Institute
Carnegie Mellon University
5000 Forbes Avenue
Pittsburgh, PA
{sopank, jlovelac, rdutt, vpratapa}@andrew.cmu.edu

Abstract

In this paper, we discuss our submission for DialDoc subtask 1. The subtask requires systems to extract knowledge from FAQ-type documents vital to reply to a user's query in a conversational setting. We experiment with pretraining a BERT-based question-answering model on different QA datasets from MRQA, as well as conversational QA datasets like CoQA and QuAC. Our results show that models pretrained on CoQA and QuAC perform better than their counterparts that are pretrained on MRQA datasets. Our results also indicate that adding more pretraining data does not necessarily result in improved performance. Our final model, which is an ensemble of AlBERT-XL pretrained on CoQA and QuAC independently, with the chosen answer having the highest average probability score, achieves an F1-Score of 70.9% on the official test-set.

1 Introduction

Question Answering (QA) involves constructing an answer for a given question in either an extractive or an abstractive manner. QA systems are central to other Natural Language Processing (NLP) applications like search engines, and dialogue. Recently, QA based solutions have also been proposed to evaluate factuality (Wang et al., 2020) and faithfulness (Durmus et al., 2020) of abstractive summarization systems.

In addition to popular QA benchmarks like SQuAD (Rajpurkar et al., 2016), and MRQA-2019 (Fisch et al., 2019), we have seen QA challenges that require reasoning over human dialogue. Some notable examples being QuAC (Choi et al., 2018) and CoQA (Reddy et al., 2019). These datasets require the model to attend to the entire dialogue context in the process of retrieving an answer. In this work, we are interesting in building a QA system to help with human dialogue.

Feng et al. (2020) introduced a new dataset of goal-oriented dialogues (Doc2Dial) that are grounded in the associated documents. Each sample in the dataset consists of an information-seeking conversation between a user and an agent where agent's responses are grounded in FAQ-like webpages. DialDoc shared task derives its training data from the Doc2Dial dataset and proposes two subtasks which require the participants to (1) identify the grounding knowledge in form of document span for the next agent turn; and (2) generate the next agent response in natural language.

In this paper, we describe our solution to the subtask 1. This subtask is formulated as a span selection problem. Therefore, we leverage a transformer-based extractive question-answering model (Devlin et al., 2019; Lan et al., 2019) to extract the relevant spans from the document. We pretrain our model on different QA datasets like SQuAD, different subsets of MRQA-2019 training set, and conversational QA datasets like CoQA and QuAC. We find that models pretrained on out-of-domain QA datasets substantially outperform the baseline. Our experiments suggest that conversational QA datasets are more useful than MRQA-2019 data or its subsets. In the following sections, we first present an overview of the DialDoc shared task (§2), followed by our system description (§3) and a detailed account of our experimental results, and ablation studies (§4, §5).

2 DialDoc Shared Task Dataset

Dataset used in the DialDoc shared-task is derived from Doc2Dial dataset (Feng et al., 2020), a new dataset with goal-oriented document-grounded dialogue. It includes a set of documents and conversations between a user and an agent grounded in the associated document. The authors provide annotations for dialogue acts for each utterance in the

Proceedings of the 1st Workshop on Document-grounded Dialogue and Conversational Question Answering, pages 103–108
August 5–6, 2021.

dialogue flow, along with the span in the document that acts as the reference of it.

The dataset shared during the shared task was divided into train/validation/testdev/test splits. Train and validation splits were provided to the participants to facilitate model development. During phase 1, the models were evaluated on testdev whereas, the final ranking was done on the performance on the test set.

Pre-processing Using the pre-processing scripts provided by the task organizers, we converted the Doc2Dial dataset into SQuAD v2.0 format with questions containing the latest user utterance as well as all previous turns in the conversation. This is in line with previous work from (Feng et al., 2020) which showed that including the entire conversational history performs better than just considering the current user utterance. Dialogue context is concatenated with the latest user utterance in the reverse time order.

The output of this pre-processing step consisted of 20431 training, 3972 validation, 727 testdev, and 2824 test instances.

3 System Description

As discussed earlier, subtask 1 of DialDoc shared task is formulated as a span selection problem. Therefore, in order to learn to predict the correct span, we use an extractive question-answering setup.

3.1 Question-Answering Model

We pass the pre-processed training data through a QA model that leverages a transformer encoder to contextually represent the question (dialogue history) along with the context (document). Since the grounding document is often longer than the maximum input sequence length for transformers, we follow (Feng et al., 2020) and truncate the documents in sliding windows with a stride. The document trunk and the dialogue history are passed through the transformer encoder to create contextual representations for each token in the input. To extract the beginning and the ending positions of the answer span within the document, the encoded embeddings are sent to a linear layer to output two logits that correspond to the probability of the position being the start and end position of the answer span. The training loss is computed using the Cross-Entropy loss function. We use the huggingface transformers toolkit in all of our experiments.

3.2 Pretraining

Recent work (Gururangan et al., 2020) has shown that multi-phase domain adaptive pretraining of transformer-based encoders on related datasets (and tasks) benefits the overall performance of the model on the downstream task. Motivated by this, we experimented with further pretraining the QA model on different out-of-domain QA datasets to gauge its benefits on Doc2Dial (Table 1).

QA Dataset	Domain	# Samples
SQuAD	Wikipedia	86k
NewsQA	News	74k
NaturalQuestions	Wikipedia	104k
HotpotQA	Wikipedia	73k
SearchQA	Jeopardy	117k
TriviaQA	Trivia	62k
MRQA-19 (Train)	Mixed	516k
QuAC	Wikipedia	70k
CoQA	Kids' Stories, Literature, Exams, News, Wikipedia	70k

Table 1: Statistics (domain, # samples) for different QA datasets used for continual pre-training.

4 Experimental Setup

In this section, we discuss our experimental setup in detail.

4.1 Pretraining Datasets

Firstly, we briefly describe the different datasets used for the continual pretraining of our transformer-based QA models.

MRQA-19 Shared task (Fisch et al., 2019) focused on evaluating the generalizability of QA systems. They developed a training set that combined examples from 6 different QA datasets and developed evaluation splits using 12 other QA datasets. We explored the effectiveness of pretraining on the entire MRQA training set as well on each of the 6 training datasets: **SQuAD** (Rajpurkar et al., 2016), **NewsQA** (Trischler et al., 2017), **NaturalQuestions** (Kwiatkowski et al., 2019), **HotpotQA** (Yang et al., 2018), **SearchQA** (Dunn et al., 2017), and **TriviaQA** (Joshi et al., 2017).

Conversational QA datasets. We also experiment with pretraining on two conversational QA datasets: **QuAC** (Choi et al., 2018)[1] and

[1] `https://huggingface.co/datasets/quac`

QA Dataset	Validation	
	EM	F1
Doc2Dial	42.1	57.8
+ SQuAD	45.0	**60.3**
+ NewsQA	**45.5**	59.8
+ NaturalQuestions (NQ)	44.2	59.9
+ HotpotQA	43.0	58.0
+ SearchQA	42.3	57.5
+ TriviaQA	43.1	58.0
+ MRQA-19 (Train)	43.4	58.9
+ SQuAD + NewsQA + NQ	43.0	59.2
+ SQuAD + NewsQA + NQ (IS)	43.8	59.4
+ QuAC	46.4	60.3
+ CoQA	**47.7**	**66.0**

Table 2: Performance (EM (%), F1 (%)) of `bert-base-uncased` on DialDoc validation set when further pretrained on different QA datasets.

QA Dataset	Validation		Testdev		Test	
	EM	F1	EM	F1	EM	F1
`bert-large-uncased-whole-word-masking`						
Doc2Dial	50.1	63.4	–	–	–	–
+ SQuAD	52.4	63.9	–	–	–	–
+ QuAC **(1)**	53.2	68.0	47.4	66.5	–	–
+ CoQA **(2)**	54.3	70.3	49.4	**68.7**	45.5	65.5
+ CoQA,QuAC **(3)**	54.2	70.1	**51.0**	68.1	–	–
`albert-xl`						
+ QuAC **(4)**	59.1	72.6	47.6	67.1	52.6	67.4
+ CoQA **(5)**	60.0	74.1	48.0	67.9	50.8	69.5
`Ensembles`						
E (4,5)	61.4	75.3	49.5	66.6	**<u>53.5</u>**	**<u>70.9</u>**
E (1,2,3,4,5)	**61.5**	**76.1**	49.5	**68.7**	52.0	69.9

Table 3: Performance (EM (%), F1 (%)) of large transformer-based QA models on DialDoc validation and testdev set when further pretrained on different QA datasets. Scores in **bold** are the best in their column; **<u>underlined</u>** are best on the official test-set.

CoQA (Reddy et al., 2019).[2] For both datasets, we filter out samples which do not adhere to SQuAD-like extractive QA setup (e.g. yes/no questions) or have a context length of more than 5000 characters.

Table 1 presents the size of the different pretraining datasets after the removal of non-extractive QA samples.

4.2 Evaluation Metrics

The shared-task relies on Exact Match (EM) and F1 metrics to evaluate the systems on subtask 1. To compute these scores, we use the metrics for SQuAD from huggingface.[3]

4.3 Hyperparameters

We use default parameters set by the subtask baseline provided by the authors.[4] However, we reduce the training per-device batch-size to 2 to accommodate the large models on an Nvidia Geforce GTX 1080 Ti 12GB GPU. We stop the continual out-of-domain supervised pretraining after 2 epochs.

5 Results

We now present the results for different experimental setups we tried for DialDoc subtask 1.

5.1 Pretraining on Different QA Datasets

Our first set of results portray the differential benefits of different out-of-domain QA datasets when used to pretrain the transformer encoder.

Experiments with `bert-base-uncased` on the validation set (Table 2) portray that pretraining on different QA datasets is indeed beneficial. Datasets like SQuAD, NewsQA, and NaturalQuestions are more useful than SearchQA, and TriviaQA. However, pretraining on complete MRQA-2019 training set does not outperform the individual datasets suggesting that merely introducing more pretraining data might not result in improved performance. Furthermore, conversational QA datasets like CoQA and QuAC, which are more similar in their setup to DialDoc, perform substantially better than any of the other MRQA-2019 training datasets.

We observe similar trends with larger transformers (Table 3). Models pretrained on QuAC or CoQA outperform those pretrained on SQuAD. However, combining CoQA and QuAC during pretraining does not seem to help with the performance on validation or testdev split.

Analyzing Different Transformer Variants Table 3 also contains the results for experiments where `albert-xl` is used to encode the question-context pair. We find that `albert-xl`-based models outperform their `bert` counterparts on validation set. However, they do not generalize well to the Testdev set, which contains about 30% of the test instances but is much smaller than validation set in size (727 samples in testdev vs 3972 in validation set).

[2] https://huggingface.co/datasets/coqa
[3] https://huggingface.co/metrics/squad
[4] https://github.com/doc2dial/sharedtask-dialdoc2021/

5.2 Results on test set

We only submitted our best performing models on the official test set due to a constraint on the number of submissions. Contrary to the trends for testdev phase, `albert-xl` models trained on conversational QA datasets perform the best. `albert-xl + QuAC` is the best-performing single model according to the EM metric ($EM = 52.60$), whereas `albert-xl + CoQA` performs the best on F1 metric ($F1 = 69.48$) on the test set.

5.3 Ensembling

We perform ensembling over the outputs of the model variants to obtain a single unified ranked list. For a given question Q, we produce 20 candidate spans, along with a corresponding probability score ps. We compute rank-scores rs for the answer-spans at rank r as $rs = \frac{1}{\log_2(r+1)}$. We then aggregate the information of the answer spans for the model variants using the following techniques.
Frequent: We chose the answer span which was the most frequent across the model variants.
Rank Score : We chose the answer span which was the highest average rank score.
Probability Score: We chose the answer span which was the highest average probability score.

We observe empirically that ensembling using the probability score performs the best and hence we report the results of ensembling using the probability score (**E**) in Table 3.

We observe the highest gains after ensembling the outputs of all the 5 model variants on the validation test and test-dev set. However, the best performance on the test set was achieved by ensembling over the `albert-xl` models pre-trained independently on CoQA and QuAC (EM = 53.5, $F1$ = 70.9). This was the final submission for our team.

5.4 Informed Data Selection

We investigate the disparate impact of pretraining on different MRQA-19 datasets on the Doc2Dial shared task. Specifically, we explored factors such as answer length, relative position of the answer in the context, question length, and context length in Table 4. We observe that the SQuAD, NewsQA, and NaturalQuestions (NQ) has compartaively longer answers than the other datasets. However, we do not observe a noticeable difference in terms of question length, context length or relative position of the answer in the context, with respect to the other datasets.

Dataset	Question	Answer	Context	Rel Pos
SQuAD	59.6	20.2	754.7	0.462
NaturalQ	47.2	23.7	804.8	0.390
NewsQA	36.8	25.0	3022.7	0.261
TriviaQA	76.1	9.7	4069.3	0.380
SearchQA	80.4	10.9	3818.7	0.392
HotpotQA	114.0	14.3	945.0	0.457
Doc2Dial	61.4	129.3	4814.2	0.427

Table 4: Statistics of Average Question Length, Average Answer Length, Average Context Length, and Average Relative Position of the Answer in the Context for Doc2Dial and different MRQA subsets.

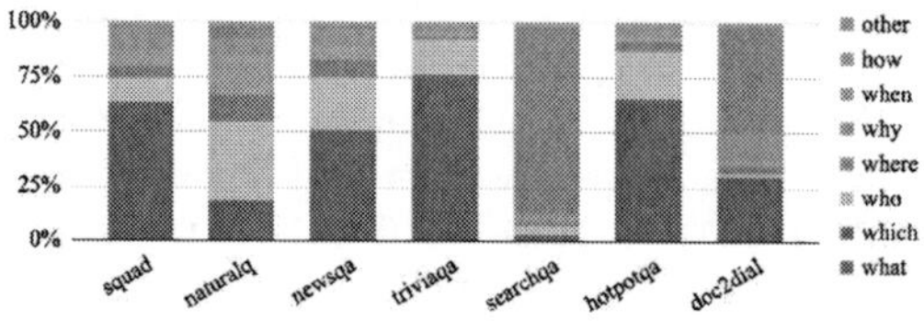

Figure 1: Distribution of Question Words for MRQA.

We also use the dataset of Li and Roth (2002) to train a BERT classifier to predict answer type of a question with 97% accuracy. The coarse-answer types are DESC (Description), NUM (Numerical), ENT (Entity), HUM (Person), LOC (Location) and ABBR (Abbreviation). We use the classifier to gauge the distribution of answer types on MRQA datasets and Doc2Dial. We observe from Figure 2 that a majority of questions in Doc2Dial require a descriptive answer. These DESC type questions are more prevelant in SQuAD, NewsQA, and NQ, which might explain their efficacy.

To ascertain the benefit of intelligent sampling, we pretrain on a much smaller subset of the SQuAD, NewsQA, and NaturalQuestions dataset, which we obtain via intelligent sampling. We select questions which satisfy one of the following criteria, (i) the answer length of the question is ≥ 50, (ii) the question includes 'how' or 'why' question word or (iii) the answer type of the question is 'DESC'. Overall, the size of the selected sample is only 20% of the original dataset, yet achieves a higher EM score than the combined dataset as seen in Table 2. Yet, surprisingly, the performance is lower than each of the individual dataset.

6 Conclusion

Our submission to the DialDoc subtask 1 performs continual pretraining of a transformer-based encoder on out-of-domain QA datasets. Experiments

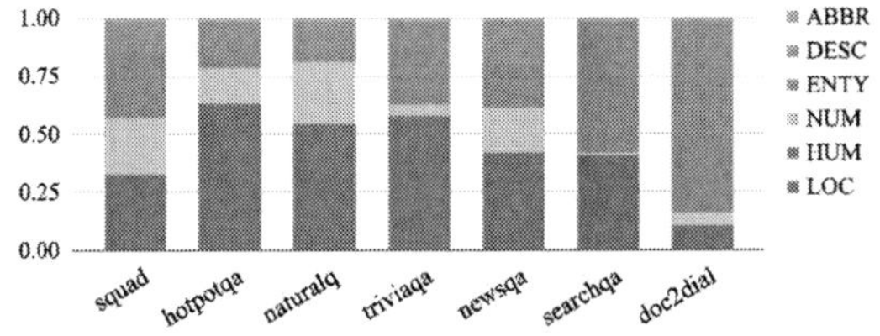

Figure 2: Distribution of Answer Types for MRQA.

with different QA datasets suggest that conversational QA datasets like CoQA and QuAC are highly beneficial as their setup is substantially similar to Doc2Dial, the downstream dataset of interest. Our final submission ensembles two AlBERT-XL models independently pretrained on CoQA and QuAC and achieves an F1-Score of 70.9% and EM-Score of 53.5% on the competition test-set.

Impact Statement

In this work, we tackle the task of question answering (QA) for English language text. While we believe that the proposed methods can be effective in other languages, we leave this exploration for future work. We also acknowledge that QA systems suffer from bias (Li et al., 2020), which often lead to unintended real-world consequences. For the purpose of the shared task, we focused solely on the modeling techniques, but a study of model bias in our systems is necessary.

References

Eunsol Choi, He He, Mohit Iyyer, Mark Yatskar, Wentau Yih, Yejin Choi, Percy Liang, and Luke Zettlemoyer. 2018. QuAC: Question answering in context. In *Proceedings of the 2018 Conference on Empirical Methods in Natural Language Processing*, pages 2174–2184, Brussels, Belgium. Association for Computational Linguistics.

Jacob Devlin, Ming-Wei Chang, Kenton Lee, and Kristina Toutanova. 2019. BERT: Pre-training of deep bidirectional transformers for language understanding. In *Proceedings of the 2019 Conference of the North American Chapter of the Association for Computational Linguistics: Human Language Technologies, Volume 1 (Long and Short Papers)*, pages 4171–4186, Minneapolis, Minnesota. Association for Computational Linguistics.

Matthew Dunn, Levent Sagun, Mike Higgins, V. U. Güney, Volkan Cirik, and Kyunghyun Cho. 2017. Searchqa: A new qa dataset augmented with context from a search engine. *ArXiv*, abs/1704.05179.

Esin Durmus, He He, and Mona Diab. 2020. FEQA: A question answering evaluation framework for faithfulness assessment in abstractive summarization. In *Proceedings of the 58th Annual Meeting of the Association for Computational Linguistics*, pages 5055–5070, Online. Association for Computational Linguistics.

Song Feng, Hui Wan, Chulaka Gunasekara, Siva Patel, Sachindra Joshi, and Luis Lastras. 2020. doc2dial: A goal-oriented document-grounded dialogue dataset. In *Proceedings of the 2020 Conference on Empirical Methods in Natural Language Processing (EMNLP)*, pages 8118–8128, Online. Association for Computational Linguistics.

Adam Fisch, Alon Talmor, Robin Jia, Minjoon Seo, Eunsol Choi, and Danqi Chen. 2019. MRQA 2019 shared task: Evaluating generalization in reading comprehension. In *Proceedings of the 2nd Workshop on Machine Reading for Question Answering*, pages 1–13, Hong Kong, China. Association for Computational Linguistics.

Suchin Gururangan, Ana Marasović, Swabha Swayamdipta, Kyle Lo, Iz Beltagy, Doug Downey, and Noah A. Smith. 2020. Don't stop pretraining: Adapt language models to domains and tasks. In *Proceedings of the 58th Annual Meeting of the Association for Computational Linguistics*, pages 8342–8360, Online. Association for Computational Linguistics.

Mandar Joshi, Eunsol Choi, Daniel Weld, and Luke Zettlemoyer. 2017. TriviaQA: A large scale distantly supervised challenge dataset for reading comprehension. In *Proceedings of the 55th Annual Meeting of the Association for Computational Linguistics (Volume 1: Long Papers)*, pages 1601–1611, Vancouver, Canada. Association for Computational Linguistics.

Tom Kwiatkowski, Jennimaria Palomaki, Olivia Redfield, Michael Collins, Ankur Parikh, Chris Alberti, Danielle Epstein, Illia Polosukhin, Matthew Kelcey, Jacob Devlin, Kenton Lee, Kristina N. Toutanova, Llion Jones, Ming-Wei Chang, Andrew Dai, Jakob Uszkoreit, Quoc Le, and Slav Petrov. 2019. Natural questions: a benchmark for question answering research. *Transactions of the Association of Computational Linguistics.*

Zhenzhong Lan, Mingda Chen, Sebastian Goodman, Kevin Gimpel, Piyush Sharma, and Radu Soricut. 2019. Albert: A lite bert for self-supervised learning of language representations. In *International Conference on Learning Representations.*

Tao Li, Daniel Khashabi, Tushar Khot, Ashish Sabharwal, and Vivek Srikumar. 2020. UNQOVERing stereotyping biases via underspecified questions. In *Findings of the Association for Computational Linguistics: EMNLP 2020*, pages 3475–3489, Online. Association for Computational Linguistics.

Xin Li and Dan Roth. 2002. Learning question classifiers. In *COLING 2002: The 19th International Conference on Computational Linguistics*.

Pranav Rajpurkar, Jian Zhang, Konstantin Lopyrev, and Percy Liang. 2016. SQuAD: 100,000+ questions for machine comprehension of text. In *Proceedings of the 2016 Conference on Empirical Methods in Natural Language Processing*, pages 2383–2392, Austin, Texas. Association for Computational Linguistics.

Siva Reddy, Danqi Chen, and Christopher D. Manning. 2019. CoQA: A conversational question answering challenge. *Transactions of the Association for Computational Linguistics*, 7:249–266.

Adam Trischler, Tong Wang, Xingdi Yuan, Justin Harris, Alessandro Sordoni, Philip Bachman, and Kaheer Suleman. 2017. NewsQA: A machine comprehension dataset. In *Proceedings of the 2nd Workshop on Representation Learning for NLP*, pages 191–200, Vancouver, Canada. Association for Computational Linguistics.

Alex Wang, Kyunghyun Cho, and Mike Lewis. 2020. Asking and answering questions to evaluate the factual consistency of summaries. In *Proceedings of the 58th Annual Meeting of the Association for Computational Linguistics*, pages 5008–5020, Online. Association for Computational Linguistics.

Zhilin Yang, Peng Qi, Saizheng Zhang, Yoshua Bengio, William Cohen, Ruslan Salakhutdinov, and Christopher D. Manning. 2018. HotpotQA: A dataset for diverse, explainable multi-hop question answering. In *Proceedings of the 2018 Conference on Empirical Methods in Natural Language Processing*, pages 2369–2380, Brussels, Belgium. Association for Computational Linguistics.

Building Goal-oriented Document-grounded Dialogue Systems

Xi Chen[¶] [*], **Faner Lin**[¶*], **Yeju Zhou**[¶*], **Kaixin Ma**[¶],
Jonathan Francis[¶§], **Eric Nyberg**[¶], **Alessandro Oltramari**[§]
[¶]Language Technologies Institute, Carnegie Mellon University
[§]Human-Machine Collaboration, Bosch Research Pittsburgh
{xc3, fanerl, yejuz, kaixinm, jmf1, ehn}@cs.cmu.edu,
alessandro.oltramari@us.bosch.com

Abstract

In this paper, we describe our systems for solving the two Doc2Dial shared task: knowledge identification and response generation. We proposed several pre-processing and post-processing methods, and we experimented with data augmentation by pre-training the models on other relevant datasets. Our best model for knowledge identification outperformed the baseline by 10.5+ *f1*-score on the test-dev split, and our best model for response generation outperformed the baseline by 11+ *SacreBleu* score on the test-dev split.

1 Introduction

There has been a recent surge of interest in building domain-specific question answering (QA) systems, in both academia and industry. Compelling real-world applications include customer services and decision-support, wherein there is strong reliance on such QA systems to be of high quality. A significant challenges for building QA systems is that domain-specific data is relatively sparse and much noisier, compared to samples from well-studied public benchmark datasets. Also, when the answer is not explicitly present in the context, models must generate new answers instead of extracting from document, adding complexity to the problem.

In this paper, we make efforts toward building domain-oriented question answering systems, by tackling the two Doc2Dial shared-tasks[1]: *knowledge identification* and *response generation*. For knowledge identification (Subtask1), the main goal is to identify the grounding knowledge, in form of a document span, for the next-agent conversational turn. For response generation (Subtask2), the main objective is to generate the next-agent response, in natural language. We experiment with various baseline models, and we developed and evaluated our proposed solutions. Some improvement strategies we tried include post-processing, hyper-parameter tuning, and pre-training on other well-known datasets such as SQuAD (Rajpurkar et al., 2016). We found that with carefully-selected hyperparameters, and with pre-processing and post-processing heuristics, the baseline model's performance can be significantly improved: our best model is able to out-perform the provided baseline by 10.5+ *f1*-score on the test-dev split for Subtask1, and our best model for Subtask2 out-performed the baseline by 11+ *SacreBleu* score on test-dev.

2 Related Work

There are many previous works that study the problem of dialogue-based question answering. Some of them only focused on answering the questions based on dialogue history alone (Ma et al., 2018; Li et al., 2020), while, for others, the dialogue and question-answer pairs are based on a document (Choi et al., 2018). Most of these tasks are extractive in nature, meaning that the exact answer can be located in the document or dialogue. Among them, CoQA (Reddy et al., 2019) is the most similar task to Doc2Dial dataset. The main objective of the CoQA challenge is to measure machine learning models' ability to comprehend text and answer related questions that appear in a conversation; also, because some answers may not appear explicitly in the document, the model may be required to synthesize the answer based on evidence. The two sub-tasks we study in this paper differ from those described above—mainly in terms of dataset attributes. The Doc2Dial dataset mostly contains long documents and dialogues that inter-connect with each other. Moreover, the ground-truth answers in Doc2Dial are usually long as well, which makes the associated prediction tasks harder to

* Equal contribution; alphabetized by surname

[1]https://doc2dial.github.io/workshop2021/shared.html

Proceedings of the 1st Workshop on Document-grounded Dialogue and Conversational Question Answering, pages 109–112
August 5–6, 2021. ©2021 Association for Computational Linguistics

tackle. Thus, the models and heuristics we have developed are mainly targeted towards handling these specific scenarios and problems.

3 Experiments

3.1 Dataset

The Doc2Dial dataset (Feng et al., 2020) contains two tasks: knowledge identification (Subtask1) and response generation (Subtask2). For knowledge identification: given a long document as the context, and a dialogue history between a user and an agent, the task is to identify a span of text in the document that serves as the knowledge which grounds for the next dialogue turn from agent. For response generation: given a full document and the dialogue history, the task is to directly generate an agent response for the next turn in natural language. We tackle both tasks in this paper and describe our approaches below.

3.2 Baselines

For Subtask1, the baseline model is the BERT-large-uncased-whole-word-masking model (Devlin et al., 2019). A span-extraction head is added on top of BERT, and the model is fine-tuned on the Doc2Dial knowledge identification dataset. For each example, an entire document is used as the context and the reverse concatenated dialogue history is used as the question.

For Subtask2, the baseline model is the BART-large-CNN (Lewis et al., 2020) model: a pre-trained BART model is first fine-tuned on the CNN summarization task, then fine-tuned on Doc2Dial response generation dataset. The entire document and full dialogue history are used as the context and the model is trained to generate the next dialogue response.

3.3 Approaches: Knowledge Identification

Based on error analysis of baseline results, we found that the model is making a lot of empty predictions. This is mainly because the documents in Doc2Dial are very long, necessitating a sliding-window approach. Consequently, if a text chunk does not contain any relevant information to the question, the model would predict *no-answer* with a very high confidence, preventing the model from choosing answers from other chunks. To alleviate this issue, we developed heuristics to post-process the prediction at inference time, to ensure that the model produces a valid answer. Specifically, we skip the empty prediction and select the candidate with the second highest probability at inference time. Also, prediction with the highest probability is extended to a longer span if another prediction candidate contains the prediction with the highest probability as sub-string and also has a higher start or end position probability. Besides post-processing, we also increase the sliding-window overlap size to 256 and max answer length to 80 during training, so as to get more positive instances. Moreover, since the Doc2dial dataset size is relatively small, we pre-trained the model on other QA datasets and then fine-tuned on Doc2dial. To this end, we selected SQuAD 1.1, because it is a widely used span-extraction dataset, and CoQA, because of its similar task structure, where models must answer questions based on both dialogue history and document-based context.

3.3.1 Approaches: Response Generation

For Subtask2, we start with error analysis of the baseline model and found that the model often generate responses based on the irrelevant content in the supporting documents. We hypothesize that this is because the document and the dialogue history are too long, thus it is hard for models to locate the relevant information and generate a response at the same time. If we keep only relevant knowledge grounding as input, the model will be able to generate better responses.

To test this hypothesis, we used the model trained on Subtask1 to select a chunk of document to feed in as Subtask2 input, instead of the full document. Since the span selection model is not perfect, it can select a completely wrong span, which would prevent the Subtask2 model from producing a valid response. Thus to increase the recall, we start with the best-selected span and iterate over the top-20 span predictions, in order to expand the selected span boundary and cover the next best prediction, if the the next best span is near the current selection boundary. Here, we set the threshold to be less than 500 characters away. For example, given the current start and end indices of (400, 520), if the next span prediction is (580, 650), we will change the boundary to (400, 650). However, if the next span prediction is (1200, 1300), we will stop iteration and return (400, 520). We also experimented with the ground-truth response grounding span, in order to find an upper bound of this approach.

Additionally, we only append the past two dialogue

turns to the supporting document in the input, instead of using the whole dialogue history as in (Reddy et al., 2019); it is found that most questions in a dialogue only have limited dependency, and including the past two dialogue turns may give comparable performance as including the complete dialogue history.
Another adjustment we make is to feed the past two turns of the dialogue to the decoder as input and the response will be generated following the past two dialogue turns. The intuition is that the decoder will also have more context to look at when generating its response, and we think this will make the task easier to learn.
Finally, we are interested in studying the effect of adding data. Thus, we re-formulated the CoQA dataset into a dialogue response task, and we pre-trained the BART model on CoQA before fine-tuning on Doc2Dial. Since the documents in CoQA are much shorter, we did not perform span selection as is proposed for Doc2Dial.

4 Result and Analysis

For Subtask1, we report *f1*-score and exact-match score on the dev set for our proposed method. For Subtask2, we report *SacreBleu* (Post, 2018) on the dev set. Finally, we report the test set results achieved with our best model, for both tasks.

4.1 Sub-task1: Knowledge Identification

The results for Subtask1 are shown in Table 1. We see that applying the post-processing heuristics improved the results by a significant margin. For pre-training the model on SQuAD and CoQA datasets, we see that the model achieves a small performance gain in both cases, suggesting that more data is helping the model learning more effectively and that the selection of these pre-training tasks does not conflict with the downstream task at hand. The advantage of CoQA over SQuAD also suggests that tasks with similar structure may transfer better. Finally, with the increased size of the overlap between each sliding-window, we see a decent improvement over the baseline, indicating the usefulness of the carefully chosen hyper-parameters. However, when we combined the larger overlap stride with pre-training on CoQA or SQuAD, we did not see further improvement; we leave the further investigation of this issue to future work.

Table 1: Model performance on Doc2Dial sub-task1. Here "Post." means post-processing.

Model	F1	EM
BERT	63.80	51.79
BERT + Post.	69.73	54.91
BERT + Post. + SQuAD	70.89	56.31
BERT + Post. + CoQA	72.15	57.18
BERT + Post. + 256 stride + 80 len	**72.74**	**58.53**

Table 2: Model performance on Doc2Dial sub-task2. "SS" means span selection and "DI" means additional decoder input.

Model	SacreBleu
BART (CNN)	17.69
BART (CNN) + SS	18.82
BART (CNN) + Gold span	24.86
BART + SS + DI	**31.61**
BART + SS + DI + CoQA	27.87

4.2 Sub-task2: Response Generation

The results for Subtask2 are shown in Table 2. We see that when using the selected span of text, instead of the full document, we achieved a small improvement on Bleu score; when using the ground-truth grounding span, we got a large improvement. This verified our hypothesis that shorter input will help the model generate relevant responses. The gap between these two settings suggest that a stronger span-selection model would further help the Subtask2 model improve.

Regarding the strategy of adding the last two dialogue turns to the decoder input: we switched from BART model pre-trained on CNN to a plain BART model, since the task setup is less like summarization and more like sentence completion. We see that, by adding the last 2 dialogue turns, the model's performance is improved by a large margin, showing that providing more context to the decoder indeed helps the model learn better. On the other hand, we see that pre-training on CoQA dataset actually leads to worse performance. We hypothesize that this is because of document length, where questions and answers for most dialogue turns in the CoQA dataset are much shorter than those of Doc2Dial datasets: models pre-trained on CoQA may not glean useful training signals for Doc2Dial.

Table 3: Results on Doc2Dial sub-task1 test splits.

Model	Test-Dev F1	Test-Dev EM	Test F1	Test EM
Baseline	59.51	45.45	-	-
Schlussstein	**70.12**	**56.57**	**67.31**	**50.32**

Table 4: Results on Doc2Dial Subtask2 test splits

Model	Test-dev	Test
Baseline	16.73	-
Schlussstein	**27.93**	**30.68**

4.3 Leaderboard Submission

We submitted our best models to both subtask leaderboards, and the results are shown in tables 3 and 4. Overall, our models out-performed baselines by large margins, and we got 8th place for Subtask1 and 6th place for Subtask2.

5 Conclusion

In this paper, we proposed several pre/post-processing heuristics that improve the model performance, on both knowledge identification and response generation tasks in the Doc2Dial challenge. We also found that pre-training on other question answering datasets only slightly improves the performance on knowledge identification, but did not help for response generation task. For future work, we think it is worth looking into other directions for improvement, including incorporating external knowledge bases (Ma et al., 2019) or synthetic data generation (Ma et al., 2021).

References

Eunsol Choi, He He, Mohit Iyyer, Mark Yatskar, Wen-tau Yih, Yejin Choi, Percy Liang, and Luke Zettlemoyer. 2018. QuAC: Question answering in context. In *Proceedings of the 2018 Conference on Empirical Methods in Natural Language Processing*, pages 2174–2184, Brussels, Belgium. Association for Computational Linguistics.

Jacob Devlin, Ming-Wei Chang, Kenton Lee, and Kristina Toutanova. 2019. BERT: Pre-training of deep bidirectional transformers for language understanding. In *Proceedings of the 2019 Conference of the North American Chapter of the Association for Computational Linguistics: Human Language Technologies, Volume 1 (Long and Short Papers)*, pages 4171–4186, Minneapolis, Minnesota. Association for Computational Linguistics.

Song Feng, Hui Wan, Chulaka Gunasekara, Siva Patel, Sachindra Joshi, and Luis Lastras. 2020. doc2dial: A goal-oriented document-grounded dialogue dataset. In *Proceedings of the 2020 Conference on Empirical Methods in Natural Language Processing (EMNLP)*. Association for Computational Linguistics.

Mike Lewis, Yinhan Liu, Naman Goyal, Marjan Ghazvininejad, Abdelrahman Mohamed, Omer Levy, Veselin Stoyanov, and Luke Zettlemoyer. 2020. BART: Denoising sequence-to-sequence pretraining for natural language generation, translation, and comprehension. In *Proceedings of the 58th Annual Meeting of the Association for Computational Linguistics*, pages 7871–7880, Online. Association for Computational Linguistics.

Jiaqi Li, Ming Liu, Min-Yen Kan, Zihao Zheng, Zekun Wang, Wenqiang Lei, Ting Liu, and Bing Qin. 2020. Molweni: A challenge multiparty dialogues-based machine reading comprehension dataset with discourse structure. In *Proceedings of the 28th International Conference on Computational Linguistics*, pages 2642–2652, Barcelona, Spain (Online). International Committee on Computational Linguistics.

Kaixin Ma, Jonathan Francis, Quanyang Lu, Eric Nyberg, and Alessandro Oltramari. 2019. Towards generalizable neuro-symbolic systems for commonsense question answering. *arXiv preprint arXiv:1910.14087*.

Kaixin Ma, Filip Ilievski, Jonathan Francis, Yonatan Bisk, Eric Nyberg, and Alessandro Oltramari. 2021. Knowledge-driven data construction for zero-shot evaluation in commonsense question answering. *In Proceedings of the 35th AAAI Conference on Artificial Intelligence (AAAI-21)*.

Kaixin Ma, Tomasz Jurczyk, and Jinho D. Choi. 2018. Challenging reading comprehension on daily conversation: Passage completion on multiparty dialog. In *Proceedings of the 2018 Conference of the North American Chapter of the Association for Computational Linguistics: Human Language Technologies, Volume 1 (Long Papers)*, pages 2039–2048, New Orleans, Louisiana. Association for Computational Linguistics.

Matt Post. 2018. A call for clarity in reporting BLEU scores. In *Proceedings of the Third Conference on Machine Translation: Research Papers*, pages 186–191, Belgium, Brussels. Association for Computational Linguistics.

Pranav Rajpurkar, Jian Zhang, Konstantin Lopyrev, and Percy Liang. 2016. Squad: 100,000+ questions for machine comprehension of text. *arXiv preprint arXiv:1606.05250*.

Siva Reddy, Danqi Chen, and Christopher D Manning. 2019. Coqa: A conversational question answering challenge. *Transactions of the Association for Computational Linguistics*, 7:249–266.

Agenda Pushing in Email to Thwart Phishing

Hyundong Cho and **Genevieve Bartlett** and **Marjorie Freedman**
Information Sciences Institute
University of Southern California
{jcho, bartlett, mrf}@isi.edu

Abstract

In this work, we draw parallels in automatically responding to emails for combating social-engineering attacks and document-grounded response generation. We lay out the blueprint of our approach and illustrate our reasoning. E-mails are longer than dialogue utterances and often contain multiple intents. To respond to phishing emails, we need to make decisions similar to those for document-grounded responses—deciding what parts of long text to use and how to address each intent to generate a knowledgeable multi-component response that pushes scammers towards agendas. We propose Puppeteer as a promising solution to this end: a hybrid system that uses customizable probabilistic finite state transducers to orchestrate pushing agendas coupled with neural dialogue systems that generate responses to unexpected prompts. We emphasize the need for this system by highlighting each component's strengths and weaknesses and show how they complement each other.

1 Introduction

The Anti-Phishing Working Group observed a doubling of phishing attacks over 2020 with business e-mail compromise scams costing an average of $75,000$ per incident (APWG, 2021). Scammers use these attacks to reach a wide audience of victims and perform targeted attacks on high-value targets. Even when not fully successful, these attacks waste victims' time and resources.

To fight back against scammers, individuals—colloquially called *scambaiters*—have demonstrated that careful engagement with scammers can waste a scammer's time, thus reducing resources for new attacks. Engaging with scammers through dialogue in the form of email also opens up opportunities to push scammers towards actions beneficial for defense and attribution, such as getting scammers to visit a specialized honeypot or divulging information. This information can aid in identifying coordinated, large-scale attack campaigns and help with attack attribution. In this paper we introduce a framework for automating dialogue engagement with scammers and pushing agendas to get scammers to take actions.

Eliciting information from scammers and continuing an email sequence to waste their time presents challenges not addressed by existing dialogue systems. Specifically, this area of automated dialogue is challenging because: 1) email conversations are significantly different from chit-chat conversations: each turn is longer and thus usually contains more information that needs to be incorporated into the response and has multiple intents/requests in a single turn that should be addressed 2) the initial dialogue topics can range greatly and change quickly and a bot must respond appropriately to new topics, goals and questions from the scammer to appear human 3) there is a high cost associated with the scammer recognizing the dialogue is automated as any work put in for trust building is lost if the attacker suspects he/she is talking to a bot and 4) the scammer's agenda is independent of the bot's agenda– thus the bot needs to maintain awareness of its own goals without ignoring the competing goals of the scammer.

Using "canned" responses chosen by following a pre-written script, or performing deep-learning over expected conversation flows for eliciting information are reasonable approaches to address the challenges of keeping responses targeted, topical and persuasive without a lapse in coherency in dialogue. However, such approaches will not meet the second challenge of being robust enough to respond to open dialogue and unexpected scamming intents in a topical and directed manner.

In this paper, we introduce our approach to address all challenges with a modular hybrid dialogue system, Puppeteer. Puppeteer uses multiple Fi-

Proceedings of the 1st Workshop on Document-grounded Dialogue and Conversational Question Answering, pages 113–118
August 5–6, 2021.

nite State Transducers (FSTs) to push and track multiple agendas in uncooperative dialogue and combines this with a neural dialogue system to keep conversation topics free-flowing and natural sounding while effectively incorporating information provided from the incoming email. We discuss our progress in building our approach and have released our framework for public use[1].

2 The Puppeteer Framework

Eliciting information from SE attackers introduces a niche but important problem space that requires a specialized dialogue system to address the distinct trade-offs and risks involved in engaging with scammers for the purpose of pushing the scammer into certain actions. In this section, we introduce our dialogue framework Puppeteer and discuss how our framework deals with open-ended dialogue, while inserting and tracking progress towards specific desired actions.

First, to carry out and track progress towards specific actions, Puppeteer uses probabilistic finite state transducers (FSTs). The FST approach enables a task-oriented framework for belief tracking and context-specific natural language understanding, which both keep the conversation moving towards specific goals and bolsters accurate interpretation of any extracted information.

Dialogue based on FSTs, however, can be inflexible and brittle in the face of open-ended conversations. An FST-based dialogue approach is not, on its own, appropriate for SMS, social media, and email conversations if the goal is to keep the conversation going without revealing the responder is a bot. To address this, the Puppeteer framework combines its FST approach with deep learning and neural generative approaches. Dialogue generated through the use of pre-trained models is folded in with responses prescribed by any active FSTs in a conversation. The goal in this hybrid approach is to "script" the persuasive dialogue designed to push agendas, while incorporating a more open-ended neural dialogue system to keep the scammer engaged. An illustrative example of this ensemble is shown in Figure 1.

Pushing Agendas with FSTs A Puppeteer agenda is defined by the states and transitions of an FST as well as the cues which indicate that a transition should be taken. The FST for an agenda captures the different pathways a conversation can go when requesting a specific action and responding to possible push-back against requests. At each turn in the conversation, the incoming message is evaluated for all cues in all active agenda FSTs. Additionally, the message is evaluated for a "non-event" for each agenda—the probability that the incoming message does not contain any cues for a particular agenda.

Each cue has a *cue detector* which recognizes when an indicator was found, and provides a confidence value for that decision. These confidence values are then combined with the non-event probability for an agenda and normalized. This normalization must support comparison between different cue detector confidence values and therefore is specific to the set of detectors used for an agenda. For each agenda's FST, Puppeteer tracks the probability distribution across all possible states in the FST as the conversation progresses, retiring agendas as they stall out or complete and adding new agendas based on policy rules dictating when and how to kick off agendas.

Determining when an agenda is complete is also based on thresholding. Ultimately, when the system reaches a high enough confidence the conversation has transitioned an agenda's FST to a terminus state, the agenda is considered complete. By default, Puppeteer does not use fixed thresholds for determining confidence for completion, but instead uses relative probabilities between states and configurable thresholds. This is because longer conversations tend to disperse total probability throughout all states over time. For agendas which are expected to complete over fewer turns, this default can be overridden.

We anticipate a wide range of agendas may be needed. The Puppeteer framework is written in Python and designed to be modular, enabling the easy addition of new agendas (backed by FSTs) and allowing for modular incorporation of nearly any natural language understanding approaches in cue detection. Additionally, defining response actions is extensible to enable differing approaches for response generation. To define a Puppeteer agenda, a user describes the state machine and any custom policy and thresholds in a YAML file. Default behaviors can be easily customized by overriding the appropriate *delegator mixin* class.

Currently, cue detectors are managed by Snips NLU (Coucke et al., 2018). For each transition cue, the user supplies a file of example sentences

[1] `https://github.com/STEELISI/Puppeteer`

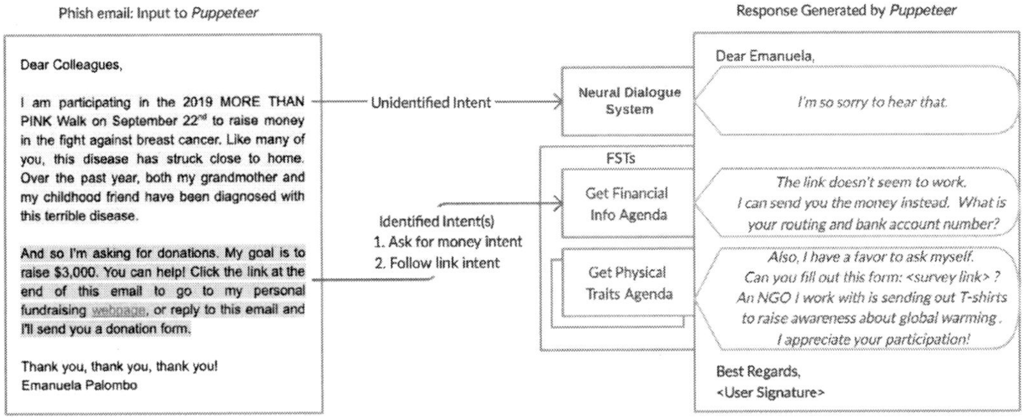

Figure 1: An example of a response generated by a neural dialogue system folded into the script indicatored by the FST to pursue an information collection agenda. Each component complements one another to generate an effective response for eliciting the attacker's information.

or phrases which indicate a transition should be taken, and optionally a file of examples for negative indicators. For example, if an cue detector is looking for text that someone lives in a location, a positive example would be "I live in New York" and a negative example would be "I want to visit New York". These negative examples help filter out false positives. These files are used to create a Snips engine which gives confidence scores on found intents in incoming messages. In practice, we have found most indicators need only 20–40 positive and negative example sentences each as cues are only employed in contexts likely to contain a small set of specific intents and need only to distinguish between "no intent" and the handful of intents in an active agenda. The framework is designed so Snips NLU can be replaced with another NLU approach. To do so, the user must supply a function to Puppeteer which takes in incoming message content and returns a confidence score a particular cue is found in the incoming messages.

Each agenda has a configurable number of associated actions with each state in its FST that can be kicked off any time the probability the conversation has reached policy thresholds for that state and threshold. The default action for all states is to pull a response from a template file, and users can provide additional functions and link these to states in their FST definition for an agenda. In use with our phishing defense system, most agendas have additional actions for states where the scammer has responded with information we pass to other functions of our phishing system such as the attribution module.

Neural Dialogue System: In our current implementation, the neural dialogue system can be chosen to be either a BERT-based question and answering system called Closed-Domain Question Answering (cdQA) or a fine-tuned GPT-2 model.

cdQA offers indirect functionality as a dialogue system by retrieving relevant segments of text to a given query. As its name suggests, it is actually closed-domain in the sense that it only retrieves answers from a given set of source documents, but the source documents can be expanded to accommodate a variety of domains.

Our GPT-2 model is SpolinBot, which can be used as a stand-alone dialogue system. SpolinBot is first fine-tuned with Personachat (Zhang et al., 2018) to adapt to the dialogue domain and then further tuned with SPOLIN to ground its response to the incoming email by learning how to incorporate the "Yes, and" principle of improvisational theatre (Cho and May, 2020). We use training details outlined by Wolf et al. (2019).

Importance of a Hybrid Approach The importance of correctly integrating the components becomes evident by observing the shortcomings of each component when used in isolation. Figure 2 demonstrates components in isolation. The FST approach is stilted in pushing an agenda as it is limited to responses for agendas deemed relevant to the conversation which does not directly address questions. The neural dialogue systems cannot push an agenda, but respond to the prompt.

In contrast, Figure 1 demonstrates the strengths of each component when they are ideally combined together to generate an effective response.

Putting them together: For each paragraph from the email other than the header and the signa-

SCAMMER: Are you interested in a job? Let's set up a meeting.

FST: Where are you based out of? What time works for you?

NDS-YESAND: Yes, I've been looking for one.

NDS-QNA: I can see what times work.

Figure 2: Examples that highlight the weaknesses of individual components. The FST approach is stilted in pushing an agenda as it does not address the question posed by the scammer. The neural dialogue system (NDS) fails to respond to specific tasks.

ture, Puppeteer currently consults the cdQA component for questions and the *yes-and bot* for non-question text and text which has no indicators for any agenda. As shown in Figure 1, the responses from the neural dialogue component and the Puppeteer agendas are naively appended in order of the parts of the email that they respond to. However, it may often be the case that some parts of the email do not necessarily need a response. Improving how and when components are called on for responses and how these responses are combined is an ongoing effort. So far, empirical results show our current combining approach does relatively well on short prompts, but this analysis is particularly challenging due to the lack of automatic evaluation metrics for neural dialogue systems and the large variance of resulting models based on different training data.

3 Related Work

Social engineering (SE) is the act of getting users to compromise information systems. Contrary to technical attacks directly on network and computer systems, SE attacks target humans with access to information and manipulate these target users to divulge confidential information (Krombholz et al., 2015). Phishing is a specific type of social engineering attack in which targets are contacted through digital channels such as e-mail, SMS or social media to lure individuals into providing sensitive data such as personally identifiable information, system log in credentials or organization details (Hong, 2012). Our work focuses on generating dialogue to engage such scammers over one or more of these digital, text-based channels.

Most research efforts addressing SE look at detection (e.g. Basnet et al. (2008); Chen et al. (2014); Singh et al. (2015)) and defending against such attacks by dropping or otherwise terminating such attacks (e.g. Chaudhry et al. (2016); Gragg (2003); Chandra et al. (2015)). An anti-phishing project by Netsafe[2] picks a curated personality and uses automated email responses to waste the attacker's time as much as possible, but its not open-sourced and little is known about how it works. Our system is similar to Netsafe's project in that it is focused on *actively engaging* scammers through automated dialogue, but Puppeteer also *pushes scammers towards actions* favorable for attribution and defense. We rely on separate detection methods to identify messages and senders the Puppeteer dialogue system should engage.

Only recently have research efforts looked at using automated text-based dialogue to respond to scammers. Li et al. (2019) leverage intent and semantic labels in non-collaborative dialogue corpora to distinguish on-task and off-task dialogue and therefore enhance human evaluation scores for engagement and coherence. We aim to achieve a similar objective with the additional goal of pushing a range of agendas and responding appropriately and topically over a broad range of open dialogue. Hobbyists and commercial developers also have looked at automatic responses to scammers. These efforts are interactive spoken-word approaches that detect silence in conversation and interject prerecorded non sequiturs to waste a scam caller's time (Oberhaus, 2018; TelTech, 2020). While one of the goals of our work is to waste scammer time, Puppeteer performs natural language understanding to engage scammers at a deeper level and push agendas with the ultimate goal of pushing scammers into actions which aid attribution.

Our hybrid system is inspired by a large body of existing work in dialogue systems. Hudson and Newell (1992) propose probabilistic FSTs for managing dialogue under uncertainty, while many dialogue systems incorporate FSTs for management functionality in spoken dialogue systems (Pietquin and Dutoit, 2003; Chu et al., 2005; Sontag, 2006; Hori et al., 2009). Recent interests in large pre-trained language models based on Transformers and open-domain question answering systems paved the way for our neural network approaches to be used as open-domain dialogue sys-

[2]`https://rescam.org`

tems, such as GPT-2 or DrQA (Vaswani et al., 2017; Devlin et al., 2019; Liu et al., 2019; Radford et al., 2018; Chen et al., 2017; Farias et al., 2019). The novelty of Puppeteer is in the combination of these two approaches to address the unique challenges of system-scammer dialogue.

4 Conclusion

In this paper we introduced email response generation for phishing as a challenging dialogue domain. Our approach draws on similarities with document-grounded response generation. As a first step to address the challenges of automating phishing response, we proposed Puppeteer and made it publicly available. Puppeteer's modular architecture makes it easy to augment or replace its components to tackle individual challenges. These components complement one another in generating suitable responses for engaging scammers and inserting agendas, but it remains an open problem to seamlessly combine response components into a composed email response.

This material is based on research sponsored by the AFRL and DARPA under agreement number FA8650-18-C-7878. The views and conclusions contained herein are those of the authors and should not be interpreted as necessarily representing the official policies or endorsements, either expressed or implied, of the AFRL, DARPA, or the U.S. Government.

References

APWG. 2021. Phishing activity trends report 4th quarter 2020.

Ram Basnet, Srinivas Mukkamala, and Andrew H Sung. 2008. Detection of phishing attacks: A machine learning approach. In *Soft Computing Applications in Industry*, pages 373–383. Springer.

J Vijaya Chandra, Narasimham Challa, and Sai Kiran Pasupuleti. 2015. Intelligence based defense system to protect from advanced persistent threat by means of social engineering on social cloud platform. *Indian Journal of Science and Technology*, 8(28):1.

Junaid Ahsenali Chaudhry, Shafique Ahmad Chaudhry, and Robert G Rittenhouse. 2016. Phishing attacks and defenses. *International Journal of Security and Its Applications*, 10(1):247–256.

Danqi Chen, Adam Fisch, Jason Weston, and Antoine Bordes. 2017. Reading wikipedia to answer open-domain questions. *arXiv preprint arXiv:1704.00051*.

Yi-Shin Chen, Yi-Hsuan Yu, Huei-Sin Liu, and Pang-Chieh Wang. 2014. Detect phishing by checking content consistency. In *Proceedings of the 2014 IEEE 15th International Conference on Information Reuse and Integration (IEEE IRI 2014)*, pages 109–119. IEEE.

Hyundong Cho and Jonathan May. 2020. Grounding conversations with improvised dialogues. In *Proceedings of the 58th Annual Meeting of the Association for Computational Linguistics*, pages 2398–2413, Online. Association for Computational Linguistics.

Shiu-Wah Chu, Ian O'Neill, Philip Hanna, and Michael McTear. 2005. An approach to multi-strategy dialogue management. In *Ninth European Conference on Speech Communication and Technology*.

Alice Coucke, Alaa Saade, Adrien Ball, Théodore Bluche, Alexandre Caulier, David Leroy, Clément Doumouro, Thibault Gisselbrecht, Francesco Caltagirone, Thibaut Lavril, et al. 2018. Snips voice platform: an embedded spoken language understanding system for private-by-design voice interfaces. *arXiv preprint arXiv:1805.10190*, pages 12–16.

Jacob Devlin, Ming-Wei Chang, Kenton Lee, and Kristina Toutanova. 2019. Bert: Pre-training of deep bidirectional transformers for language understanding. In *NAACL-HLT*.

André Farias, Félix Mikaeliean, Matyas Amrouche, Théo Nazon, and Olivier Sans. 2019. cdqa: Closed domain question answering. `https://github.com/cdqa-suite/cdQA`.

David Gragg. 2003. A multi-level defense against social engineering. *SANS Reading Room*, 13.

Jason Hong. 2012. The state of phishing attacks. *Commun. ACM*, 55(1):74–81.

Chiori Hori, Kiyonori Ohtake, Teruhisa Misu, Hideki Kashioka, and Satoshi Nakamura. 2009. Statistical dialog management applied to wfst-based dialog systems. In *2009 IEEE International Conference on Acoustics, Speech and Signal Processing*, pages 4793–4796. IEEE.

Scott E Hudson and Gary L Newell. 1992. Probabilistic state machines: dialog management for inputs with uncertainty. In *Proceedings of the 5th annual ACM symposium on User interface software and technology*, pages 199–208. ACM.

Katharina Krombholz, Heidelinde Hobel, Markus Huber, and Edgar Weippl. 2015. Advanced social engineering attacks. *Journal of Information Security and applications*, 22:113–122.

Yu Li, Kun Qian, Weiyan Shi, and Zhou Yu. 2019. End-to-end trainable non-collaborative dialog system. *arXiv preprint arXiv:1911.10742*.

Yinhan Liu, Myle Ott, Naman Goyal, Jingfei Du, Mandar Joshi, Danqi Chen, Omer Levy, Mike Lewis, Luke Zettlemoyer, and Veselin Stoyanov. 2019. Roberta: A robustly optimized bert pretraining approach. *arXiv preprint arXiv:1907.11692*.

Daniel Oberhaus. 2018. The story of lenny, the internet's favorite telemarketing troll.

Olivier Pietquin and Thierry Dutoit. 2003. Aided design of finite-state dialogue management systems. In *2003 International Conference on Multimedia and Expo. ICME'03. Proceedings (Cat. No. 03TH8698)*, volume 3, pages III–545. IEEE.

Alec Radford, Karthik Narasimhan, Tim Salimans, and Ilya Sutskever. 2018. Improving language understanding by generative pre-training. *URL https://s3-us-west-2. amazonaws. com/openai-assets/researchcovers/languageunsupervised/language understanding paper. pdf*.

Priyanka Singh, Yogendra PS Maravi, and Sanjeev Sharma. 2015. Phishing websites detection through supervised learning networks. In *2015 International Conference on Computing and Communications Technologies (ICCCT)*, pages 61–65. IEEE.

Daniel Sonntag. 2006. Towards combining finite-state, ontologies, and data driven approaches to dialogue management for multimodal question answering. In *Proceedings of the 5th Slovenian First International Language Technology Conference (IS-LTC 2006)*.

TelTech. 2020. Robokiller, the app that stops spam calls forever.

Ashish Vaswani, Noam Shazeer, Niki Parmar, Jakob Uszkoreit, Llion Jones, Aidan N Gomez, Łukasz Kaiser, and Illia Polosukhin. 2017. Attention is all you need. In *Advances in neural information processing systems*, pages 5998–6008.

Thomas Wolf, Victor Sanh, Julien Chaumond, and Clement Delangue. 2019. Transfertransfo: A transfer learning approach for neural network based conversational agents. *arXiv preprint arXiv:1901.08149*.

Saizheng Zhang, Emily Dinan, Jack Urbanek, Arthur Szlam, Douwe Kiela, and Jason Weston. 2018. Personalizing dialogue agents: I have a dog, do you have pets too? In *Proceedings of the 56th Annual Meeting of the Association for Computational Linguistics (Volume 1: Long Papers)*, pages 2204–2213.

Can I Be of Further Assistance? Using Unstructured Knowledge Access to Improve Task-oriented Conversational Modeling

Di Jin
Amazon Alexa AI
djinamzn@amazon.com

Seokhwan Kim
Amazon Alexa AI
seokhwk@amazon.com

Dilek Hakkani-Tur
Amazon Alexa AI
hakkanit@amazon.com

Abstract

Most prior work on task-oriented dialogue systems are restricted to limited coverage of domain APIs. However, users oftentimes have requests that are out of the scope of these APIs. This work focuses on responding to these beyond-API-coverage user turns by incorporating external, unstructured knowledge sources. Our approach works in a pipelined manner with knowledge-seeking turn detection, knowledge selection, and response generation in sequence. We introduce novel data augmentation methods for the first two steps and demonstrate that the use of information extracted from dialogue context improves the knowledge selection and end-to-end performances. Through experiments, we achieve state-of-the-art performance for both automatic and human evaluation metrics on the DSTC9 Track 1 benchmark dataset, validating the effectiveness of our contributions.

1 Introduction

Driven by the fast progress of natural language processing techniques, we are now witnessing a variety of task-orientated dialogue systems being used in daily life. These agents traditionally rely on pre-defined APIs to complete the tasks that users request (Williams et al., 2017; Eric et al., 2017); however, some user requests are related to the task domain but beyond these APIs' coverage (Kim et al., 2020a). For example, while task-oriented agents can help users book a hotel, they fall short of answering potential follow-up questions users may have, such as "whether they can bring their pets to the hotel". These beyond-API-coverage user requests frequently refer to the task or entities that were discussed in the prior conversation and can be addressed by interpreting them in context and retrieving relevant domain knowledge from web pages, for example, from textual descriptions and frequently asked questions (FAQs). Most task-oriented dialogue systems do not incorporate these external knowledge sources into dialogue modeling, making conversational interactions inefficient.

To address this problem, Kim et al. (2020a) recently introduced a new challenge on task-oriented conversational modeling with unstructured knowledge access, and provided datasets that are annotated for three related sub-tasks: (1) knowledge-seeking turn detection, (2) knowledge selection, and (3) knowledge-grounded response generation (one data sample is in Section B.1 of Supplementary Material). This problem was intensively studied as the main focus of the DSTC9 Track 1 (Kim et al., 2020b), where a total of 105 systems developed by 24 participating teams were benchmarked.

In this work, we also follow a pipelined approach and present novel contributions for the three subtasks: (1) For knowledge related turn detection, we propose a data augmentation strategy that makes use of available knowledge snippets. (2) For knowledge selection, we propose an approach that makes use of information extracted from the dialogue context via domain classification and entity tracking before knowledge ranking. (3) For the final response generation, we leverage powerful pre-trained models for knowledge grounded response generation in order to obtain coherent and accurate responses. Using the challenge test set as a benchmark, our pipelined approach achieves state-of-the art performance for all three sub-tasks, in both automated and manual evaluation.

2 Approach

Our approach to task-oriented conversation modeling with unstructured knowledge access (Kim et al., 2020a) includes three successive sub-tasks, as illustrated in Figure 1. First, knowledge-seeking turn detection aims to identify user requests that

Proceedings of the 1st Workshop on Document-grounded Dialogue and Conversational Question Answering, pages 119–127
August 5–6, 2021.

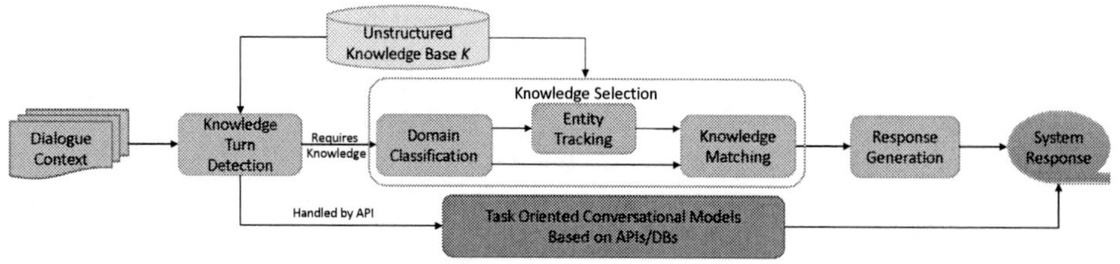

Figure 1: Task formulation and architecture of our knowledge-grounded dialog system.

are beyond the coverage of the task API. Then, for detected queries, knowledge selection aims to find the most appropriate knowledge that can address the user queries from a provided knowledge base. Finally, knowledge-grounded response generation produces a response given the dialogue history and selected knowledge.

DSTC9 Track 1 (Kim et al., 2020b) organizers provided a baseline system that adopted the fine-tuned GPT2-small (Radford et al., 2019) for all three sub-tasks. The winning teams (Team 19 and Team 3) extensively utilized ensembling strategies to boost the performance of their submissions (He et al., 2021; Tang et al., 2021; Mi et al., 2021). We follow the pipelined architecture of the baseline system, but made innovations and improvements for each sub-task, outlined in detail below.

2.1 Knowledge-seeking Turn Detection

We treat knowledge-seeking turn detection as a binary classification task, given the dialogue context as the input, and fine-tuned a pre-trained language model for this purpose. The knowledge provided in the knowledge base constitutes a set of FAQs. We augmented the available training sets by treating all questions in the knowledge base as new potential user queries. Furthermore, for all questions in this augmentation that contain an entity name, we created a new question by replacing this entity name with "it". In this way, we obtained 13,668 additional data samples. In contrast to the baseline, we found that replacing GPT2-small with RoBERTa-Large (Liu et al., 2019) improved the performance. The other changes we made include feeding only the last user utterance instead of the whole dialogue context into the model and fine-tuning the decision threshold t_{ktd} (when the inferred probability score $p > t_{ktd}$, the prediction is positive, otherwise negative) to optimize the F1 score on the validation set, both of which helped achieve better performance.

2.2 Knowledge Selection

For knowledge selection, the baseline system predicts the relevance between a given dialogue context and every candidate in the whole knowledge base, which is very time-consuming especially when the size of knowledge base is substantially expanded. Instead, we propose a hierarchical filtering method to narrow down the candidate search space. Our proposed knowledge selection pipeline includes the following three modules: domain classification, entity tracking, and knowledge matching, as illustrated in Figure 1. Specifications of each module are detailed below.

2.2.1 Domain Classification

In multi-domain conversations, if the system knows what domain a given turn belongs to, the search space for knowledge selection can be greatly reduced by taking the domain-specific knowledge only. The DSTC9 Track 1 data includes the augmented turns for "Train", "Taxi", "Hotel", and "Restaurant" domains in its training set, where the first two domains have domain-level knowledge only, while the others can be further subdivided for each entity-specific knowledge. To improve the generalizability of our filtering mechanism for unseen domains, we merged the domains which require further entity-level analysis into an "Others" class and defined this task as a three-way classification: {"Train", "Taxi", and "Others"}.

We implemented a domain classifier by fine-tuning the RoBERTa-Large model which takes the whole dialogue context and outputs a domain label. Considering that a new domain (i.e., "Attraction") is introduced in the test set, we augmented the training data with 3,350 additional samples of the "Attraction" domain, which were obtained from the MultiWOZ 2.1 (Eric et al., 2020), the source of the DSTC9 Track 1 data (all augmented samples are labeled as "Others"). More specifically, we first find out those dialogues for "Attraction" in the training set of the MultiWOZ 2.1 dataset (this dataset contains seven domains including "Attraction") by selecting dialogue turns that contain "Attraction" related slots. We then replace the original "Attraction" related slots with entities of the "Attraction" domain in the knowledge base K. Meanwhile we replace the last user utterances in the dialogues with the knowledge questions that belong to the replaced new entities. Table 1 gives one example for explanation. In this example, we replace the original entity of "funky fun house" with a new entity of "California Academy of Science" randomly selected from the "Attraction" domain of the knowledge base. Besides, we replace the original last user utterance with a knowledge question randomly selected from the FAQs of this new entity "California Academy of Science".

2.2.2 Entity Tracking

Once the domain classifier predicts the 'Others' label for a given turn, the entity tracking module is executed to detect the entities mentioned in the dialogue context and align them to the entity-level candidates in the knowledge base. We adopt an unsupervised approach based on fuzzy n-gram matching whose details can be referred to Section A.2 of the Supplementary Material. After extracting these entities, we determined the character-level start position of each entity in the dialogue context and selected the last three mentioned entities as the output of this module.

2.2.3 Knowledge Matching

The knowledge matching module receives a list of knowledge candidates and ranks them in terms of relevance to the input dialogue context. We concatenated the dialogue context, domain/entity name, and each knowledge snippet into a long sequence, which is then sent to the fine-tuned RoBERTa-Large model to get a relevance score.

To train the model, we adopted Hinge loss, which was reported to perform better for the ranking problems (Wang et al., 2014; Elsayed et al., 2018) than Cross-entropy loss used in the baseline system. For each positive instance, we drew four negative samples, each of which is randomly selected from one of four sources: 1) the whole knowledge base, 2) the knowledge snippets in the ground truth domain, 3) the knowledge snippets of the ground truth entity, and 4) the knowledge snippets of other entities mentioned in the same dialogue. In the execution time, we fed the knowledge candidates filtered by the predicted domain and entity from Section 2.2.1 and 2.2.2, repectively. Then, the module outputs a list of the candidates ranked by relevance score.

2.3 Response Generation

For response generation, we compared the following three pre-trained sequence-to-sequence (seq2seq) models: T5-Base (Raffel et al., 2020), BART-Large (Lewis et al., 2020), and Pegasus-Large (Zhang et al., 2020). Each model inputs a concatenated sequence of the whole dialogue context and the knowledge answer and then outputs a response. The ground-truth knowledge answer is used in the training phase, while the top-1 candidate from the knowledge selection result is used in the test phase.

3 Experiments and Results

We used the same data split and evaluation metrics as the official DSTC9 Track 1 challenge. All model training and dataset details are summarized in the Section B of the Supplementary Material.

3.1 Knowledge Seeking Turn Detection

Table 2 compares the knowledge seeking turn detection performance between our proposed models and the best single model and ensemble-based systems from the DSTC9 Track 1 official results.[1] The results show that our proposed data augmentation method helped to improve the recall of our detection model and led to the highest F1 score among all the single models in the challenge.

3.2 Knowledge Selection

Our domain classification and entity tracking modules achieved 99.5% in accuracy and 97.5% in recall, respectively. The data augmentation method helped to improve the domain classification accuracy from 97.1% to 99.5%.

Table 3 summarizes the knowledge selection performance of our system based on the proposed hierarchical filtering mechanism using the results from both domain classification and entity tracking modules. Our proposed system outperformed the challenge baseline in all three metrics with a largely reduced execution time from more than 20 hours by the baseline to less than half an hour to process the whole test set with a single V100 GPU.

[1]There are up to five entries submitted by each team in the competition and we report only the best entries by a single model and ensemble-based systems.

Speaker	Original Dialogue	New Dialogue
User	I was hoping to see local places while in Cambridge. Some entertainment would be great.	I was hoping to see local places while in Cambridge. Some entertainment would be great.
Agent	I got 5 options. which side is okay for you?	I got 5 options. which side is okay for you?
User	It doesn't matter. Can I have the address of a good one?	It doesn't matter. Can I have the address of a good one?
Agent	How about funky fun house, they are located at 8 mercers row, mercers row industrial estate.	How about California Academy of Sciences, they are located at 8 mercers row, mercers row industrial estate.
User	Could I also get the phone number and postcode?	Is WiFi available?

Table 1: An example of data augmentation for domain classification. The left dialogue is the original dialogue from the MultiWOZ 2.1 dataset while the right one is synthesized by replacing the original entity and last user utterance highlighted by red with a new entity and knowledge question from the knowledge base highlighted by blue.

	Precision	Recall	F1
Our proposed model	0.9920	0.9344	0.9623
+ data augmentation	0.9903	<u>0.9833</u>	<u>0.9868</u>
DSTC9 Track 1 Systems:			
Baseline	0.9933	0.9021	0.9455
Team 17†	<u>0.9933</u>	0.9748	0.9839
Team 3‡	**0.9964**	**0.9859**	**0.9911**

Table 2: Test results on task 1: knowledge-seeking turn detection. † and ‡ denote the best DSTC9 Track 1 systems with a single model and model ensemble, respectively. Overall highest scores are made bold while highest scores for single models are underlined.

	MRR@5	Recall@1	Recall@5
Our proposed model	<u>0.9461</u>	<u>**0.9251**</u>	<u>0.9702</u>
DSTC9 Track 1 Systems:			
Baseline	0.7263	0.6201	0.8772
Team 7†	0.9309	0.8988	0.9666
Team 19‡	**0.9504**	0.9235	**0.9840**

Table 3: Test results on task 2: knowledge selection.

Compared with the best knowledge selection results from the challenge, our model achieved higher performances than the best single model-based system in all metrics, and even surpassed the best ensemble model in recall@1. To be noted, recall@1 is the most important metric, since the response generation is grounded on only the top-1 result from knowledge selection.

3.2.1 Ablation Study

First of all, Table 5 summarizes the ablation results by imposing two kinds of changes based on our full knowledge matching model: instead of concatenating the dialogue context, domain name, entity name, and knowledge question and answer pair as the input to the model, we only concatenate the dialogue context and knowledge question and answer pair (w/o entity names); we replace the Hinge loss with Cross-entropy loss (w/o Hinge Loss). To be noted, we should pay more attention to the Recall@1 score in the Table 5, which is the most important metric. And we can see that adding the domain and entity names are beneficial and the use of Hinge loss for optimization is better than Cross-entropy for this ranking problem.

As above-mentioned, for training the knowledge matching module, we need to sample several negative samples for each position sample and instead of using only one negative sampling strategy, we used a mixed strategy. More specifically, for sampling each negative sample, we randomly adopted one of the following four strategies:

1. Randomly select from all knowledge snippets;
2. Randomly select from the knowledge snippets of entities that are the in the same domain as the ground truth one (i.e., the entity of the positive sample);
3. Randomly select from the knowledge snippets of the ground truth entity;
4. Randomly select from the knowledge snippets of entities that are mentioned in the same dialogue as the ground truth one.

Each strategy $i \in \{1, 2, 3, 4\}$ is sampled at a certain sampling ratio p^i_{ns}. We tuned this sampling ratio by trying several combinations, and the results are summarized in Table 6. From it, we can see that: (1) Strategy 4 is the most effective among all four ones; (2) Mixing four strategies is better than using only one of them; (3) Allocating higher ratio to strategy 4 is better than uniform ratios for every strategy.

3.3 Response Generation

Table 4 summarizes the automated evaluation results for the generated responses with different seq2seq models. Our fine-tuned T5-Base model achieved lower BLEU scores than BART-Large and Pegasus-Large, while its METEOR score is

	BLEU-1	BLEU-2	BLEU-3	BLEU-4	METEOR	ROUGE-1	ROUGE-2	ROUGE-L
Our Systems:								
BART-Large	0.3743	0.2428	0.1620	0.1098	0.3869	0.4163	0.1992	0.3639
T5-Base	0.3575	0.2432	0.1685	0.1155	**0.4379**	0.4139	0.2103	0.3536
Pegasus-Large	0.3808	0.2531	0.1727	**0.1192**	0.4013	0.4237	0.2099	0.3656
DSTC9 Track 1 Systems:								
Baseline	0.3031	0.1732	0.1005	0.0655	0.2983	0.3386	0.1364	0.3039
Team 15†	0.3779	0.2532	**0.1731**	0.1175	0.3931	0.4204	0.2113	0.3765
Team 3‡	**0.3864**	**0.2539**	0.1692	0.1190	0.3914	**0.4332**	**0.2115**	**0.3885**

Table 4: Test results on task 3: knowledge grounded response generation.

Settings	MRR@5	Recall@1	Recall@5
Original model	**0.9811**	**0.9693**	**0.9936**
w/o entity names	0.9788	0.9656	0.9933
w/o Hinge Loss	0.9734	0.9613	0.9905

Table 5: Ablation study of the knowledge matching module for knowledge selection by removing entities and hinge loss. Scores are reported on the validation set.

Sampling ratios	**MRR@5**	**Recall@1**	**Recall@5**
Original model			
[0.1,0.1,0.1,0.7]	**0.9811**	**0.9693**	**0.9936**
[0.25,0.25,0.25,0.25]	0.9761	0.9615	0.9929
[1.0,0.0,0.0,0.0]	0.9712	0.9514	0.9933
[0.0,1.0,0.0,0.0]	0.9559	0.9248	0.9906
[0.0,0.0,1.0,0.0]	0.9728	0.9540	0.9933
[0.0,0.0,0.0,1.0]	0.9751	0.9596	0.9929

Table 6: Ablation study of the knowledge matching module for knowledge selection by tuning the mixed negative sampling ratio. Scores are reported on the validation set. The sampling ratio is represented in the format of $[p^1_{ns}, p^2_{ns}, p^3_{ns}, p^4_{ns}]$.

substantially higher than the others. Note that our generation system does not perform any model ensemble, and it surpasses the best single system in the DSTC9 Track 1 for half of the metrics.

Following the official evaluation protocol in the challenge, we performed human evaluation to compare our system with the top systems from the challenge[2], as shown in Table 7. Specifically, we hired three crowd-workers for each instance, asked them to score each system output in terms of its "accuracy" and "appropriateness" in five point Likert scale, and reported the averaged scores. We have three findings: (1) T5 achieves higher accuracy, while Pegasus is slightly better for appropriateness; (2) our systems generates more accurate responses than the top DSTC9 systems, while the appropriateness scores is comparable (confirmed by significance testing in Section C.2 of Supplementary Material); (3) the final average scores of our systems rank the highest. We present several examples of the generated responses by our system compared against the baseline and top 2 systems in Section C.3 of Supplementary Material.

Systems	Accuracy	Appropriateness	Average
Our Systems:			
T5-Base	**4.5994***	4.4572†	**4.5283***
Pegasus-Large	4.5451†	4.4591†	4.5021†
DSTC9 Track 1 Systems (Top-2):			
Team 19	4.4979 (4.3917)	**4.4698** (4.3922)	4.4838 (4.3920)
Team 3	4.4524 (4.3480)	4.4064 (4.3634)	4.4294 (4.3557)

Table 7: Human evaluation results of the test set for response generation. Numbers within the parentheses are official scores from DSCT9 (Kim et al., 2020b). The symbol * means our score is significantly higher than the best previous system while † means our score is not significantly different from the best previous system, according to paired t-test with $p < 0.05$.

4 Conclusions

In this work, we propose a comprehensive system to enable the task-orientated dialogue models to answer user queries that are out of the scope of APIs. We significantly improved the system's capability of finding the most relevant knowledge snippets, consequently providing excellent responses by introducing a novel data augmentation method, incorporating domain and entity identification modules for knowledge selection, and utilizing mixed negative sampling. To demonstrate the efficacy of our approach, we benchmark our system on the DSTC9 Track 1 challenge dataset and report the state-of-the-art performance.

[2]https://github.com/alexa/alexa-with-dstc9-track1-dataset/tree/master/results

References

Gamaleldin Elsayed, Dilip Krishnan, Hossein Mobahi, Kevin Regan, and Samy Bengio. 2018. Large margin deep networks for classification. In *Advances in Neural Information Processing Systems*, volume 31, pages 842–852. Curran Associates, Inc.

Mihail Eric, Rahul Goel, Shachi Paul, Abhishek Sethi, Sanchit Agarwal, Shuyang Gao, Adarsh Kumar, Anuj Goyal, Peter Ku, and Dilek Hakkani-Tur. 2020. MultiWOZ 2.1: A consolidated multi-domain dialogue dataset with state corrections and state tracking baselines. In *Proceedings of the 12th Language Resources and Evaluation Conference*, pages 422–428, Marseille, France. European Language Resources Association.

Mihail Eric, Lakshmi Krishnan, Francois Charette, and Christopher D. Manning. 2017. Key-value retrieval networks for task-oriented dialogue. In *Proceedings of the SIGDIAL 2017 Conference*, pages 37–49.

Huang He, Hua Lu, Siqi Bao, Fan Wang, Hua Wu, Zhengyu Niu, and Haifeng Wang. 2021. Learning to select external knowledge with multi-scale negative sampling. *arXiv preprint arXiv:2102.02096.*

Seokhwan Kim, Mihail Eric, Karthik Gopalakrishnan, Behnam Hedayatnia, Yang Liu, and Dilek Hakkani-Tur. 2020a. Beyond domain APIs: Task-oriented conversational modeling with unstructured knowledge access. In *Proceedings of the 21th Annual Meeting of the Special Interest Group on Discourse and Dialogue*, pages 278–289, 1st virtual meeting. Association for Computational Linguistics.

Seokhwan Kim, Mihail Eric, Karthik Gopalakrishnan, Behnam Hedayatnia, Yang Liu, and Dilek Hakkani-Tur. 2020b. Beyond domain apis: Task-oriented conversational modeling with unstructured knowledge access. *arXiv preprint arXiv:2006.03533.*

Mike Lewis, Yinhan Liu, Naman Goyal, Marjan Ghazvininejad, Abdelrahman Mohamed, Omer Levy, Veselin Stoyanov, and Luke Zettlemoyer. 2020. BART: Denoising sequence-to-sequence pretraining for natural language generation, translation, and comprehension. In *Proceedings of the 58th Annual Meeting of the Association for Computational Linguistics*, pages 7871–7880, Online. Association for Computational Linguistics.

Yinhan Liu, Myle Ott, Naman Goyal, Jingfei Du, Mandar Joshi, Danqi Chen, Omer Levy, Mike Lewis, Luke Zettlemoyer, and Veselin Stoyanov. 2019. Roberta: A robustly optimized BERT pretraining approach. *CoRR*, abs/1907.11692.

Haitao Mi, Qiyu Ren, Yinpei Dai, Yifan He, Jian Sun, Yongbin Li, Jing Zheng, and Peng Xu. 2021. Towards generalized models for beyond domain api task-oriented dialogue. *AAAI-21 DSTC9 Workshop.*

Alec Radford, Jeff Wu, Rewon Child, David Luan, Dario Amodei, and Ilya Sutskever. 2019. Language models are unsupervised multitask learners.

Colin Raffel, Noam Shazeer, Adam Roberts, Katherine Lee, Sharan Narang, Michael Matena, Yanqi Zhou, Wei Li, and Peter J. Liu. 2020. Exploring the limits of transfer learning with a unified text-to-text transformer. *Journal of Machine Learning Research*, 21(140):1–67.

Liang Tang, Qinghua Shang, Kaokao Lv, Zixi Fu, Shijiang Zhang, Chuanming Huang, and Zhuo Zhang. 2021. Radge relevance learning and generation evaluating method for task-oriented conversational system-anonymous version. *AAAI-21 DSTC9 Workshop.*

Jiang Wang, Yang Song, Thomas Leung, Chuck Rosenberg, Jingbin Wang, James Philbin, Bo Chen, and Ying Wu. 2014. Learning fine-grained image similarity with deep ranking. In *Proceedings of the IEEE conference on computer vision and pattern recognition*, pages 1386–1393.

Jason D. Williams, Kavosh Asadi, and Geoffrey Zweig. 2017. Hybrid code networks: practical and efficient end-to-end dialog control with supervised and reinforcement learning. In *Proceedings of the 55th Annual Meeting of the Association for Computational Linguistics (ACL 2017).*

Thomas Wolf, Lysandre Debut, Victor Sanh, Julien Chaumond, Clement Delangue, Anthony Moi, Pierric Cistac, Tim Rault, Remi Louf, Morgan Funtowicz, Joe Davison, Sam Shleifer, Patrick von Platen, Clara Ma, Yacine Jernite, Julien Plu, Canwen Xu, Teven Le Scao, Sylvain Gugger, Mariama Drame, Quentin Lhoest, and Alexander Rush. 2020. Transformers: State-of-the-art natural language processing. In *Proceedings of the 2020 Conference on Empirical Methods in Natural Language Processing: System Demonstrations*, pages 38–45, Online. Association for Computational Linguistics.

Jingqing Zhang, Yao Zhao, Mohammad Saleh, and Peter Liu. 2020. PEGASUS: Pre-training with extracted gap-sentences for abstractive summarization. In *Proceedings of the 37th International Conference on Machine Learning*, volume 119 of *Proceedings of Machine Learning Research*, pages 11328–11339. PMLR.

A Methods

A.1 Entity Extraction

Specifically, we first normalize the entity names in the knowledge base using a set of heuristic rules, such as replacing the punctuation "&" with "and". Table A.1 summarizes the full list of normalization rules and we give an example for each rule as illustration. Then we perform the fuzzy n-gram matching between an entity and a certain piece of dialogue context. For example of an entity of "Alexander Bed and Breakfast", it is a four-gram, therefore we extract all four-grams from the dialogue context and match each of them against it. And the process of matching is to first find out the longest contiguous matching sub-sequence and then calculate the matching ratio by the equation of $2M/T$, where M is the length of the matched sub-sequence while T is the total length of the two n-grams to be matched.[3] If this ratio is higher than 0.95, we deem this pair of n-grams as matched. In this way, we can find out which entities in the knowledge base are mentioned in a certain dialogue.

B Experiments

B.1 Data Samples & Statistics

Table B.2 shows an example conversation with unstructured knowledge access. The user utterance at turn $t = 5$ requests the information about the gym facility, which is out of the coverage of the structured domain APIs. However, the relevant knowledge contents can be found from the external sources as in the rightmost column which includes the sampled QA snippets from the FAQ lists for each corresponding entity within domains such as train, hotel, or restaurant. With access to these unstructured external knowledge sources, the agent manages to continue the conversation with no friction by selecting the most appropriate knowledge.

The data statistics are summarized in Table B.3.[4] The main data is an augmented version of MultiWOZ 2.1 that includes newly introduced knowledge-seeking turns in the MultiWOZ conversations. A total of 22,834 utterance pairs were newly collected based on 2,900 knowledge candidates from the FAQ webpages about the domains and the entities in MultiWOZ databases. To be noted, for the test set, other conversations collected from scratch about touristic information for San Francisco are added. To evaluate the generalizability of models, the new conversations cover knowledge, locale and domains that are unseen from the train and validation data sets. In addition, this test set includes not only written conversations, but also spoken dialogues to evaluate system performance across different modalities.

Table B.4 gives the statistics of the knowledge base, which is a collection of frequently asked questions (FAQs). To be noted, there are no entities for the "Train" and "Taxi" domains while for "Hotel", "Restaurant", and "Attraction" domains, each entity has its corresponding list of FAQ pairs. Besides, the knowledge base for the test set covers the train & validation sets and is further expanded by adding one more domain of "Attraction" and more entities.

B.2 Experimental Details

We implemented our proposed system based on the DSTC9 Track 1 baseline provided by Kim et al. (2020b) and the transformers library (Wolf et al., 2020). For all sub-tasks, the maximum sequence length for the dialogue context and the knowledge snippet is both 128. For the knowledge seeking turn detection sub-task, the model is fine-tuned for 5 epochs with the batch size of 16, while for other sub-tasks, 8 epochs and the batch size of 4 are used. A model checkpoint is saved after each epoch, and the best checkpoint is picked based on the validation results. For decoding process of the response generation model, we replaced the nucleus sampling in the baseline to beam search (beam width is 5), which achieved higher performances in the validation set.

C Results

C.1 Significance Testing for Human Evaluation

Since those scores of human evaluation for response generation are quite close to each other, we resort to significance testing to confirm our system's superior performance. Table C.5 summarizes the significance testing p-value between our systems and the top-2 submitted systems in the DSTC9 challenge for the accuracy, appropriateness, and average scores, respectively. From it, we can see that T5-Base is significantly higher than the competing systems in terms of accuracy ($p < 0.05$). Besides,

[3] https://towardsdatascience.com/sequencematcher-in-python-6b1e6f3915fc

[4] Data can be downloaded from: https://github.com/alexa/alexa-with-dstc9-track1-dataset

Normalization rules	Examples
Replace the punctuation "&" with "and"	Bay Subs & Deli → Bay Subs and Deli
If the entity contains any symbol of " - ", ", " or "/", split this entity by this symbol and remove the second part	Hard Knox Cafe - Potrero Hill → Hard Knox Cafe
Replace "guesthouse" with "guest house"	ARBURY LODGE GUESTHOUSE → ARBURY LODGE GUEST HOUSE
If the entity contains a place name such as "Fisherman's Wharf" and "San Francisco" in the end, remove it (since the entities in the knowledge base do not contain these place names)	Bay Bridge Inn San Francisco → Bay Bridge Inn
Replace numbers with corresponding English words	Pho Huynh Hiep 2 → Pho Huynh Hiep Two

Table A.1: Entity normalization rules and the corresponding examples.

Turn	Speaker	Utterance	Sampled Knowledge Snippets from FAQs
1	User	I'm looking for a place to stay in the south of town. It doesn't need to have free parking.	
2	Agent	There are 4 hotels that are in the area you are looking for. Would you prefer a 3 or 4 star rated hotel?	
3	User	I don't care about the star rating as long as it's expensive.	
4	Agent	The ***Lensfield Hotel*** is the only expensive hotel in the south area. Would you like any more information on this location?	
5	User	I'm interested in knowing, do they have a workout facility on the premises?	
6	Agent	There are both a fitness center and gym available on the premises. Does this sound ok?	Q1: Do you have room service for your guests? A1: Yes, the Lensfield Hotel provides room services. **Q2: Is there a gym available at your location?** **A2: There is both a fitness center and gym available on the premises.** Q3: Can I bring my dog? A3: Pets are not allowed at the Lensfield Hotel.
7	User	That is perfect can you book that for me please.	
8	Agent	The Lensfield Hotel is located in the South. It has a 3 star rating and is expensive. There is free parking and internet. I have booked it for you.	
9	User	Great, thank you!	

Table B.2: Examples of task-oriented conversations with unstructured knowledge access. Three sampled FAQ pairs for the entity "Lensfield Hotel" are listed in the rightmost column for turn 5 which is beyond the coverage of API and needs external knowledge support. The most appropriate FAQ pair to address turn 5 is highlighted in bold font.

Split	Source	# dialogues	# samples	# knowledge seeking turns
Train	MultiWOZ	7,190	71,348	19,184
Valid	MultiWOZ	1,000	9,663	2,673
Test	MultiWOZ	977	2,084	977
	SF Written	900	1,834	900
	SF Spoken	107	263	104

Table B.3: Statistics of the data divided into training, validation, and test sets. The test set contains three sources of samples: MultiWOZ, San Francisco tourism in written English, and San Francisco tourism in spoken English, which is different from train and validation sets.

Domain	Train & Val		Test	
	# Entities	# Snippets	# Entities	# Snippets
Train	–	26	–	26
Taxi	–	5	–	5
Hotel	33	1,219	178	4,346
Restaurant	110	1,650	391	7,155
Attraction	–	–	97	507
Total	143	2,900	666	12,309

Table B.4: Statistics of the knowledge base (the list of FAQs). "Train" and "Taxi" domains do not have any entities and there is no "Attraction" domain for the knowledge base in train and validation sets.

	Accuracy		Appropriateness		Average	
	T5-Base	Pegasus-Large	T5-Base	Pegasus-Large	T5-Base	Pegasus-Large
Team 19	1.86×10^{-6}	1.45×10^{-1}	6.07×10^{-1}	5.56×10^{-1}	1.96×10^{-3}	4.25×10^{-1}
Team 3	1.21×10^{-16}	8.01×10^{-7}	2.89×10^{-4}	5.68×10^{-5}	8.31×10^{-15}	2.48×10^{-8}

Table C.5: Significance Testing p-values between our systems and top-2 systems in the DSTC9 competition for the accuracy, appropriateness, and average score of response generation. Paired t-test is used.

	Example
Dialogues	**User:** I need a train to Broxbourne, that arrives by 20:30. **Agent:** Certainly. Can I assume you're leaving from Cambridge? **User:** Yes, that is correct. **Agent:** There is a train leaving at 5:01, would you like a seat? **User:** Is that leaving on Sunday? **Agent:** I have the TR8991 leaving at 19:01 and arriving by 20:01. Would you like me to book that for you? **User:** Not yet but I also need a restaurant that serve mediterranean food and should be in the centre of town. **Agent:** I have a few restaurants that fit your criteria. The Gardenia, La Mimosa, and Shiraz Restaurant. Which one are you interested in hearing about? **User:** Tell me about The Gardenia. **Agent:** It's a cheap restaurant located at 2 Rose Crescent City Centre. Phone number and postcode are 01223356354 and cb23ll. Do you need anything else? **User:** Does the restaurant offer live music on the weekend? **Agent:** Sorry, there is no live music at The Gardenia. What else can I help you with? **User:** Does the train have a data limit for wifi usage?
Knowledge Answer	Data is limited to 50MB per day with no option of additional data.
Our systems:	
T5-Base	Data is limited to 50MB per day with no option of additional data. Is there anything else I can do for you today or would you like to make a reservation?
Pegasus-Large	Data is limited to 50MB per day with no option of additional data. Is there anything else I can help you with?
Top-2 submitted systems:	
Team 3	No, there is no additional data available to purchase. Anything else I can do for you?
Team 19	No, the train does not have a data limit for wifi usage. Anything else I can do for you?

Table C.6: Qualitative comparison between our system with previous strong competitors. Knowledge answer is the answer part of the ground truth knowledge snippet. We are comparing against the top-2 systems submitted to the DSTC9 competition.

T5-Base and Pegasus-Large are comparable to the best previous system in terms of appropriateness. Finally, with regards to the average score, our T5-Base significantly rivals the previous best system.

C.2 Qualitative Examples of Responses

Table C.6 gives one qualitative example to compare our system's responses against those of the top-2 submitted systems in the DSTC9 competition (i.e., Team 3 and 19)[5]. Overall, we can see that our system's responses are more accurate. Taking the example in Table C.6, our responses can exactly answer the user query and it is strictly aligning with the ground truth knowledge, while the response from Team 19 is totally wrong and that from Team 3 does not address the user query at all.

[5]https://github.com/alexa/alexa-with-dstc9-track1-dataset/tree/master/results

Author Index